Baggett, J
19
abitat fo
Humanit

HABITAT FOR HUMANITY®

HABITAT FOR HUMANITY®

BUILDING PRIVATE HOMES,

BUILDING PUBLIC RELIGION

Jerome P. Baggett

 Temple University Press

PHILADELPHIA

Temple University Press, Philadelphia 19122
Copyright © 2001 by Temple University
All rights reserved
Published 2001
Printed in the United States of America

Library of Congress Cataloging-in-Publication Data

Baggett, Jerome P., 1963– .
    Habitat for Humanity® : building private homes, building public
religion / Jerome P. Baggett.
        p.   cm.
    Includes bibliographical references and index.
    ISBN 1-56639-802-9 (cloth : alk. paper) — ISBN 1-56639-803-7
(pbk. : alk. paper)
    1. Habitat for Humanity®, Inc.   2. Voluntarism—Religious aspects—
Christianity.   I. Title.

BV4407.63.B34   2001
267'.13–dc21
                                                          00-037806

In loving memory of
Thomas Patrick Baggett, Jr.

Contents

Preface

If a brother or sister is ill-clad and in lack of daily food, and one of you says to them, "Go in peace, be warmed and filled," without giving them the things needed for the body, what does it profit? So faith by itself, if it has no works, is dead.

James 2:14–17

I believe we're saved by grace—you don't earn your way into heaven. But believing in Jesus has got to be more than a verbal proclamation. If somebody says in a sermon, "Love your neighbor as you love yourself," everybody would say, "Amen!" When you look at the reality of their lives, though, they are laying up big, big treasures for themselves but are not willing to be that concerned for their neighbors.

Millard Fuller, founder and president of Habitat for Humanity®

abitat for Humanity®, a grassroots house-building ministry founded in 1976 by evangelical Christians, is one of the best-known and most estimable nonprofit organizations in the United States today. Americans acquainted with the organization often associate it with its most famous volunteer, former President Jimmy Carter, and less so with its energetic founder, Millard Fuller. Other notable public figures have had a part in spreading the word about Habitat as well. During the 1992 presidential campaign, candidate Bill Clinton, his running mate, Al Gore, and their families volunteered at a house build, a ritual that is becoming more commonplace for candidates at all levels of government. Through their involvement they hope to demonstrate their interest in local communities and in the personal responsibility purportedly molded by self-help efforts like Habitat. On the Republican side, former President Gerald Ford served on the organization's board of advisors, former HUD Secretary Jack Kemp currently sits on its board of directors and is an outspoken supporter, and former House Speaker Newt Gingrich once financed a house built in his home county in Georgia.

Celebrities from the entertainment world who have financially supported and publicly endorsed Habitat include singers Amy Grant, Reba McEntire, and Willie Nelson, humorists Bob Hope and Garrison Keillor, and actors Jane Fonda, Gregory Hines, and Paul Newman. The latter has donated hundreds of thousands of dollars in proceeds from his Newman's Own specialty foods business. One nationally televised promotion featured a house building with NFL football players on Super Bowl Sunday, and the organization has been scripted into the highly rated sitcom *Home Improvement*. Habitat's popularity is also enhanced by local TV news stations throughout the country eager to report on a nonprofit doing work that is more colorful and less controversial than that of many others.

Although impressive and still growing, Habitat's popularity is neither its most interesting feature nor the original stimulus for this study. The epigraphs appearing above suggest a more fundamental attraction. The first, one of the most frequently quoted scripture passages at Habitat, mandates Christians to put their faith into practical action by attending to the basic needs of others. Millard Fuller essentially affirms this mandate when he asserts that "believing in Jesus has got to be more than a verbal proclamation." Both quotations reflect the prevailing understanding within the organization that Habitat is intended to serve as a kind of institutional vessel in which action can be mixed with proclamation, where works are blended with grace. Habitat's religious roots and tenor are what make the organization so interesting.

Contrary to the widely accepted Enlightenment paradigm, which forecasts the inexorable privatization of institutional religion and thus its increasing irrelevance for inciting civic participation, Habitat exists as a distinctly public manifestation of religious conviction that is compelling enough to mobilize thousands of American volunteers each year. Explaining how Habitat is able to do this and how its supporters understand their involvement with the organization is the intent of this book. In a sense, the main question to be addressed in these pages is a derivation of the one so memorably posed by the second-century theologian, Tertullian of Carthage: "What does Jerusalem have to do with Athens?" What does religious faith, in other words, have to do with stirring the broad civic participation and commitment to the common good that many see as necessary for sustaining a democratic society? The full answer to this question is clearly not a simple one. Yet, if nothing else, the example of Habitat indicates that religious ideas and symbols remain influential for shaping citizens' sense of responsibility to the public at large.

The challenges to Habitat's efforts in shaping such citizens and the nuances of its organizational culture cannot be fully understood unless one realizes that the organization exists within a more encompassing social ecology. In the first half of Chapter 1, I identify Habitat's place within this social ecology as the voluntary sector, the institutional niche in which people act through associations and nonprofit organizations in order to advance specific nonrationalized, expressive values in public. Insofar as Habitat is concerned with enabling people to act upon their religious convictions and their compassion for inadequately housed families, it primarily institutionalizes expressive values, not those geared to more instrumental, calculative ends. However, to say that voluntary groups like Habitat exist within a broader social ecology means that they reside alongside entities from the much larger state and market sectors.

This reality is critical to keep in mind because these two sectors can impinge upon voluntary-sector organizations in ways that may undermine their ability to operate according to the expressive values upon which they were originally founded. That this tendency is a pronounced one within Habitat is one of the two central claims of this book. Even though its leadership has been wary of the state's potential influence on its house-building ministry, it has been far less reflective about how the inequitable and rationalized capitalist market has subtly affected its organizational culture. Indeed, after describing the history and structure of the organization in Chapters 2 and 3, I demonstrate in Chapters 4 and 5 the tensions inherent in Habitat's citizenship ideal and its susceptibility to being co-opted by the class divisions and instrumental logic that are the hallmarks of the market sector.

In the latter half of the first chapter, I note that the expressive values institutionalized within the voluntary sector are often derived from distinctly religious worldviews. This sector would not exist if it were not for the initiatives undertaken by people of faith in the past; and without them today it would not be nearly as vibrant and eclectic as it is. Habitat's success illustrates the power of religious convictions to stir people to activism in their communities. It also exemplifies the growing importance of a social form of religion that is often referred to as a paradenominational organization. Briefly stated, these are typically ecumenical agencies, grounded in religious values and drawing upon church-based constituencies for support, that seek to have an impact on the public at large though social service provision, political mobilization, and consciousness raising. These organizations, I will argue, are gaining in number and significance because they represent a social form of religion uniquely adapted to the secular tendencies of the modern world.

This is the second of the two central claims of this study. I tease out some of the implications of this claim in Chapters 6 and 7 by investigating how it plays out among Habitat volunteers and staff. In essence, I contend that Habitat provides an institutional space for a distinctly pragmatic, nondoctrinal, and individual-based kind of religiosity that is well suited to the secular climate of modernity and, consequently, is tremendously attractive to the growing numbers of Americans involved in its ministry. Adaptation has its costs, though. Ironically, the kind of religiosity largely responsible for Habitat's growth appears to be less able to sustain the shared religious language and values that can marshal an ideological resistance to the market's problematic effects on the organization. Put differently, the example of Habitat reveals the tensions faced by this social form of religion as it endeavors to maintain its religiously derived expressive values while, at the same time, doing work that exposes those values to pressures from the broader societal context.

Before embarking upon this course, a word about methodology may be useful. The research for this study employed standard methods of qualitative sociological analysis. I performed an extensive review of Habitat's publications, promotional materials, internal records (when permitted), and archives as well as an analysis of survey data generated by the organization itself. I also conducted semi-structured interviews (ranging from one to three hours in length) with Habitat staff (forty-eight interviews), volunteers (thirty interviews), and homeowners (eight interviews), nearly all of which I taped and later transcribed. With the exception of the Marin County group, all of the local affiliates in my sample had staff members, and I interviewed most, if not all, of them.

Among those employed by Habitat International, I interviewed five people from two different regional offices and also sixteen staff members employed at the organizational headquarters in Americus, Georgia. Approximately half of my interviewees working at both the local affiliates and Habitat International had actually begun their involvement with the organization as volunteers. The volunteers I interviewed were either people I met during my participant observation or, more often, people reputed to be seriously involved with the organization and referred to me as such. Affiliate staff members referred some of the homeowners I interviewed to me; I met others at various affiliate-sponsored events. Finally, I undertook participant observation at numerous Habitat meetings, training sessions, celebrations, and construction sites at the locations I visited. At such events, I made no effort to conceal my identity as an openly note-jotting sociologist and was forthcoming about my research to all Habitat staff and to the few (among those I did not interview) volunteers and homeowners curious enough to inquire about it. For the most part, I simply fit in and, like others, entered into each event as fully as I could by remaining attentive at meetings and training sessions (although I never contributed to these), looking on as an audience member at celebrations, and employing my decidedly inconspicuous carpentry skills during a few builds.

These data were collected during a period of two years (1994–96) at Habitat's international headquarters in Americus, Georgia, and from Habitat affiliates at the following locations: Marin County, California; Oakland, California; Redwood City, California; San Francisco, California, Walnut Creek, California; Twin Cities, Minnesota; and Sioux Falls, South Dakota. I was also fortunate in attending two Habitat International–sponsored events: the week-long 1994 Jimmy Carter Work Project in Eagle Butte, South Dakota, and the organization's three-day, eighteenth-anniversary celebration and conference held in Los Angeles the same year. These research sites, while necessarily (due to budget constraints) modest in number, were selected in order to provide a clear sense of the practices and ethos embedded within Habitat International and within local affiliates varying in size, stage of organizational development, productivity level, and, to a lesser extent, geographic region. Except for Millard Fuller and David Williams, Habitat's president and senior vice president respectively, all interviewees have been given pseudonyms, and in some cases their biographical particulars have been altered to ensure confidentiality.

With more than fifteen hundred local affiliates mobilizing thousands of volunteers each year in the United States alone, Habitat does not easily lend itself to comprehensive analysis. Nor is that what this study was designed to provide. Instead, it conveys an understanding of Habitat's organizational culture, the élan of seemingly average Americans coming together, caring for others, living out their religious (or perhaps not so religious) convictions, and, not infrequently, hammering away feverishly during their spare time. The compelling story of Habitat is told in these pages. That story, moreover, is linked to two pervasive cultural realities that, in ways unprecedented among advanced industrialized nations, are deeply ingrained within American life. The first is an impressive tradition of voluntarism that has established the voluntary sector as an important feature of our social ecology. The second is the exceptional degree of religious fecundity responsible for bolstering that voluntary sector and engendering such social forms of religion as the paradenominational organization. Since the emergence of Habitat seems unthinkable without the considerable influence of these larger realities, turning to each of them is an appropriate way to begin.

Acknowledgments

The original impetus for this study came from my work as a research assistant on the Discipleship/Citizenship Project funded by the Lilly Endowment and administered by the Center for Ethics and Social Policy (CESP) at the Graduate Theological Union. That project was both a formative and exciting one for me, due largely to my experience of working with several people, including: John A. Coleman, S.J., the project's principal investigator and my esteemed teacher; fellow research assistants Christopher Adams, Suzanne Holland, Thomas Leininger, and Donna McKenzie; CESP office manager Lynne Jerome; and fellow researcher Richard Wood and project coordinator Barry Stenger, both of whom were kind enough to read this work carefully and offer invaluable suggestions.

This book, originally my doctoral dissertation at the Graduate Theological Union in Berkeley, could never have been completed without the support, insight, and inspiration I received from my dissertation committee, to whom I am extremely grateful: John Coleman, Loyola Marymount University; Clare Fischer, Starr King School for the Ministry; and Ann Swidler, University of California at Berkeley.

Others who have read all or part of an early draft of my manuscript and deserve much thanks for their assistance are Veronica M. Baggett, Mark Chmiel, and Lyman Hostetler. I am indebted to Michael Ames and Elizabeth Johns for their editorial expertise and to many others at Temple University Press, especially production coordinator Jennifer French, for skillfully assisting me in bringing this project to completion. I am also grateful to Jim Trudnowski and Mary Kunnary at Carroll College for their logistical and, frequently, personal support.

It would be impossible to thank sufficiently all of the many people associated with Habitat for Humanity® who generously gave their time and shared parts of their life stories with me. They have taught me much, not least that, despite its many failings and injustices, we still inhabit a society in which apparently average people endeavor to act upon a profound concern for others. Habitat personnel who have been particularly helpful in introducing me to the organization and providing me with information and contacts are Joel Mackey, Patricia St. Onge, Stephen Seidel, David Snell, and Michael Wagner.

Finally, Sheri Hostetler, my partner for the past fourteen years (as well as my computer consultant, editor, confidante, therapist, and best friend) deserves more thanks than my middling prose can convey. Whatever sensitivity I may have to the solicitude, compassion, and generosity displayed within Habitat is no doubt the result of her making these qualities so thoroughly familiar within our own home.

1

The Voluntary Sector and American Religion

There are nonprofits whose assets exceed those of several
nations, such as the Ford Foundation, Harvard University,
and the J. Paul Getty Trust, and there are nonprofits that
conduct intense civic campaigns out of someone's kitchen
with volunteer labor and never more than $500 in the bank.
There are associations dedicated to saving the world from
nuclear war and associations dedicated to promoting the
values of birdwatching. There are organizations such as the
Democratic and Republican parties, which want to get all
their candidates elected; and there is Mikes of America, which
wants only to get anyone named Mike elected president of
the United States. There is Mensa, an association for people
with IQs of over 132; and there is Densa, "for all the rest of
us." There are 350,000 churches, synagogues, and mosques
for the religious; and there is Atheists Anonymous for those
of a different persuasion.

Michael O'Neill, *The Third America*

The Value of the Voluntary Sector

O n one Saturday morning in October, in the auditorium of a
large Lutheran church in downtown Minneapolis, the local
Habitat for Humanity® affiliate celebrated both its tenth
anniversary and the completion of its hundredth house. The
event included a devotional service, informational seminars,
program reports from affiliate staff and board members,
plenty of Habitat promotional literature, videos, and T-shirts,

and, finally, a hearty lunch for scores of volunteers and new home-owners—all signs of the vitality of this international housing ministry. As the celebration came to a close, an older woman named Amanda, a retired music teacher turned volunteer house builder, stood to offer a story about a man who inadvertently fell into a deep ditch. Fortunately for him, she explained, this was a ditch next to a well-trodden road, so he was noticed by a passing government official. The official, of course, was willing to help but regretted he would have to place the man on a waiting list, as well as ask him to fill out a few legal forms and undergo extensive counseling before and after his removal from the ditch. Dissatisfied, the man in the ditch was pleased to see a businessman approach. The businessman gloated that he could easily remove the man from the ditch more quickly than the official, but made it very clear that this service would be expensive. Needless to say, the man in the ditch was enraged and began reciting a litany of curses that was silenced only by the sight of a small girl who, moved by sympathy, had dragged a ladder from her nearby home to help him. "Habitat is doing the work of that little girl," Amanda concluded. Then she sat down.

No further explanation was given, yet it was apparent that the story was well understood by those gathered around her. Perhaps the appreciative audience responded to the Good Samaritan motif or to the politically correct depiction of a man (read: not a "welfare queen") who receives some assistance but does the work of climbing out of the ditch himself. Whatever the case, there seemed to be a shared understanding that Habitat provides an important social space, distinct from the workings of business and government, where people's deeply held sympathies and values can find expression through collective efforts to enhance the life of their communities. Amanda's story and the knowing smiles and nods that it elicited from her audience seemed to indicate that the significance of this social space is recognized by the people who contribute to it during their day-to-day lives.

Social scientists, purportedly among the keenest observers and chroniclers of people's day-to-day lives, have long acknowledged this social space, the so-called voluntary sector. In his Jacksonian-era classic, *Democracy in America*, Alexis de Tocqueville famously marveled at the proclivity of Americans to form associations designed to enhance the public good. "Nothing, in my view," he claimed, "more deserves attention than the intellectual and moral associations in America."[1] More than 160 years later, our attentiveness remains warranted. Today voluntary associations, which are groups united to pursue an interest or promote a cause, are as heterogeneous as they are countless. They include people united on the basis of a common hobby or by a collective desire to alleviate anything from personal addiction to some perceived social malady; their organizations range from Alcoholics Anonymous to Zero Population Growth. They can also be as informal as a monthly science fiction reading group and as temporary as a political demonstration; or they may be more formal and lasting, like the nation's 1.1 million nonprofit organizations falling into any one of the twenty-six Internal Revenue Service categories for federal tax exemption.

Among their number are approximately 350,000 religious organizations, 64,000 human-service agencies, 18,000 hospitals and health-care facilities, 36,000 private schools (of which 1,873 are colleges and universities), 41,000 civic, social, and fraternal organizations, 30,000 foundations, and thousands more advocacy, cultural, and mutual-benefit organizations.[2] Whatever else they may represent, these numbers suggest that the United States remains, as historian Arthur Schlesinger once put it, a "nation of joiners" and that a casual bifurcation of our social ecology into "public" government and "private" business sectors is too simplistic. While it is perhaps less visible than the other two, we overlook this third, voluntary sector at our analytical peril. "They exist in a sense in the interstices of the structures of authority and materiality," wrote Waldemar Nielsen of nonprofit agencies in his influential book on the topic, "and most of their products are essentially intangible, as unmeasurable as compassion, inspiration, or dissent . . . the Third Sector has remained an invisible presence, a kind of Holy Ghost of the American Trinity."[3]

By distinguishing it from the "structures of authority and materiality," Nielsen suggests what many consider to be the voluntary sector's essential value to modern society. If we conceive of sectors, as sociologist Robert Wuthnow does, as defined by the "dominant principles of association" by which collectivities pursue various ends, then voluntary associations and nonprofits are commonly seen as operating according to different principles than do institutions within the other sectors.[4] Consider, for instance, the state. As most people are aware, it is composed of elected officials and accompanying administrative bureaucracies and, taken as a whole, constitutes the legitimate authority within any democratic society. Usually less reflected upon is the fact that, since it monopolizes the right to enforce compliance to its directives through the courts, police, and the military, its operative principle is coercion. Many of the ways in which these coercive powers are exercised are obvious. They are even evident in the state's provision of the same kinds of social services also offered within the other two sectors. That welfare programs are "mandated" by the state is actually another way of saying that it employs its coercive apparatus to delimit the number of qualified beneficiaries of these programs as well as to transfer income in the form of taxes to pay for them. Furthermore, because such programs are legitimated by majoritarian will, they are governed by an instrumental logic that adheres to highly rationalized and bureaucratic procedures focusing on public accountability, efficiency, and demonstrable effectiveness.

A similar argument can be made for the market sector, which serves to allocate private goods and services within a society through exchange mechanisms. Here the governing principle is profitability, which is secured through entrepreneurship, efficiency, and complex systems of supply and demand. Since the flip side of the coin of profit is competition, businesses are inevitably steered by an instrumental concern for self-preservation. This does not mean that the sorts of services provided by the state and voluntary sectors cannot be supplied by proprietary firms. They often are, as the recent entrance of for-profit enterprise in the nursing-home "industry" demonstrates. But the market is comparable to the state in the sense that it too is governed by a rationalized logic more attuned to the imperatives of the system than to the needs of particular individuals. Rather than full persons, they are "consumers" entitled to precisely the level of care their private resources can afford (and not a bit more), or they are faceless, scrupulously catalogued "clients" benefiting (within the bounds of means-tested qualifications and now specified time limits) from the supposed largesse of the state.

In contrast, the voluntary sector, as illustrated by Amanda's story, is an arena of freely chosen activity, and its initiatives are relatively free of bureaucratic and pecuniary constraints. To say its dominant principle is voluntarism means that people are free to enter into (and exit from) participation with those voluntary associations that best reflect their own values. This is clearly not the case for the other sectors, which are actually *involuntary* in the sense that no one living in a given territory is exempt from its statutory laws, and not even the most monastic among us can totally avoid buying and selling on the capitalist market.

Voluntarism also implies that the freely chosen, expressive values upon which voluntary associations are typically founded actually drive their everyday activities. There is a certain nonrationalized quality to voluntarism. Even when people behave instrumentally and try to get things done in the voluntary sector, the means by which they do so are much less settled upon than in the other sectors. These means typically entail considerable in-depth reflection among volunteers and staff upon the people whose needs they are attempting to meet. Those people are also more likely to be treated not only as full persons but as persons with actual voices capable of directing the specific voluntary association or nonprofit in question.

This, in the eyes of innumerable dedicated participants and scholarly observers, is the real value of the voluntary sector. By institutionalizing expressive values and operating according to a noninstrumentalized organizational logic, voluntary associations generate a sense of moral obligation to others that far surpasses perceiving and treating them as mere clients or consumers. As Alan Wolfe explained in *Whose Keeper*, his important book on civil society, "moral obligation ought to be viewed as a socially constructed practice, something we learn through the actual experience of trying to live together with other people."[5] If this is the case, then voluntary associations, at their best, can contribute to an expanded notion of obligation to others by carving out a social niche for such practices as open discussion, shared responsibility, community leadership, and even personal sacrifice. Voluntary-sector organizations do this by keeping expressive values like compassion and justice from being simply vague, ethereal notions. The values that instill a concern for human rights, fire safety, or adequate housing, for instance, will not get a full hearing in society unless they are institutionalized in groups that range from Amnesty International to the local volunteer fire department to Habitat. Such values might no longer be part of our social ecology, and no longer stimulate the imaginations and incite the energies of even the most socially concerned, if they are not institutionalized within the voluntary sector.

"We form institutions," wrote Robert Bellah and his colleagues in *The Good Society*, "and they form us every time we engage in a conversation that matters."[6] Thus, voluntary associations not only provide individuals with numerous and manageable volunteer roles to enact their deepest values; they are also institutional bearers of evocative narratives and language (biblical, civic, humanistic, and so forth) through which those values come to make sense and actually obligate people to behave in accordance with them. In ways that are rare in other areas of our busy lives, they present opportunities, even expectations, for us to engage publicly in the conversations that matter most to us. Voluntary associations are, in the words of Peter Berger and Richard John Neuhaus, "the value-generating and value-maintaining agencies in society" because they contribute to forming us and allowing us to reach beyond the narrow confines of our own private interests.[7] In sum, they facilitate the construction of a fuller sense of moral obligation to others by providing the practices through which busy people can live out their highest values and by creating the cultural templates and conversations that enable them to discern authentic meaning in those practices.

The Scope of the Voluntary Sector

While certainly instructive, Amanda's story may lull one into conceiving the voluntary sector as less expansive and organized than it actually is. The personal, homespun nature of her story gives no hint that, as reported in a 1981 study, the cash outlays from nonprofits in the United States astonishingly exceeded the gross domestic products (GDP) of all but seven nations in the world.[8] Four decades ago no more than seven thousand new nonprofits applied to the IRS for tax-exempt status each year and, all told, they accounted for about 2.1 percent of the U.S. national GDP. Now organizations are becoming tax-exempt by the tens of thousands annually and they constitute more than 6 percent of the American economy. Voluntary-sector growth is outpacing that of both the state and market sectors, which make up 14 and 80 percent of the GDP respectively.[9]

Even though about one out of every fifteen American workers is currently employed by a nonprofit organization, the amount of *unpaid* labor within the voluntary sector is one of its most remarkable assets.[10] The research institute Independent Sector found that in 1993 nearly half of all Americans eighteen years or older had volunteered within the previous year and more than one in four volunteered five or more hours per week.[11] With a combined average of 4.2 hours per week, these 89 million adult volunteers contributed approximately 19.5 billion hours of work in a single year. Nearly a quarter of these hours went to such informal activities as helping a neighbor, babysitting, or baking cookies for a school fundraising drive. The remaining three-quarters involved formal volunteering at nonprofit organizations, and it represented the equivalent of 8.8 million full-time workers whose estimated value, if paid, would have reached $182 billion.

Support to the voluntary sector is not restricted to contributions of time. Charitable donations are a huge part of its success as well. For the nearly three-quarters of American households that gave money to various causes in 1993, the average total amount for the year was $880 or 2.1 percent of household income. Forty-four percent of these contributing households gave at least 1 percent of their annual income, and a full 12 percent gave 5 percent or more. As one would expect, contribution rates depend on such variables as gross income, marital status, and educational attainment. One of the more striking findings, however, is that these rates are also affected by the level of volunteering in the household. The nearly one-third of all American households that made charitable contributions, but did not volunteer, donated an average of 1.1 percent of their annual income. This figure more than doubles (2.6 percent of annual income) for those households that both gave money and volunteered. The actual number of volunteer hours is also a decisive factor. Households that volunteered less than one hour per week gave an average of 2.4 percent of their annual incomes, while those that volunteered at least five hours per week contributed 3.9 percent. In addition to cautioning us against sounding a cynical death-knell for generosity in the United States, these data suggest that the practices of volunteering and charitable giving tend to be mutually reinforcing.[12]

The support the voluntary sector receives from ordinary working people becomes most evident if one considers that individual households are responsible for nearly nine-tenths of all private giving in the United States. Currently foundations account for only 6 percent of all private funding for nonprofits, while businesses—despite the oft-publicized magnanimity of corporate philanthropists—contribute a scant 5 percent.[13] Perhaps even more surprising is the fact that, although a sturdy pillar of the voluntary-sector edifice, all private giving combined generates only about one-quarter of the total nonprofit revenues in the United States. The other two pillars are actually the state and market sectors. Due largely to what has been dubbed the "new federalist" approach to social welfare, whereby government (at all levels) contracts with nonprofits to deliver programs to its citizens, the state has in recent years become the source of another quarter of all nonprofit revenues.

Meanwhile, a full 45 percent is derived from nonprofits' activity within the market.[14] Whether their revenues come from membership fees, payment-for-service contracts, or such commercial activities as investments and subsidiary enterprises, it appears that few nonprofits can afford to be inattentive to the bottom line.

Nonprofit organizations function within a complicated social ecology that seldom exempts them from the cost-benefit considerations that preoccupy business firms nor entirely deprives them of the public funds that support state-mandated programs and entities. While altruism and voluntarism are undeniable elements of the social world, it is important to remember that they do not exist in a world of unfettered, spontaneous do-goodism, isolated from the state and market. When nonprofit organizations are given government funds to deliver various services to the public and, in the process, get weighed down by the same sorts of red tape, accountability requirements, and bureaucratic structure that are the scorned features of state agencies, then one realizes that the voluntary sector is not immune from familiar organizational patterns and pathologies. And should anyone doubt that the voluntary sector is at the mercy of the same economic uncertainties as businesses are, then the decreases in individual (and especially corporate) giving and volunteering that accompany recessions should suffice to make them think otherwise. Certainly businesses do not fail to notice the commercial nature—and, at times, substantial market shares—of many nonprofit organizations. As the increasing number of unfair competition lawsuits filed by the Small Business Association against nonprofits attests, business firms are quick to see in such organizations kindred spirits doing what they can to remain fiscally viable.[15]

The voluntary sector, while characterized by people's commitments of time and money to associations promoting their freely chosen values, is not entirely free of the systemic imperatives so prominent in the state and market sectors. This realization complicates the picture somewhat. It would be easier to think of these sectors as the institutional equivalents of a Scylla and Charybdis, between which reputable nonprofits like Habitat are always able to navigate successfully. But this is not the case, and a failure to understand this comes at the cost of being blind to important organizational dynamics occurring within most nonprofits. In the specific case of Habitat, seeing such dynamics more clearly also requires one to recognize the prominent role played by religion within the voluntary sector.

The Voluntary Sector and the Religious Factor

The importance we thus attribute to the sociology of religion does not in the least imply that religion must play the same role in present-day societies that it has played at other times. In a sense, the contrary conclusion would be more sound. Precisely because religion is a primordial phenomenon, it must yield more and more to the new social forms which it has engendered.

Emile Durkheim, *Année sociologique*

Introducing the Lay of the Land

If the voluntary sector can be likened to a plot of fallow soil from which institutions bearing expressive values may burgeon forth, then only the dullest of observers could fail to observe that the fruits of religious sentiments and concerns have been perennially its highest yield. Indeed, planted within the most sizable section of this plot are the 350,000 churches, synagogues, and mosques to which 40 percent of all American adults flock during any given week.[16] But these institutions, as important as they are, are hardly the only outgrowths of religious values in the United States today. Recent studies, for example, indicate that 86 percent of all students receiving private elementary or secondary education are enrolled in religiously based schools, while more than three-quarters of the accredited private colleges and universities have a religious affiliation. Similar observations can be made about other parts of the voluntary sector as well. At least one-third of all child-care agencies, for instance, are church based. Many health-care organizations, particularly hospitals, have been founded by religious groups. Most of the largest international aid and relief organizations have religious affiliations.[17] Finally, in the absence of their founding religious visions such prominent social service organizations as the YMCA, Big Brothers and Big Sisters, the Salvation Army, and the United Way would likely never exist.

Despite evidence of the religious bounty within it, scholarship on the voluntary sector has persisted in portraying it as something of a secular wasteland. Consider, for instance, Daphne Layton's 1987 annotated bibliography of 2,195 books and articles on voluntarism and philanthropy, which, although admirably comprehensive, listed only fifty-seven publications (a mere 2.1 percent of the total) that specifically dealt with religion.[18] Clearly, a significant component of the voluntary sector is not being observed. But, one hastens to caution, this does not necessarily mean that the published researchers in this field ought to be written off as dull observers. It is more likely that their analytical faculties have been meticulously sharpened by Enlightenment categories that equate religious traditions with superstition, prerational need fulfillment, and authoritarianism—all of which are deemed incompatible with public discourse and shared conceptions of the common good. As religiosity enters the pluralistic realm of the voluntary sector, the typical assumption proceeds, it must divest itself of its particular beliefs and practices and behave as instrumentally as all the other institutions that are simply trying to accomplish their goals. This assumption, incidentally, is not without empirical support. The YMCA, after all, has long dropped its "C" in favor of preaching the Good News of Nautilus equipment and Jazzercise, and the members of the Salvation Army still proudly wear their militaristic uniforms but, at times, seem to have removed the threads of salvation that once bound their organization together so tightly.

While notable, this process is neither universal nor inexorable. Researchers who have given short shrift to the salience of religion within the voluntary sector tend to neglect three critical points. First, the very existence of the sector is a result of religiously inspired dissent occurring at the outset of the modern era. Second, people's religious convictions have invigorated the voluntarism, charitable giving, interpersonal networks, and basic, everyday compassion that are the lifeblood of the voluntary sector as a whole. Finally, these observers overlook the fact that, even though many religious nonprofits have been secularized, scores of new ones are sprouting up within the voluntary sector, seemingly at every moment. One important innovation is what this study will call paradenominational organizations, of which Habitat is a provocative example. These are essentially religiously based organizations founded to mobilize their constituencies in pursuing a decidedly public agenda or in promoting some kind of social change. In addition to institutionalizing expressive values in public, these groups—to the extent that involvement in them functions as authentic expressions of individuals' faith commitments—also represent, as Durkheim stated it in the epigraph above, one of the irrepressible new social forms that religious sensibilities may assume. The remainder of this chapter will address in order each of these three analytical lacunae regarding religion in the voluntary sector.

Tilling the Soil: The Consequences of Religious Dissent

As land needs to be tilled in preparation for new growth, so too has the voluntary sector been readied by people who, in a sense, have turned the ground from which the seeds of voluntary associations have sprouted and grown to maturity. Within Western societies, in other words, religion typically provided the initial motivation for forming, and the legitimation for maintaining, groups of believers united in accordance with principles of association distinct from those of the "principalities and powers" of the world. The religious principle that has contributed most to the burgeoning of the voluntary sector is the biblical notion of the covenant.[19] Central to both Christianity and Judaism, it depicts a God actively engaged in the struggles of history and insistent that people abide by ethical norms that supersede civil law. The covenant envisions a God concerned with human affairs, just as it presumes associations of the faithful called to privilege the "higher law" of divine mandate over temporal authority.[20] One of the founding figures in sociology, Max Weber, emphasized this theme in his groundbreaking study *Ancient Judaism*. In it, he described the Jewish prophets as early exemplars of religious leaders able to create the sort of social space from which kings' prerogatives could be criticized on the basis of alternative, frequently dissident, interpretations of God's will.[21] Similar observations have been made regarding the early Christian church. Commenting upon Jesus' admonition to render to God what is God's, Alfred North Whitehead got to the crux of the issue by noting incisively that "however limited may be the original intention of the saying, very quickly God was conceived as a principle of organization in complete disjunction from Caesar."[22]

Without question, the single most important development in curbing what would hence be rendered unto Caesar was the Radical Reformation of sixteenth- and seventeenth-century Europe, which spawned sectarian movements seeking to surpass the reforms achieved by Lutheranism and Calvinism. In addition to advocating intense moral purity and promoting a millennial expectation that served to relativize state authority, these more radical groups also disagreed with the ecclesiology embedded in those two main branches of Protestantism. Groups like the Baptists, Quakers, and Presbyterian Independents, to name the most influential, regarded their congregations as "free" or "gathered" churches constituted by authentic believers who had experienced spiritual regeneration. They were not state-established churches into which the masses were simply born. To the sects, Protestant ecclesiology generally smacked too much of a sinful Constantinianism, which elided church and state and did not sufficiently emphasize a freely chosen and rigorous understanding of church membership. They, on the other hand, were essentially voluntary associations made up of religious virtuosi who were expected to take very seriously their identities as members of covenanted communities. Indeed, the prolonged religious persecution and warfare that marked much of early modern European history is indicative of the seriousness with which these groups clung to their convictions.

Over time, the right to religious dissent came to be widely accepted. The Free Churches became tolerated and gained a level of autonomy from state control that, as other religious and secular groups followed suit, ultimately led to the emergence of the voluntary sector as a distinct component of the social ecology.

The Radical Reformation's impact in establishing a pluralistic voluntary sector does not end there. Stating the case baldly, James Luther Adams, who has done some of the most influential work on this topic, argues that "Nonconformity in modern religious history has made a decisive contribution to the achievement of freedom of association and the development of modern democracy."[23] This, he contends, is because the Free Churches engendered certain practices and ideas through which they functioned as a kind of seedbed of democracy. Four features of these churches were particularly influential. First, the congregational form of polity by which these churches governed themselves meant that each local church was entirely autonomous and sustained by the active participation and decision-making of its members. Second, they incorporated a separation of powers into their internal structures. The laity, commensurate with the idea of the "priesthood of all believers," not only ordained their own clergy but also reserved for themselves the power to make important decisions at congregational meetings. Third, their contention that collective decisions were made through the counsel of the Holy Spirit meant that significant attention was typically devoted to achieving consensus. Even when this was not possible, this pneumatic emphasis meant that minority views were at least listened to and taken seriously since they had the potential of being divinely inspired.[24] Finally, as these ideas and practices instilled the habits of self-governance, these churches often formed new voluntary associations extending beyond themselves. Originally these were formed to disseminate their ideas among members of the established churches in a manner similar to the modern interest group or political action committee, but soon this movement came to include associations for social reform as well.[25] The Free Churches, in sum, did not simply advance the cause of freedom of *religious* association. They also precipitated the demand for freedom of association in general, which in turn allowed the cultivation of democracy to proceed in earnest.

Fertilizing the Soil: Religion and Social Capital

Theorists have long stressed the importance of a healthy voluntary sector for sustaining democracy, and Alexis de Tocqueville's reflections on this question are still among the most memorable. Commenting upon an associative urge he considered unique to the United States, he writes:

> Americans of all ages, all stations in life, and all types of disposition are for-
> ever forming associations ... Americans combine to give fêtes, found semi-
> naries, build churches, distribute books, and send missionaries to the
> antipodes. Hospitals, prisons, and schools take shape in that way. Finally, if
> they want to proclaim a truth or propagate some feeling by the encourage-
> ment of a great example, they form an association. In every case, at the head
> of any new undertaking, where in France you would find the government or
> in England some territorial magnate, in the United States you are sure to find
> an association.[26]

While this may sound politically salubrious, Tocqueville was cautiously aware that the same "condition of equality" among American citizens that precipitated their democracy could also manifest itself as a perva-sive individualism potentially threatening to the continued viability of the republic. By retreating into their own private avocations and mate-rial pursuits, individuals without a sense of public responsibility, he feared, would leave the governing of social affairs to a centralized state, which would mark the de facto demise of democracy.

The most important safeguard against this threat of administrative despotism was, for Tocqueville, the mores (*moeurs*)—or "habits of the heart"—of the people. These include the ideas, dispositions, and habit-ual practices (such as volunteering and charitable giving) necessary for producing virtuous citizens and thus a strong tradition of participatory democracy. He considered religion fundamental for pushing those mores in the direction of public responsibility. "Religion is considered the guardian of mores," he writes, "and mores are regarded as the guarantee of the laws and pledge for the maintenance of freedom itself."[27] Put differently, religion tempers individualism by inculcating the notion that recognizing and fulfilling obligations to others is actually in one's own long-term self-interest. This is not moral heroism to Tocqueville but simply "self-interest properly understood." "Every religion," he elaborates, "also imposes on each man some obligations toward mankind, to be performed in common with the rest of mankind, and so draws him away, from time to time, from thinking about himself."[28] Given religion's capacity to deepen people's sense of public obligation and stimulate civic participation, it is little wonder he considered Americans' religiosity to be "the first of their *political* institutions." The health of the voluntary sector and the vigor of both the religious and secular institutions within it, he suggests, are compromised without a citizenry tutored by religious sensibilities.

The validity of Tocqueville's argument for the present day rests upon the fact that religious institutions provide what, in a widely influential article, political scientist Robert Putnam calls "social capital."[29] Defined as the "networks, norms, and social trust that facilitate coordination and cooperation for mutual benefit," social capital provides people with the resources that encourage and enable them to become more politically engaged citizens. Religious and other voluntary groups, he maintains, put people into contact with one another such that they are recruited into further civic activity, gain information about public issues and events, acquire a sense of generalized reciprocity and group loyalty, and develop feelings of personal efficacy by which their own efforts toward enhancing the common good are deemed worthwhile. Social capital, then, protects democracy because it empowers citizens. Because religious groups build social capital they, at least potentially, perform Tocqueville's role of enhancing democratic participation. Or, to use the aforementioned agrarian analogy, religion—along with performing the historical labor of tilling the soil—serves as a kind of fertilizer that stimulates the outcroppings of civic virtue and participation without which our communities would become ominously barren.

The evidence for this is truly compelling. One-third of Americans' volunteer labor and a remarkable two-thirds of all charitable giving by individuals are directed to religious organizations.[30] About half of this time and money is devoted to specifically religious activities such as liturgical ministry or catechetical education; the rest spills out into local communities in numerous ways.[31] For instance, 90 percent of congregations in the United States sponsor at least one social-service program.[32] Church members exceed nonmembers in volunteering and giving—not only to religious but to secular nonprofits as well. Among Americans currently active in social movements, a stunning two-thirds of them describe their motivations as being primarily religious.[33] One notable study actually discovered religious involvement to be the single best predictor of people's sense of attachment to their own communities.[34] Comparing the self-described most religious with the least religious, this survey revealed the former to be seven times more likely to attend a community meeting and about 50 percent more likely to vote in local elections, to discuss political issues with friends, and even to pay their own neighbors an occasional visit.

Evidence abounds to support Tocqueville's contention that religion contributes to the fecundity of the voluntary sector and molds people into more socially engaged citizens. Who could deny—and who does not have an ample supply of anecdotal evidence—that religion accounts for those "habits of the heart" encouraging people to gather together, forgive trespasses against them, walk the extra mile, turn the other cheek, discuss pressing social issues (usually over bland coffee) in the basements of churches throughout the land, and accept that we are indeed one another's keepers? Who, furthermore, could deny that these expressive values are truly religiously informed ones? What many are unsure about is precisely how religious organizations generate social capital among the citizens affiliated with them.

There are no magical formulas. One of the very basic things that churches (and synagogues and mosques) do is provide congregants with transferable skills enabling them to participate more fully and confidently in civic activities elsewhere. That churches can function as a kind of training ground for civic skills has been demonstrated by one national survey. It discovered that 12 percent of all adult members had written a letter and 18 percent had made a public presentation on behalf of their church, 32 percent had attended a church meeting where decisions were made, and 17 percent had actually planned such a meeting.[35]

Of course, such skills would remain underutilized if people did not actually *want* to employ them. Creating this desire is another forte of churches. No one has been more attentive to this than Robert Bellah and his co-authors, who, concerned that we are increasingly shaped by the "first language of American individualism," regret that typically in the United States "we put our own good, as individuals, as groups, as a nation ahead of the common good."[36] From the churches, though, shine glimmers of hope. Sustained within these "communities of memory" Bellah and his colleagues detect the "second languages" of the biblical and republican cultural traditions that may yet color our imaginations and direct our interests beyond ourselves. Political scientist James Reichley agrees. "From the standpoint of the public good," he maintains, "the most important service churches offer to secular life in a free society is to nurture moral values that help to humanize capitalism and give direction to democracy."[37] Churches can do this because they bring together groups of people who share expectations of altruistic behavior. They also coalesce stories that—depicting everything from fiery prophets denouncing social injustice to widows selflessly parting with their last mites to head-shaven bodhisattvas modeling the essence of compassion—function as cultural templates making such behavior both imaginable and desirable.

Making people aware of various social issues is a way churches parlay the desire to do something into actual doing. Pastors' sermons, congregational publications, and informal interactions are all means by which people gain information about community needs from their churches. For example, a National Election Studies survey measured the frequency with which church members reported that their pastors "speak out" on selected social issues. Three-fifths said their pastors addressed the problem of low-income housing, nearly two-fifths indicated their pastors spoke about disparate economic issues, and one-fifth said their pastors voiced their opinions on the topic of nuclear disarmament.[38] And the people in the pews seem to be listening. Consider a study of church members in Indiana.[39] Among those who indicated that their churches encouraged them to help others, a full nine-tenths said the churches did so by providing them with information about community needs.

Another way churches transform people's desire to help into actual helping is by serving as loci for recruitment into various forms of civic participation. For their nationwide survey on voluntarism, political scientists Sidney Verba, Kay Schlozman, and Henry Brady queried people about whether and where they had been asked to vote for a particular political candidate or to take some other political action (such as signing a petition, writing a letter, or contacting a public official) regarding a pressing issue. Fully one-third of Americans had been asked to do one or both of these things at their churches, whereas less than one-fifth were asked at their jobs and fewer than one in ten were asked at the other (nonpolitical) voluntary associations with which they were affiliated.[40] The impact of such appeals should not be underestimated since people who are asked to donate their time to various causes are actually about four times more likely to do so than those who are not asked at all.[41]

Churches, therefore, generate social capital by making their members more skilled, willing, and informed and by recruiting them into active roles within the voluntary sector. One final and critically important point is that churches also perform these functions more democratically than any other major institution in the United States today. Evidence for this too has been compiled by Verba and his colleagues. The title of their book, *Voice and Equality*, reminds us that—even though American politics operates according to strict one-person, one-vote equality—the degree to which different groups can voice their concerns to government varies by social class. Better-off citizens, for instance, can write checks to make sure their political opinions are heard. They are also disproportionately represented within civic organizations and within occupations that provide the requisite skills and opportunities for political engagement. In stark contrast, however, this research found that it is primarily the churches that do this for nonelite and thus politically underrepresented groups of people. In a nation with relatively weak labor unions and virtually no class-based political parties, their data reveal religion to be not the "opium of the people," as Karl Marx once disdainfully characterized it, but a kind of political amphetamine helping to mobilize less advantaged people within the voluntary sector.

New Harvest: A Bumper Crop of Paradenominational Organizations

In addition to creating the voluntary sector and enriching it with social capital, the influence of religion is apparent in the new institutions that continue to emerge there. This development tends to be overlooked by observers who focus on more familiar organizational harvests. Robert Putnam, for example, has correctly perceived religious institutions as generative of social capital. Yet he depicts them as sharing the declines in activism evident in politics, labor unions, parent-teacher associations, civic and fraternal organizations, and—despite the greater numbers of people bowling than ever before—even organized bowling leagues.

His is a warning that should not be taken lightly. Our essential interdependence with others and thus our responsibility to be informed
about issues affecting the common good surely unfolds in the company
of our fellows or not at all. Cultivating a dense civic culture is important if we are to avoid living in an "all against all" social milieu where
self-interests trump our altruistic impulses. But there is reason to pause.
The fact that fewer people are joining bowling leagues does not necessarily mean that they, as Putnam fears, are "bowling alone." Perhaps
they are bowling with people from their workplaces or neighborhoods,
or perhaps—exerting commendable efforts to solidify the purportedly
disintegrating family—they are using bowling alleys as places to recon-
nect with loved ones. Or it may even be that bowling leagues have
become too rigid or competitive and, therefore, bowlers who leave them
actually demonstrate a greater, more authentic commitment to the
game.

Similar caveats can be made about religious institutions. Putnam rue-
fully informs his readers that "net participation by Americans, both in
religious services and in church-related groups, has declined modestly
(by perhaps a sixth) since the 1960s."[42] Yet he does not notice the emergence of new social forms of religion that may not be so church-
centered. People, he seems to imply, must be doing everything from
praying alone to (if it is possible) apostatizing alone. Little heed is paid
to the possibility that they might be living out their religious values in
different contexts, in different company—but not alone—and perhaps,
as was suggested with the case of bowling, demonstrating a greater,
more authentic commitment to those values all the while.

Paradenominational organizations are an important example of a
social form of religion to which Putnam and other theorists have given
little consideration. These are religiously inspired, though usually ecumenical, voluntary associations with explicitly public missions. They
include organizations that stir social activism such as Bread for the
World, a lobbying group on hunger issues, and Pax Christi, an advocacy group for peace and disarmament. They include organizations like
the Saint Vincent DePaul Society and Habitat for Humanity®, which
attend to people's basic needs. Within the community of the religious
right, they promote everything from moral family-policy legislation
(Focus on the Family) to the charismatic gifts of glossolalia and faith
healing (the Full Gospel Business Men's Fellowship). They represent
the concerns of various occupational groups through the National

Association of Church Business Administrators, the Christian Legal Society, the Christian Chiropractors Association, and the Fellowship of Christian Athletes. They advocate for the social rights of such disparate groups as women (Task Force on Equality of Women in Judaism), gays and lesbians (Dignity, Affirmation), the elderly (Catholic Golden Age), African Americans (American Baptist Black Caucus), and numerous others. The list could go on indefinitely. The key point is that these paradenominational groups are manifestations of an increasingly significant social form of religion in the United States today. It is also a form that appears to be just as much a product of people's authentic, religiously informed commitments as it is a vehicle by which those commitments are invigorated and institutionalized within the larger society.

The scholar perhaps most attentive to this social form of religion has been sociologist Robert Wuthnow.[43] He notes that while religious voluntary associations like the prayer-meeting movement and abolitionist movement emerged during the early nineteenth century, they were never structured into formal organizations. The forerunners of paradenominational groups were thus the foreign and domestic mission societies also formed during that time. Organizations like the American Bible Society (1816), the American Tract Society (1823), the American Sunday School Union (1824), the American Education Society (1826), and the American Temperance Union (1836) qualify as the first paradenominational groups insofar as they focused on narrowly defined objectives, tended to transcend denominational barriers in attracting supporters, and had some centralized coordination of local chapters, which were often dispersed nationally.

Fully enumerating these groups today, Wuthnow concedes, would be an unmanageable undertaking since they are so varied and pursue their goals in such a vast array of institutional settings. Looking only at the most prominent, he discovered 800 paradenominational groups with IRS tax-exempt status as religious nonprofits and ministries of national scope. This is certainly a impressive number. It looms even larger in light of the fact that no more than several dozen such groups existed at the close of the Civil War, less than 150 had been formed by the turn of the century, and only half of the present number were in operation immediately following World War II. The public's participation in these groups is also significant, although this too is difficult to quantify since these organizations seldom keep records of their constituencies. But there is national survey data on the public's involvement in ten different categories of social ministries, into which most paradenominational groups are likely to fall.[44] Making use of this data, Wuthnow found that most American adults have heard of these ministries and a surprising one-third of them had participated in an organization belonging in one of the ten categories. To put things into perspective, this is a larger proportion of the population than that which attends religious services on a regular weekly basis. Consider also that the impressive 7 percent of Americans who report involvement in world hunger ministries, for example, is comparable to the 7 percent who are members of churches in the Southern Baptist Convention, the nation's largest Protestant denomination.[45]

There are discernible reasons for the proliferation of these groups. First, the increased professionalization of religious workers means they are now increasingly inclined to form organizations attending to their own concerns (recall the National Association of Church Business Administrators) as well as to the needs of the people they are trained to serve. The growing tendency for religious people to form organizations imitating or challenging other groups is another factor. To give an illustration, groups like Catholic Women for the ERA imitate some of the work of the secular National Organization for Women (NOW), but their efforts are countered by other paradenominational groups, such as the largely evangelical American Coalition for Traditional Values. None of these groups could approach their actual levels of influence if it were not for a third factor: technological innovation. Computers, direct-mail capabilities, and the mass media have permitted organizations to spread their messages more widely. That average citizens are now capable of responding more effectively to these messages due to higher levels of educational attainment and increased affluence is a fourth factor. Next, and very importantly, the postwar expansion of the state's role in such areas as education, social welfare, and equal-rights legislation has meant, first, that religious constituencies wanting to have a significant say in policy decisions have had to form paradenominational groups to do so. Second, given the previously mentioned "new federalist" structure of social welfare, paradenominational groups have also emerged as prominent delivery conduits for government-funded services and entitlement programs.[46]

There is one final, specifically religious reason to consider. These groups have become more popular because they are a means by which people "put legs to" their religious commitments and infuse the secular public sphere with a language and sensibility attuned to the sacred. In a manner that differs from congregations and denominational structures, paradenominational groups have become important institutional vehicles by which the sacred is publicly represented for people through their own everyday actions within the voluntary sector.[47]

Representing the sacred is no trivial matter. Indeed, even defining it is problematic since it refers to those things that are considered most holy, numinous, and set apart. According to sociologist Emile Durkheim, religion itself is based upon the distinction people inevitably make between things that, by virtue of being embedded in the routines of everyday life, are profane and those that are imbued with the extraordinary character of the sacred.[48] When perceived by individuals, the sacred confers a sense of the transcendent, of something beyond the self that seems to put ordinary life into an all encompassing context and provide it with greater meaning.

Whether this sense of sacredness is linked to a supernatural being is a theological question that for many remains shrouded in mystery. Still, the sense of the sacred that intermittently insinuates itself into people's everyday realities and consciousnesses needs to be adequately represented in order to be a feature of the social world. Without places to reside, the sacred has no home in a given society and is ultimately evicted from people's minds, which are left to ponder the clatter of busy quasi-certitudes, routinized tasks, and perhaps a future appointment or two. Institutions provide the residential structures for the sacred, and paradenominational groups are becoming important for that purpose. They advocate rights, champion causes, evangelize the populace, pursue avocations, lobby Congress, raise awareness, convene the public, and even build houses—all on the basis of religious beliefs and concerns. In that sense, they represent something beyond the confines of the ordinary. They point to values and motivations that transcend the practical concerns of the people who contribute to and participate with them. Paradenominational organizations, then, represent the sacred because they remind us that goodness and obligation and service continue to exist in the world and that we are better than our daily, relatively profane activities require us to be.

These groups function as emblems of personal transcendence even when we are not involved with them. They make the evening news, they occupy the free time (and maybe the conversations) of our neighbors, and their slogans and entreaties for support decorate the bumpers of the cars that surround us in traffic jams. Even if we rarely get off our living room couches, these groups tell us that we live in a society replete with a transformative power for benevolence, as evidenced by the fact that others are somehow moved to get off their couches. For people active in these organizations, the sacred becomes a reality in their lives because it is institutionalized. Paradenominational groups make the sacred real because they mobilize resources that make people effective, they establish practices that people enact, they devise social roles that people fill, and they enliven the religiously informed symbolic frameworks people use to interpret and find meaning in their voluntary efforts. By institutionalizing an appreciation of the sacred, these groups make it an objectifiable component of the social world. As this appreciation enters people's awareness or incites their active commitment, it can become a part of their subjective identities as well. Institutions such as these construct a home for the sacred within our society. Paradoxically, it is a home that individuals construct while, at the same time, this sense of the sacred constructs individuals who are accustomed to the presence in their midst of something larger than themselves.

Paradenominational Organizations as Religious Adaptations to the Climate of Modernity

Positing that paradenominational groups are gaining in significance as the public face of American religion because they represent the sacred does not mean that other kinds of religiously affiliated institutions do not perform a similar function. The key point is that this paradenominational form of religious commitment is growing for a reason: It is well adapted to the climate of modernity.

Without attempting casually to sum up the modern climate (or what some see as a burgeoning "postmodern" era), we can specify certain changes that have led to the success of paradenominational groups within the voluntary sector. At the most basic level, it is critical to understand that modern societies are institutionally differentiated societies.[49] The separation of such social entities as the state, market, science, and religion into autonomous institutional spheres, with their own values and means for performing their respective roles, was a dramatic shift from prior social arrangements.[50] In medieval society, a more unified schema prevailed, held together by the hegemonic worldview of

Western Christendom. In general, this was a profoundly undifferentiated social arrangement. Kings ruled by divine mandate, not by more inclusive political processes. Collecting interest was considered usury and therefore sinful, not a legitimate return on a financial investment. Galileo, among others, could be tried by Church tribunals for having the effrontery to disprove false cosmological theories. Religion, in short, was not only inseparable from the other institutional spheres, it dictated the very means by which they could operate.

That is not the case today. Rather than denoting an overall decline in religious belief and practice—something that the data thoroughly refute for the American context—the notion that ours is a secular society means that religion has become one differentiated sphere among others. Secularization basically amounts to an inability of religious authority and values to influence the other social spheres as thoroughly as they did in the past.[51] But how does this historical process account for the kind of climate in which paradenominational groups can emerge and thrive? Asking this question requires consideration of three additional characteristics of the modernization process: rationalization, pluralization, and subjectivization. They are consequences of societal differentiation; directly related to the issue of religious change, they are also prominently featured within the sociological literature on secularization.[52] Here I will summarize them briefly and explain how they have contributed to the emergence of paradenominational groups in the United States today.

Rationalization

The differentiation of modern society means that, as well as being untethered from one another, these distinct institutional spheres gravitate in the direction of incremental rationalization. This term, rationalization, refers to the tendency for both individuals and organizations to plan their actions so as to maximize the efficiency and effectiveness of the means used to reach a particular end. As discussed earlier, the state and market spheres are directed toward rationalized methods of wielding power and accruing profit. Rational control systems can also be found in other institutions. Think, for instance, of the bureaucratized and results-oriented character of knowledge that predominates when colleges become transformed into "research" institutions. What rationalized institutions have in common is an instrumental ethos that discourages such nonrationalized expressive values as caring, meaningfulness, and piety, which are typically considered irrelevant to their daily functioning.

This reality has important consequences for religious belief. The rationalization of public institutions demands that modern people assume an analytic and pragmatic cognitive style often at odds with the experience of the sacred that is characteristic of religious worldviews. As heirs of the Enlightenment and the scientific revolution, people today have generally come to assume that all phenomena can be explained rationally, and they are less likely to rely upon magic, myths, miracles, holy objects, or religious authorities to negotiate their everyday lives. Because a rationalist cognitive style governs the major institutional spheres of society, it largely undermines the credibility of religious meaning systems and religious ways of determining truth. Faced with what has been referred to as the "disenchantment of the world,"[53] individuals remain free to keep their own private lives enchanted with as many religious beliefs and practices as they like. But when interacting with the larger social world, they are significantly constrained to do so on the world's own rationalized terms.

This might seem to make modern societies increasingly uninhabitable for religious institutions intent upon engendering a sense of the sacred in public. Yet such an assessment would underestimate the adaptability of religion. Rather than being corrosive to religious commitments, disenchanted institutional domains have actually proven to be catalysts for paradenominational groups. People do not form such groups for the purpose of determining the extent to which Jesus was fully human or fully divine. We do not receive direct-mail solicitations requesting support for groups organized to determine the truth of certain miracle stories found in the gospels or to persuade the public of their position regarding the virginity of Mary. There are no official taskforces charged with ascertaining, once and for all, the precise number of angels that can dance upon the end of a pin. Such issues may have mobilized the energies of people in the past, but modern people are left with primarily secular concerns to move them toward action. Involved as they are with rectifying political and economic injustices, perceived cultural maladies, and threats to individual rights, paradenominational groups are overwhelmingly oriented to this secular, disenchanted world, but in ways that do not exclude religious values.[54] The sacred, in a sense, is discovered and represented—inhaled and exhaled—within the atmosphere of secularity itself.

In addition to influencing the social settings in which paradenominational groups operate, rationalization also informs the methods by which they operate. Even when they are not functioning particularly well or meeting individual needs, denominations and congregations can still count on the financial support of people who are denominationally loyal or who have strong neighborhood ties. This is much less true of paradenominational groups. They win support by virtue of their own merits and, unlike those other religious institutions, have to compete with secular organizations doing similar things. Since most paradenominational groups stay afloat by appealing to the public for financial assistance with specific projects, they usually feel pressed to accomplish those projects as expediently as possible in order to justify future contributions.[55] As anyone who reads the promotional literature of such groups can attest, they often make special efforts to assure their constituencies just how efficient and resourceful they are and how little they spend on operating costs (for staff, office space, and the like) that could detract from their stated goals. The implied message: The sacred is most clearly manifest in purposive, instrumental endeavors to get things done within the workaday world. It is about the effective, no-nonsense activity of people who know what to do and have learned—mostly through their secular educations and occupational experiences—how to do it. This understanding of the sacred is not necessarily any less sacred than that expressed in theological doctrine, both of the past and present, but it is different. And, to the extent that sacredness is borne by paradenominational groups, it exists amid a critical tension. These groups provide a glimpse of the sacred for those with eyes to see while also risking the possibility that it may ultimately be lost as the blinders of efficiency and public accountability become affixed to their organizational cultures.

Pluralization

While the cognitive style associated with widespread societal rationalization presents a problem *for* religious belief, another characteristic of modernity, cultural pluralism, presents the problem *of* religious beliefs for paradenominational groups. In the absence of any single worldview able to claim monopoly status, myriad ideologies and traditions have proliferated within modern society. Increased urbanization, mass communications, and greater opportunities for travel have brought diverse subcultures into proximity with one another to an extent previously unimaginable. The consequences for religious belief have been tremendous. Rather than being acquainted with a single religion endowed with a taken-for-granted aura of certainty, the modern person is exposed to a plurality of religious and secular worldviews that, insofar as they appear to be plausible ways of seeing the world, undermine the unquestioned adherence to any one of them.[56]

Let us look at this situation more closely. Surrounded by a multitude of feasible worldviews, people are accosted with what Peter Berger called "the heretical imperative," the necessity of choosing a particular belief system while cognizant that it is one possible choice among others. This makes for a precarious, tentative venture. Instead of giving us continual social reinforcement for our religious convictions, pluralization brings regular interaction with individuals holding divergent views. Their ways of life and perspectives on the world are likely to be so different that they fail to provide the kind of social confirmation that subjective and inevitably chosen beliefs require to be believed without question. And question them we do. The pluralistic climate of modernity brings us to the realization that our own perspective on truth is just that: a single perspective among many others. With the noted seventeenth-century mathematician and philosopher Blaise Pascal, we are brought (sometimes dragging our feet) to the realization that truth on one side of the Pyrenees is error on the other.[57] Thus, increasingly aware of the short distance between truth and error, people tend to cling less dogmatically to what they consider to be the truth and are generally more conciliatory toward others who appear to dwell—although fewer of us can be sure—in error.

Paradenominational groups once again prove themselves to be adaptive to this modern situation. In giving pride of place to their public ministries they, in effect, sidestep theological precepts and instead accentuate the ethical ramifications of diverse religious beliefs. They set aside dogmatism in an attempt to better meet the needs of a pluralistic society. For example, an evangelical Christian and her unchurched neighbor may be involved with the same hunger-relief organization. One may ground her commitment on Jesus' Sermon on the Mount while the other may have been moved by a United Nations report on rampant malnutrition in certain parts of the world or by a TV commercial featuring Sally Struthers. Whatever the case, the neighbors are able to reach a rapprochement because their shared ethical convictions are given priority over the divergent belief systems that they may hold rather loosely.

The sacred, paradenominational groups seem to suggest, is most adequately represented by ethical mandates largely derivable from common sense rather than from distinct theological doctrines. It is not the province of any one religious worldview to monopolize ultimate truth. These groups sacralize their ethical causes and make them accessible to ordinary people with a diversity of motivations. They are thus ideal organizations for mobilizing ordinary and diverse people within a pluralistic society. As with the issue of rationalization, however, pluralism tends to precipitate a critical tension within these groups. They must find a balance between the virtue of being nondogmatic and the vice of being so inclusive that they are no longer distinguishable from the larger society. Without the powerful symbols and narratives provided by particular normative traditions, they may fail to capture the imaginations and commitment of supporters If that is the case, paradenominational groups may generate the kind of sound and fury that not only signifies nothing extraordinary but that accomplishes nothing at the same time.

Subjectivization

At one time common wisdom held that, because of the increasing rationalization of social institutions, religious beliefs and values would recede from public affairs and become sequestered in the realm of private life. Religion, it was thought, would take the form of saying grace before meals, baptizing and marrying off children, and burying those loved ones we happen to outlive. It would function, as they say, merely as a "haven in a heartless world." But this purported common wisdom is actually neither. It was never particularly wise because the adaptability of religion has confounded the prognostications about its future. Nor was it ever particularly common since, if nothing else, the proliferation of paradenominational groups in the United States indicates that it is just as common for people to cast their religious commitments into the fray of public concerns.

Although not entirely privatized, a more nuanced look reveals religion to be quite subjectivized within modern society. No doubt this is partly due to the way cultural pluralism has loosened the grip of "objective" religious truth. It may also reflect an emerging (especially since the 1960s) "expressive individualism" in American culture exalting the unrestrained pursuit of new experience, personal autonomy, and self-realization.[58] Whatever the case, it is clear that a focus on the self now tends to dominate the other, once-prominent emphasis in American religion—community belonging. Discerning meaning in the major events of the life cycle, enjoying a sense of emotional and psychological well-being, experimenting with various paths to self-fulfillment, "finding oneself"—these concerns focused on the self are rife among people professing to have religious sensibilities.

This third element of the modern religious climate is also partly responsible for the astounding growth of paradenominational groups. To understand this, keep in mind that transformations in the self need to be felt in order to be real. Little wonder that more and more people are flocking to religious forms that provide them with distinct, sometimes powerful, personal experiences of the sacred.[59] Immediately springing to mind are the spiritual practices associated with Eastern religions (such as meditation, yoga, and macrobiotic diets) and branches of the human-potential movement (*est*, Scientology), which have become popular by holding out promises of deeper, if not more esoteric, religious experiences. The same is true of the rapidly growing Pentecostal churches, for which ecstatic experiences are normative and understood within an explicitly Christian framework as gifts of the Holy Spirit. These examples and others suggest that the experiential is becoming more than the means to a spiritual end; it is becoming an end in itself. It is also something paradenominational groups offer their constituencies. Whether it is by building houses with Habitat or holding mass outside of a missile site with Pax Christi, these groups accost people with experiences they seldom have in everyday life. Even if their group is involved in more mundane activities—say a letter-writing campaign—when done in the company of others, people feel a more palpable sense of their own convictions. Participation, putting time into timeless ethical values, making a difference in a seemingly indifferent world—these are the kinds of experiences that make these groups popular and allow people to feel like the subjects of their own religious lives.

This emphasis on the self is also apparent in people's sense of entitlement to religious "preference," where once they would have remained in the faith communities into which they were born.[60] Sociologically speaking, the limits to this kind of religious enfranchisement were once set by ascription. People's social and cultural backgrounds helped determine the faiths they would claim for themselves and, therefore, functioned to restrict the possibility or even the desire for religious selectivity. But such sociocultural attachments have weakened considerably since World War II. Rising educational levels, opportunities for class and geographic mobility, and family instability have all slackened traditional communal ties, including people's loyalties to religious communities. Now people "happen to be" a member of this or that religious community if they claim membership at all.[61] And even when they do associate with a particular religious institution, it is much more likely than in days past that they will privilege their own spiritual journeys over adherence to group norms. People are now free to choose among religious institutions and teachings, as if at a smorgasbord, rather than accept them as a single, unified set of values handed on by a community of believers.

Paradenominational organizations have adapted to this world of finicky religious consumers. By bringing specific ethical values into the public sphere, they appeal to people who hold those same values but do not want them to be mixed into a conglomeration of others they may not hold. The vast diversity of paradenominational groups, all engaged in religiously informed ethical pursuits, allows religious beliefs and values to be segmented into distinct units able to be picked and chosen from to suit individual spiritual needs.

Herein lies the danger of subjectivization for paradenominational groups. Their willingness to voice religiously derived expressive values in public can serve as a corrective for a retreat into the private realm and for a religious fixation on the self. If they succeed in this mission, there is reason to believe that these groups can become institutional sources for social capital, passing on a greater knowledge of public affairs, imbuing individuals with civic virtue, and convincing them that the rationalized social structures that shape our lives are not impervious to religious values emphasizing human dignity over instrumentality. As salutatory as this sounds, there is another possibility to ponder. These organizations may simply become vehicles for enhancing the personal well-being and self-realization of their participants and may jettison the larger communal purposes they usually claim to advance. Participants' expressive individualism may become separated from public obligation and degenerate into a therapeutic discourse that, despite the occasional religious platitude, is principally centered upon ensuring that they all feel good about themselves.

While some might say that the result would be an insipid, self-indulgent brand of religiosity, that is not the point. The crux of the issue is that sacralizing the individual self can lead, ironically, to the dehumanization of society. No one saw this more clearly than sociologist Thomas

Luckmann, who argued that self-realization had become the "invisible religion" of modernity. But, he continued, it came at the cost of leaving rationalized social structures unchecked and thus increasingly inimical to human flourishing. He offers few consolations regarding the kind of future that religious subjectivization may herald: "The modern sacred cosmos legitimates the retreat of the individual into the 'private sphere' and sanctifies his subjective 'autonomy.' Thus it inevitably reinforces the autonomous functioning of the primary institutions. By bestowing a sacred quality upon the increasing subjectivity of human existence it supports not only the secularization but also what we called the dehumanization of the social structure."[62] At their very best, paradenominational groups, bugling religious values and narratives, embolden individuals and mobilize them so that they are not satisfied with a retreat into the private sphere. In good Tocquevillian fashion, these groups may shape people's mores by moving individuals to see their own good as wedded to that of the others around them. Contrary to Luckmann's pessimistic expectation that religious values would become invisible and innocuous features of personal identities, they may actually become visibly institutionalized by paradenominational groups and thus capable of stimulating people's imaginations and patterning their actions.

Perhaps these things will happen. It would be speculative to suggest anything more definite because subjectivization presents these groups with an unsettling and unsettlable tension between an expressive infatuation with the self and a contrary insistence that religious values entail public responsibility. This is a tension just as rationalization presents these groups with the tension between discerning religious meaning within the secular world and being co-opted by secular organizational methods. Another tension is that accompanying pluralization, between an inclusive embrace of different values and a potentially anemic adherence to any set of particular religious values. Tensions abound in any organization. These tensions are particularly compelling within paradenominational organizations because they have assumed part of the burden of representing the sacred in our society. Obviously, they do not do this alone; churches, denominational structures, religious schools, monasteries, and public rituals all still have a role to play. Yet the role of paradenominational groups has expanded—not by divine fiat but because they represent a social form of religion that has steeled itself to the secular chill of modern times. As some might put it, while modernity constrains some institutional structures from growing successfully, it enables others to do so as long as they are able to take advantage of whatever opportunities and resources the new conditions afford.[63] Paradenominational groups have done this by relocating the sacred within a modern world that, marked by the constraints of rationalization, pluralization, and religious subjectivization, many have considered to be successfully exorcised.

Religion abounds now, as it long has, in a voluntary sector created historically by religious dissent and enriched by a steady provision of religiously derived values and social capital. This sector has nurtured various social forms of religion as well as more secular associations, all of which have borne expressive values that, like seeds carried by the air, seldom grow on the rockier ground of the state and market sectors. Paradenominational groups are among the voluntary sector's most interesting and vibrant yields; this much has been discussed. The further question of how successful such groups are in enabling religious values to flourish and to escape being beaten down by other considerations is one that cannot be answered from afar. Rather, it is preferable to stop among their thick rows, stoop toward one of them, and examine it more closely. This is the primary intent of the following chapters, which will consider Habitat for Humanity, a paradenominational group that has grown so rapidly and extensively that it could hardly fail to capture the eye of anyone accustomed to lingering in this vast voluntary field.

2

The Founding Vision of Habitat for Humanity®

Rosalynn and I are often asked, "Why do you work with Habitat? What do you get out of it?" I was president of the U.S. for four years, but I get a lot more recognition for building houses in partnership with poor people in need than I have ever gotten before. Habitat is not a sacrifice that we make for others. It is a blessing for those of us who volunteer to help others. It gives me a life of excitement and pleasure, and adventure and unpredictability, to put it mildly.

Former President Jimmy Carter

A Scene from the Dakota Prairie

When Habitat's best-known volunteer discusses the cause of low-cost housing construction, he sounds no different from most people who have experienced the personal rewards that come from helping others. Yet his uniqueness becomes apparent when he sets aside a week to employ his reportedly considerable carpentry skills in building modest homes, and draws a full 1,575 other volunteers from forty-eight states and five countries into the same task. This is precisely what occurred during the 1994 Jimmy Carter Work Project in Eagle Butte, a small town located within the Cheyenne River Indian Reservation in South Dakota.[1] The townspeople, mostly members of the Lakota Sioux tribe, had become familiar with Habitat for Humanity® when a local affiliate established an office in town about a year before. But because the Okiciyapi Tipi (translated "helping each other build homes") affiliate had still not built or rehabilitated a single house, the town was hardly familiar with the sort of frenetic activity that Habitat could generate during a single week in mid-July.

This was to change soon enough. Weeks prior to this intensive house-raising project—a "blitz build," in Habitat vernacular—building materials had been trucked in, the land was surveyed and cleared, sewage and electrical lines were installed, and a horseshoe-shaped road was constructed in order to connect what would soon be thirty new three- and four-bedroom homes into a single neighborhood. Rather than resting upon the concrete slabs typical of much Habitat construction, these dwellings were designed to provide protection against severe winter conditions and to accommodate extended families, which meant that basements also had to be dug and poured in advance.

With this work complete, the scene at this initial stage of the building process had an eerie readiness about it. Thirty huge concrete-lined ditches were waiting to function as the foundations for newly built houses and, according to most expectations, for the newly invigorated lives of their occupants as well. Signs in front of each lot, two-thirds of an acre in size, announced the names of the new residents and of the groups that financed and would typically send volunteers to help with the construction of that particular house. These included such private corporations as Dow Chemical, Coldwell Banker, and Fannie Mae, various foundations, a number of civic groups both within the tribe and without, and religious groups ranging from the Sisters of the Presentation to the Church of the Latter Day Saints. Enormous stacks of construction materials—two-by-fours, plywood sheets, boxes of shingles, vinyl siding, interior drywall, windows and doors, preassembled triangular roof trusses—were all assembled in readiness. The yellow and white circus-sized tent for morning prayer and noon lunches, the portable sheds housing all manner of building tools, the water jugs and consequently the rows of port-a-potties, the smaller tents used for selling Habitat books and other paraphernalia and for attending to inevitable first-aid needs—everything smacked of quiet potential. The only thing moving or even slightly audible was a warm evening wind unexpectedly stirring the prairie dust like some grand, heaving breath.

Things sprang to life on the Sunday afternoon before the blitz week began. Arriving seemingly from every direction, volunteers clustered at the local elementary school, where the registration process was being facilitated by scores of staff members from Habitat's international head-quarters in Americus, Georgia. The mood was electric. These people had applied months in advance for the privilege of donating their $150 registration fee and a week of hot, dirty, and often strenuous labor, and they seemed to consider themselves fortunate for being among the half of all applicants who had been chosen to do so. Wherever one looked, people were introducing themselves to one another, laughing, and shaking hands. Some came in groups, some with their families, and some alone. They were men and women of all ages (although predominantly white), and they wore Habitat hats and T-shirts with the names of local affiliates from all over the country. Scurrying about was a legion of reporters and camera operators, drawn primarily to President and Mrs. Carter and, later in the week, to such hammer-swinging notables as news anchor Tom Brokaw, a native South Dakotan, and the then-Secretary of Housing and Urban Development, Henry Cisneros. At one point that afternoon, approximately 150 bicyclists—one group riding from Minneapolis and another from Winnipeg—pedaled into town with a group of Lakota runners leading the way to show the tribe's respect. The cyclists, after all, had raised more than $120,000 through pledges to be used for building Habitat houses, both in their own cities and in Eagle Butte.

The excitement only grew when the volunteers met in the school auditorium to be addressed by Habitat's energetic founder, Millard Fuller, President Carter, key project leaders, and a number of representatives from the tribal community. There was a festive, pep-rally air to the proceedings, but the main focus was unmistakably the work that needed to be done and how best to go about it. Participants had already been assigned a house to work on for the week; now they were reminded to meet with their house leader and fellow builders after the general meeting and early the following morning. Mandatory safety rules were enumerated. The week's building schedule was outlined. Admonitions against shoddy labor were made. Emphasis was placed equally on the imperatives of keeping busy and of interacting with others, especially with the eventual homeowner families, who would work with the volunteers. The point was to create a sense of community as well as to complete the building project. A nearly palpable feeling of exhilaration mixed with a let's-get-this-job-done seriousness. Even as a purportedly "objective" participant observer, it was difficult for me to avoid getting caught up in the camaraderie that comes when people unite for a shared purpose. Arguing for the social necessity of voluntarism and philanthropy in the nineteenth century, philosopher William James once called for a "moral equivalent of war" to eradicate poverty and other obstacles to full human flourishing.[2] The Habitat volunteers in that auditorium appeared to be girding themselves for an engagement of warlike ferocity: an overwhelming assault upon the substandard housing conditions afflicting thirty Native American families. The approximately six hundred two-person dome tents they set up on the school grounds that afternoon reinforced this impression, resembling the encampment of an invading force preparing to spring to action at the morrow's first light.

Is this description too panegyrical, too uncritical? Maybe. This book will offer a critical, yet appreciative, analysis of this paradenominational group, but it is impossible to understand the success of annual events like this one, and perhaps of Habitat more generally, without suspending one's criticisms long enough to gain a feel for the organization. In the process, it becomes clear why the people I interviewed described Habitat in such acclamatory terms, as a "sexy organization" or a "public relations heaven" or an "unbelievably contagious experience." Take the first day of building, for instance. By 7:30 Monday morning, most volunteers and all of the Habitat staff had eaten breakfast and were assembled within and around the imposing yellow and white tent at the worksite. However different their everyday lives may have been, on that morning they appeared like a single corps. Clad in a motley assortment of work clothes, each wore a work belt from which dangled a hammer and perhaps a carpenter's square, as well as sundry leather pouches for nails, tape measures, and other necessities. Among their ranks were skilled builders who, as frequent volunteers at Habitat events, were accustomed to sipping coffee from a Styrofoam cup and engaging in nonchalant conversation before a day of physical labor. Most of the others, if honest, would count themselves among the construction novices; they exhibited the eagerness and perhaps trepidation that come with novel experiences.

As happened every morning of "the build," things quieted down with the beginning of devotions. Hats were removed and heads bowed as Millard Fuller drew parallels between the work they were about to undertake and that of Jesus, the carpenter and rabbi from Nazareth. Then all guffawed at Fuller's reminder of Habitat's single theological doctrine: Anyone driving around in a car without a Habitat bumper sticker is living in sin. While not always so humorous, such assurances that theological differences matter less than the unifying power of "love in action" are ritualized aspects of most of Habitat's engagements with the wider public. This message was not lost on one of the tribal spiritual leaders, Arvol Looking Horse, whose opening prayer acknowledged the capacity for such action to help overcome cultural differences and even lead to widespread reconciliation between the white and Native American populations. The very reservation within which the volunteers stood was testimony to the injustice wrought from that clash of cultures. But on that particular morning, he raised his voice to assure everyone present: "On behalf of the Lakota people, I want to say that what you are doing here is creating a good environment. I am really happy to see it. I pray that we would continue to help each other and heal." More nods of assent and then a chorus of amens filled the air. In a society grappling with seemingly insuperable differences between people—with multiculturalism, identity politics, religiously waged culture wars—it is small wonder that many would be drawn to a cause that, in its sheer practicality and common sense, supersedes those differences and provides rituals of common purpose for them to enact.

When, on that first day, devotions ended and the group dispersed, some running, in thirty slightly different directions, another reason for Habitat's appeal became clear—the energy. Soon the volunteers had jumped pell-mell into the fray, and the senses came alive with the to-and-fro of questions and commands, the smell of newly cut wood, and eventually sweat stinging the eyes, accompanied all the while by the quickened syncopation of hammering. In time the buzz of activity at the work site became practically dizzying—people hammering on rooftops, painting porches, sawing boards to the side; others rushing off to find sixteen-penny nails or maybe another roll of insulation; an older gentleman inquiring if you would like some Gatorade while four sorority sisters carrying a bathtub simultaneously cast an impatient glare in your direction as if to say, "Hey, this thing's heavy, move it or lose it!" Particularly on the first day, during which each site was speedily transformed from a hollow foundation to an entirely framed and boarded house, the event took on the spirit of an old-fashioned barn raising. The results were immediately discernible. It all seemed so basic, so cooperative. Every now and then, someone would catch another's eye, notice that they were both covered with dirt or paint or some species of spackling dust, and simply start laughing. Maybe they would sit on a sawhorse and talk for a moment or two.

This also is part of Habitat's appeal. People who might not ordinarily interact with one another find an opportunity to do so. Evangelical Christians and agnostic seekers, CEOs and college students, rural folk and city dwellers, skilled carpenters and everyone else—all seemed uniformly intent on such basic, but critical, concerns as getting the nails in straight and keeping the vinyl siding from taking flight in an occasional afternoon squall. The whole project, similar to a rock concert or tent revival, was a "happening." It took on the feel of a ritualized public drama in which distinctions based on race, class, or status seemed to be momentarily suspended by an equalizing collective energy. Anthropologist Victor Turner refers to such experiences of immediate, non-hierarchical relatedness within groups as "communitas." In his view, it is usually a temporary state but one that is important for critiquing the patterns of social power operative at all other times.[3]

The most obvious example of communitas was provided by the homeowner families, children included, who helped to build their own homes (as well as a central playground area) alongside the overwhelmingly middle-class volunteers. Working feverishly at house number eight were José and Sonya Anaya and their five children. The entire family was living in a small tent with duct tape covering its many holes, but they seemed to blend in comfortably with the group from the San Francisco–based PMI Mortgage Insurance Company. At house number ten, E. J. Gunville, a substitute teacher, janitor, and father of four, was amazed at the satisfaction the volunteers from the Larson Foundation derived from helping him to build his family a home. "They kept telling me," he later mused, "that they got more out of it than I did. I thought to myself, 'they must really be feeling good.'"[4] Everyone blends in and everyone can get something out of this work, the basic message reads. No one symbolizes this better than President Carter who, with the former First Lady, spent the week working at house number one with Isaac and Cindy Brown Bear and their four children. His well-known impatience with reporters, disdain for fanfare or interruptions, and his willingness to spend late nights kneeling in a homeowner family's bathroom laying tile or preparing the walls for volunteers to paint the following day are all treasured bits of Habitat lore. They symbolize that there are no distinctions here. Everyone is divested of their social roles, even those bearing incomparable political power, and they become, albeit temporarily, part of a greater whole of concerned people. The Sioux elders who, during the ceremony at the conclusion of the building week, bestowed an eagle feather upon Carter and adopted him into their tribe understood this. After careful consideration, they also gave him a new name, Waihakta, which is translated as "He waits for us." In apparent agreement with the general Habitat ethos, they seemed to equate greatness not with striking out on one's own in some distinctive way but rather in waiting for others, agreeing to be part of the greater community, and then endeavoring to strike out together.

The downplaying of individual differences, the high energy, and the flouting of social hierarchy are all ritualized aspects of the blitz build that function to prioritize the importance of caring for others over other, lesser concerns. Christian or Jew, conservative or liberal, white or Native American—it does not matter, so lend a hand. The work site is charged with activity because America's housing needs are urgent and require the sort of energy generated when people unite to meet a problem head on. Former residents of the White House and future residents of Habitat houses look surprisingly alike in their overalls, flannel shirts, and work boots. Their shared effort in meeting human needs is more noticeable than whatever status or privileges they do not share. Service and caring for others are the heart of the Habitat ethos, and nothing represents and enacts these values more vividly than a project such as this one.

This is not to romanticize. Mixed in with these laudable, other-regarding values are surely many others. Volunteers from sponsoring corporations spoke of the public-relations and team-building gains that were derived from the experience, both of which could redound in future profits. Church groups, in somewhat parallel fashion, marveled about their heightened sense of fellowship. Individuals listed a number of considerations, including admiration for Jimmy Carter, interest in Native American culture, desire to challenge themselves, a hankering to acquire carpentry and home-maintenance skills, a longing for adventure and, of course, their commitment to serve and care for others. Occasional moments of flirting at the work site suggested that the event was a good place to meet potential partners. Glimpses of a couple of tummy-toners underneath T-shirts and a woman wearing ankle weights seemed to indicate that helping to alleviate substandard housing might also help reduce one's love-handles or tighten flabby thighs. And to anyone recalling the Southern evangelical tenor of Habitat's early years, the raucous volunteers crowding Eagle Butte's three bars each night should be proof that the organization has tapped into different spirits and new sources of public support. In short, this was not some Grail quest that only those with the purest and most singular of motives could undertake. Millard Fuller's original vision for the organization, while attractive to many, is not the only vision. People, quite naturally, brought additional motives and interests with them to South Dakota; they brought their own complicated selves. Nonetheless, this public ritual seemed to be a powerful enough experience to grab a good many of them and create a certain esprit de corps that was truly compelling.

It was also productive. At the completion of the first day, which for many volunteers went well into the evening, thirty newly fashioned structures serrated the once razor-straight horizon west of town. Professional plumbing, electrical, and heating contractors worked most of the night doing the trade work for which most volunteers were unqualified. Each of the days following saw, to say the least, impressive progress. Shingling the roofs, insulating exterior walls, and creating interior walls with eight-foot panels of sheetrock—the height of all Habitat rooms to avoid wasted material—was the goal for Tuesday. Wednesday's work was sanding smooth and double coating those walls (which were plastered the night before) with paint, constructing back porches, and covering the outside of each house with medium gray or slate blue vinyl siding. Thursday was dedicated to finishing those painstaking jobs begun the previous day and attending to such interior detail work as putting in doors, baseboards and trim, kitchen cabinets and bathroom fixtures, and tile. Finally, volunteers spent the day on Friday laying carpet, doing landscaping chores, meticulously cleaning up each site, and adding other finishing touches where necessary.

The sore muscles, sunburnt noses, and blackened fingers and thumbs from inexperienced swings of the hammer were all emblems of what was, for most, a very long week. The final ceremony at the tribe's pow-wow grounds was the emotional finale of the project. The Carters and Fullers, standing on buffalo robes and each draped in a star quilt, were honored by the tribe. In accordance with Habitat practice, the homeowner families were each given bibles and keys to their new homes, a ceremony that was met with enthusiastic and, especially among the volunteers who worked with each family, tear-filled applause. Particularly moved was Tribal Chairman Doug Highland. "What you have done for my people is too great," he informed the volunteers in the bleachers.

"You have done what the Bible says: Love one another. You have done that. You have loved my people." With that, the night's celebration began in earnest.

But even that was not the most memorable part of the project. The blitz build's memory has since been kept alive with the birth of an active grassroots organization. One year after the Jimmy Carter Work Project, Amy Nicolson, the volunteer coordinator for the Okiciyapi Tipi Habitat affiliate, insisted, "What the community saw last year was a huge media blitz. Now they are seeing that this is an ongoing ministry. People in the community feel good about Habitat."[5] Evidence for this statement is easily found. The affiliate hired a Native American executive director, and financial contributions from the local community in 1995, while a modest three thousand dollars, were triple that of the previous year. By the end of 1995, the affiliate selected seven additional homeowner families to work on and eventually occupy the four new homes they built and the three boarded-up HUD houses they acquired from the government and rehabilitated. A Habitat homeowner association has also been quite active in taking ownership of their shared neighborhood as well as their individual homes. Working together, the residents have written a grant proposal for the construction of a basketball court and picnic pavilion as well as for the installation of three streetlights. Then they wrote another proposal to acquire trees from a state forestry program. Things appear to have come a long way in a single year. Before, the prospective homeowners confided about harboring such dreams as moving out of two-bedroom apartments shared by a dozen or so family members or no longer having to sleep in their automobiles. Now word has it that gardens are growing here and there, just as those dreams have grown to include basketball games at night, wind blowing through trees, safe neighborhoods, children's college educations, and probably plenty more.

Millard Fuller's "New Frontier in Christian Missions"

To understand the success of the 1994 Jimmy Carter Work Project and of Habitat more generally requires a look back to the founding of this ministry. One of the interesting things about Habitat is that, although usually identified with a former president known for at least occasionally shunning the residual trappings of political power in favor of serving others, its owes its beginnings to another man's willingness to relinquish his substantial economic assets. Given his humble beginnings in the small cotton-mill town of Lanett in rural eastern Alabama, it would be easy to assume that Millard Fuller's road to financial success must have been a long one. However, by the time he graduated from Auburn University and then from law school at the University of Alabama in 1960, he had already amassed quite a bit of money. He and a fellow student began a birthday cake service, sold everything from desk blotters to holly wreaths, and even purchased about half a city block, upon which they put mobile homes and an old army barracks to rent out to other students. After graduation, they eventually opened a law office in Montgomery. But practicing law took a back seat to their driving ambition of getting rich off the tractor cushions, door mats, toothbrushes, candy, and especially cookbooks that fueled their thriving mail-order business. In time, they found themselves running a business with 150 employees, and Fuller realized before his thirtieth birthday that he was worth well over one million dollars.

By all appearances, this ambitious country lawyer—with the flailing arms and lanky gait of a drawling Ichabod Crane—was a success, the American Dream incarnate. A big house with a maid located on two thousand acres of land, a Lincoln Continental for which he paid cash, a cabin on the lake with two speedboats for good measure, a loving wife and two children (four eventually)—who could ask for anything more? He could. By his own admission, Fuller had become a workaholic obsessed with accumulating greater and greater wealth. The only things he failed to calculate scrupulously were the costs of this success. Among these were a slipping moral compass and deteriorating health evidenced by kidney problems, persistent neck and back aches, and alarming episodes during which he could scarcely catch his breath. Something was wrong. Yet he was not willing to right it until his wife, Linda Fuller, revealed her feelings of neglect and discontent with their marriage and, the very next day, left for New York City to seek guidance from a minister she knew. She wanted a divorce, and he was left feeling confused and empty. Characteristically, though, Fuller was compelled to do something: He went to New York to save his marriage. The account of their ensuing reconciliation would make a fitting conclusion for a fairy tale except for the fact that this was really only the beginning of the story.

Sharing responsibility for a lifestyle that had undermined their relationship, cherished values, and strong religious faiths, the couple decided to make a radical change. With the exception of a small amount Fuller, coincidentally, spent repairing his own father's house, they gave away all of their money to various charities. This was the turning point in their lives. "We had gone too far down the wrong road to be able to correct our direction with a slight detour," explained Fuller. "We simply had to go back and start all over again, but this time we would let God choose the road for us."[6] That, he steadfastly asserts, is precisely what God did the following month. Friends thought they were crazy, but, having escaped the hold of their own money, the Fullers found themselves authentically happy and decided to celebrate with a family vacation in Florida. While returning, they found themselves on a Georgia road near Koinonia Farm, an intentional Christian community a few miles from Americus. Since its founding in 1942, the community was widely known for its pacifism, economic sharing, and racial integration—qualities that roused disfavor and precipitated some violence among its ardently anticommunist and segregationist neighbors, the most threatening of whom were members of the Ku Klux Klan. The bold, some say prophetic, witness the people at Koinonia presented to the injustices they saw around them has since been widely acknowledged.[7] But when Fuller turned the corner onto Route 2 to pay an impromptu visit to two friends living there, he discovered that the community had dwindled to a fraction of its original membership.

That scarcely mattered to him, though. The individual who would have the single most important influence on Fuller's life and future ministry was still there, and when they arrived he was seated on an apple crate in the concrete-block house where the community gathered for midday meals. This was the founder of Koinonia Farm, a Southern Baptist preacher and farmer with a doctorate in Scripture studies named Clarence Jordan. He was known to Fuller for his radical communalism, modeled after the depiction of the early church in the Acts of the Apostles, and for his popular "Cotton Patch" translations of the New Testament, in which biblical stories were placed into the context of the American South. Accepting his invitation to join the community for lunch, Fuller had expected to stay for a couple of hours. Enthralled by Jordan's wisdom and powerful personality, he kept his family at the community for more than a month. "God led me to Clarence in my hour of greatest need," he would later recall. "This man of tremendous depth and intellect, possessed of the keenest spiritual insights of any person I've ever known, lovingly nurtured me back to emotional and

spiritual health when we were at the farm in December of that year."[8]
Fuller had experienced a kind of conversion the previous month that
had emptied him of his materialism, competitiveness, and obsession
with business. Jordan, whom Fuller has described as "the greatest man
I ever met,"[9] appears to be the person most responsible for filling him
back up again, this time with a new vision and direction more worthy
of his considerable zeal.

By all accounts, the two men were practically inseparable during that
month, with Fuller arranging work assignments so he could milk the
community's cows and tend to its vast pecan groves in the company of
his older, newfound friend. Jordan was quite a study. Like the Old Testament prophets whom he admired, he had gained a reputation for rail-
ing against religious ceremonialism and hypocrisy, the haughtiness of
the powerful, and their indifference to the injustices suffered by those
who were poor or otherwise oppressed. Endeavoring to follow in these
prophetic footsteps, he minced few words. He had nothing but disdain
for "Kleenex Christians," who were all piety but no social action, and
for churches that had "gone awhoring" with Mammon and had thus
given birth to a new generation of Christians devoted primarily to making money. Jordan told a pastor who boasted of a ten-thousand-dollar
cross atop his new church that he had been cheated on the price, characteristically bristling, "Time was when Christians could get those
crosses for free."[10] For Jordan Christianity was not about pomp and new
crosses, it was about faithfulness, obedience, and living out the mandates
of the Gospel in the modern world. The churches neglected to preach
this, he claimed, because, in their rush to worship Jesus as the Son of
God, they downplayed his humanity and, therefore, his acute awareness
of and incessant concern for the real human needs of others. In vintage
form, he once declared from a pulpit, "People reject the incarnation by
the deification of Jesus. We create in our minds an image of him as a
super-being, and thus safely remove him from our present experience
and his insistent demands on us."[11]

Jordan's this-worldly, socially active image of Jesus was one that
would thereafter guide Fuller's vision of his own ministry, and it came
with some radical implications. Convinced that "the present structure
of capitalism is wrong," Jordan preached that solutions to the problems
of social injustice needed to go beyond the reformist policies of the
American welfare state combined with the occasional casting of charitable crumbs from the tables of the affluent. Recalling Saint Augustine's

dictum "He who possesses a surplus possesses the goods of others," Jordan called for the personal transformation of the wealthy, whom, when unrepentant, he considered no more than common thieves. Moreover, he felt that the conversion of individuals had to be matched by a restructuring of society such that it better approximated biblical conceptions of justice. "We need to return to the Old Testament idea that the earth is the Lord's," he demanded. "It's still God's property—no person can give you a clear title. If you trace the title back far enough, somebody stole it."[12] In his eyes, capitalism was founded upon people taking from others, and it perpetuated itself by transmitting the imperatives of competition and acquisition to successive generations. This pattern, thought Jordan, had to be destroyed. Because capitalism separated people from one another, the only way to overcome it was to accept our common humanity before God. It is not competitiveness, not the hoarding of wealth, but this commonality that overshadows all the petty distinctions between people and makes partnership possible. Jordan elaborated upon this theme frequently and vividly: "The era of competition, each man like a snarling wolf trying to get his little bit of carcass, must pass away and a new era of partnership with each other must be allowed to break through. White must quit being 'White,' black must quit being 'Black,' rich must quit being 'Rich,' poor must quit being 'Poor,' nation must quit being 'Nation'—and we must be people together, partners under God."[13]

Fuller had been a wolf, a particularly carnivorous one in fact; but he had turned his back on the wilds of the capitalist market, a decision his mentor helped him render comprehensible. Fuller and his family realized this was also a decision requiring concrete action. After leaving Koinonia, they moved into a small apartment above a gas station just outside of New York City. There he had taken a fund-raising position with the small, predominantly black Tougaloo College, located near Jackson, Mississippi, but which had a development office in New York. Fuller wished to take a stand, as a white Southerner, against the racial divisiveness that seemed to be coming to a turbulent head in 1960s America. He was successful at this job, which, given his past, was not unexpected. Yet, after two years there, he wanted to do more, and this, he knew, would involve Koinonia Farm. "I have just resigned my job with Tougaloo," he jotted to Jordan in the spring of 1968. "What have you got up your sleeve?"[14]

"Maybe God has something up His sleeve for both of us," was the immediate reply, along with an invitation for Fuller to meet Jordan in

Atlanta to talk about what that might be.[15] They met and, according to Jordan's recollection, their discussion centered upon their shared "feeling that modern man's greatest problems stem from his loss of any sense of meaningful partnership with God."[16] To combat this, they devised a new ministry they called Koinonia Partners. It would consist of "communicating" the social message of the Gospel to the broader public, "instructing" groups of concerned Christians at Koinonia Farm, and "applying" their beliefs by assisting the poor in the immediate area. This third component meant that, in addition to partnering with God, the ministry would concern itself with partnering with people in need. In other words, Koinonia would allow low-income people to farm its lands ("partnership farming"), operate its already productive pecan-shelling plant, fruitcake bakery, candy kitchen, and mail-order business ("partnership industries"), and build homes on tracts of land that would ultimately be made available to them ("partnership housing"). The money for these ventures—especially for the houses—would come from the voluntary contributions of those with means, collected in a "Fund for Humanity" and dispensed as no-interest loans to those without sufficient means.

This Fund for Humanity was the centerpiece of their bold idea. Two of its features are particularly noteworthy. First, this ministry was to be a partnership between the "haves" and the "have nots," since both were considered to possess complementary needs that must be met in order for them to flourish as whole persons. Jordan expressed this idea in his typically piquant manner in a letter to the Koinonia community at the outset of this new ministry: "What the poor need is not charity but capital, not caseworkers but co-workers. And what the rich need is a wise, honorable and just way of divesting themselves of their overabundance. The Fund for Humanity will meet both of these needs."[17] This was never supposed to be a giveaway program—it was justice. It was expected to contribute to righting the relationship between the rich and poor as well as between a distorted, competitive social order and the God of justice whose creation was intended for the benefit of all. This leads to a second feature of the fund, namely, that it was biblically based. From the very first, they identified their plan with the mandate from the Book of Exodus: "If you lend money to any of my people who are poor, do not act like a moneylender and require him to pay interest" (Ex. 22:25).[18] Although the Fund for Humanity did not make much sense from a cost-benefit perspective, Jordan and Fuller were convinced that, by providing the poor with a dignified form of assistance, it made definite scriptural sense.

This was all that mattered to them, and they were intent on prioritizing "faithfulness" to the biblical vision of justice over what they scorned as mere "successfulness." Yet not long after they began to implement that vision later the same year, it became clear that the housing component of their ministry would become quite successful. The enormous number of dilapidated shacks without running water or electricity in Sumter County alone—Koinonia Farm's own back yard—ensured that the demand for this kind of assistance would be nothing less than incredible. In addition, this ministry proved itself to be viable because it was self-perpetuating. Contributions and no-interest loans to the Fund for Humanity were used to purchase building materials for houses that, in turn, were surprisingly inexpensive because they were constructed with volunteer labor (including that of the eventual occupants), financed without charging interest, and sold without profit. Not only could low-income families afford these homes but, by making their flat monthly payments (usually over a twenty-year span), they would replenish the Fund for Humanity and provide the ministry with a continuous stream of capital for further building projects. It sounded so simple, and, in time, building "simple, decent homes" for people in the surrounding area became the primary focus of Koinonia Partners.

Such a bold undertaking was also a suitable match for Fuller's newfound enthusiasm and dedication to a life of Christian ministry. After Clarence Jordan's untimely death in October 1969, Fuller assumed a greater leadership role within the community and oversaw all of its building operations. Soon the first homeowners moved into their new house, which was built next to the run-down shack they once called home; during the next winter, the old home provided them with a source of firewood. At a cost of $25 per month for twenty years ($6,000 in total), the family's modest new concrete house well exceeded their expectations; the husband happily signed their mortgage with an "X." By the early 1970s, twenty-six other families experienced the same satisfaction, and Fuller came to realize that his faithfulness had resulted in a success that was beyond his expectations as well.

Tensions between Fuller and other members of the Koinonia community, coupled with his desire to see whether this innovative approach to substandard housing could work in other contexts, eventually left Fuller restless with the work he was doing. He and his wife had visited

Zaire (now the Democratic Republic of Congo) in the 1960s, so when the Disciples of Christ offered them the opportunity to head a community-development project there in 1973, they took it without hesitation, believing it to be God's will. For the next three years they, with their children, worked in the equatorial city of Mobutu on the Zaire River, accumulating a Fund for Humanity and building houses. The land for the project, donated by the Zaire government, had once been the official dividing line separating the white colonists in the region from the townspeople, who were not permitted to cross it. This narrow, overgrown field had deservedly been left with the ignominious name Bokotola, roughly translated as "man who does not care for others." Fuller was determined to transform it into a symbol of hope and the care that people, imbued with a spirit of partnership, could have for one another. The results were dramatic. By the time the Fullers left Africa in the summer of 1976, eighty families had moved into new homes, thirty-four other houses were under construction, and plans were underway for a second project in the village of Ntondo, ninety miles to the south. These concrete houses with tin roofs, built with materials from the block-making factory established by Fuller and costing between $1,000 and $2,500, turned a once-empty field into a vibrant community in the center of the city.

Whatever else Fuller learned from his years abroad, it was clear that the basic idea behind this new ministry could be successful. Building homes with the unpaid labor of the new homeowners and concerned volunteers, selling them at no profit and no interest, recycling monthly house payments into a Fund for Humanity used to finance new construction—the idea was sound. Now he wanted to expand its scope, something that could best be accomplished by returning to the United States, where personal contacts and capital were more easily accessible.

Another reason for returning home was his insistence, which he shared with (and perhaps learned from) Jordan, that the opulence of the wealthy and the suffering of the poor were directly related. The wealthy, in his opinion, needed to recognize this relation. They needed to understand that their privilege came with a responsibility to actively assist others. If provided with a sound way of helping others—such as his house-building idea—he believed that most people would naturally be willing to do so. People, in other words, are not morally bereft or apathetic about the plight of others; they simply need to be actively shown how they can make a difference. He felt that he had come up with such a way.

Perhaps his optimism was a function of his faith; perhaps he was simply naïve. Or perhaps he realized that his own metamorphosis from Millard Fuller the self-absorbed millionaire to Millard Fuller the indefatigable, house-building missionary had been a relatively quick one, one that merely required some redirection. Thus it may have seemed logical that other people, other snarling wolves, could be brought to lie down with their lamb-like better selves if given similar opportunities to redirect their lives. This may be little more than speculation. The fact remains that Fuller wanted to begin an international housing ministry based on principles, successfully tested at Koinonia and then in Zaire, that he believed could be widely effective throughout the United States.

In September 1976, within weeks of returning from Africa, Fuller summoned a number of "committed Christian friends" from throughout the country to Koinonia Farm to help him discern how best to proceed with this ambitious enterprise. Twenty-seven people attended the three-day conference, during which they "prayed and dreamed and discussed and brainstormed together."[19] According to the conference records, the central question they deliberated upon was, "What is God calling us to do with this idea?"[20] This was not a matter to be taken lightly; it was a question that warranted and apparently received bold responses. In fact, leading one of the devotional periods that preceded each discussion session, Fuller quoted some telling lines from renowned architect Daniel Hudson Burnham:

> Make no little plans; they have
> no magic to stir men's blood;
> they probably themselves
> will never be realized.
> Make big plans; aim high in hope and work,
> remembering that a noble diagram,
> once recorded, will never die, but
> long after we are gone will be a
> living thing.[21]

No one could deny that "big plans" were made during that weekend. All agreed to establish and support the newly named Habitat for Humanity®, an organization that would be thoroughly ecumenical and financed at the grassroots level by a Fund for Humanity created by each local affiliate. More than two decades later, about 1,500 of these affiliates currently exist throughout the United States, and in excess of 300 more are scattered within sixty-four other countries. The 90,000 houses they have built worldwide—including 29,000 built or rehabilitated in the United States—now provide shelter for approximately 450,000 people. These numbers suggest that, indeed, no little plans were made at Koinonia Farm that weekend. According to *Professional Builder* magazine's April 2000 "giant 400 survey," Habitat now ranks number 21 among the largest home-building operations in the United States (based on closings) and, not surprisingly, number one among "lower price" builders.[22]

This is a sensational achievement, but it is only part of the larger story. Habitat is more than a nonprofit construction company. At its founding conference nearly twenty-five years ago, Fuller made it clear that he envisioned the work of Habitat becoming a "new frontier in Christian missions" that would necessarily entail a clear religious orientation.[23] The Christian faith—as understood and articulated by Fuller and others associated with Habitat—provided the "noble diagram," to use a phrase from the poem quoted above, that would guide the organization's mission and growth well into the future. As a paradenominational organization, one would expect Habitat to be founded upon, or at least be sympathetic to, selected religious values. Still, the theological ideas that provided the blueprint for Habitat's religious vision are particularly innovative and are worth examining closely, since they are responsible for erecting the distinctive organizational edifice that would make the ministry increasingly successful through the years.

Building on Faith: Habitat's Religious Vision

The Centrality of Partnership

It is impossible to understand Habitat without first being cognizant of the organization's avowedly theological understanding of itself. It is interesting that much of the religious language that one now hears at different Habitat affiliates and, of course, reads in the promotional literature was used during the organization's early years as well. This is because the lion's share of it originated with Jordan and especially Fuller, both of whom have demonstrated a knack for expressing religious ideas in accessible and even catchy ways. The perduring appeal of this religious language has had the effect of keeping the organization close to its original charism and preventing it from being perceived as just another low-income housing developer. The houses, so says the typical refrain, should not overshadow the religious convictions of those who put hammer to nail in building them.

Habitat's mission statement is the most obvious illustration of this concern. It reads: "Habitat for Humanity® works in partnership with God and people everywhere, from all walks of life, to develop communities with God's people in need by building and renovating houses, so that there are decent houses in decent communities in which people can grow into all that God intended."[24] A more theological grounding for an organization would be difficult to find. It attests to a conviction that people have a real relation with God ("God's people"), they are imbued with a divinely intended purpose that does not include anything less than decent living conditions ("grow into all that God intended"), and they can choose to cooperate with God's plan for humanity by assisting those in need of better living conditions ("partnership with God"). Over and beyond building houses, in other words, the importance of Habitat for many of its participants lies in the belief that they are cooperating with God's own work. Such a belief, in itself, does not distinguish Habitat from most paradenominational groups or many other kinds of religious collectivities. However, if one scratches the surface a bit, a unique interpretation of its particular cooperative mission becomes noticeable.

For example, it is not unexpected to see the word *partnership* in the mission statement because it is such a prominent theme within the organization. As previously suggested, Jordan and Fuller founded Koinonia Partners because they bemoaned humanity's lost sense of partnership with God and, in competitive capitalist societies, with other persons. Habitat was very consciously founded in order to continue the work of reestablishing that crucial "dual partnership." Fuller, at nearly every available opportunity, states the case clearly:

> First, we're in partnership with God. If Habitat were primarily a movement of individuals, there would be nothing lasting to it. But this is God's movement, and there's nothing that can stop it. Second, we're in partnership with each other. One of the most exciting features of Habitat for Humanity® is that people who don't normally work together at all are coming together everywhere to work in this cause. . . . With this dual partnership as our foundation, we are going to arouse the consciences of individuals and organizations around the world, challenging them to join in this cause. And together, we are going to get rid of the shacks. *All of them!*[25]

Get rid of *all* the shacks? The boldness of the ministry is striking—
intentionally so. Fuller revels in telling the story of being interviewed
on a radio talk show, during which he was asked to describe the goal of
his then five-year-old ministry. Never having been posed that question
before, he almost inadvertently uttered, "To eliminate poverty housing
from the face of the earth."[26] It has been Habitat's endlessly repeated
raison d'être ever since. And it is not simply Pollyannaish wistfulness.
The immodesty and, to be frank, the impossibility of this goal is pivotal because it functions to highlight the centrality of the organization's
oft-announced partnership with God. The result: Habitat's brash goal
is rendered legitimate by framing it as part of God's irresistible will for
humankind and, therefore, it only *appears* immodest and impossible in
the eyes of the outsider.

This notion of being in partnership with God also accounts for two
characteristic themes embedded within Habitat's religious vision. The
first, derived from Jesus' parable of the mustard seed, is the assurance
that even though small acts of voluntarism and charitable giving may
seem inconsequential, relative to the awesome scope of the world's problems, they are actually efficacious in many, often unforeseeable ways.
Succumbing to a paralyzing despair before the challenge of the world's
overwhelming housing needs may be a temptation, but it is ultimately
unacceptable because one person, one dollar, or one house *can* make a
difference. Partnering with God, the message continues, means that
one's own efforts are multiplied to unanticipated proportions, such that
even Habitat's unimaginable goal becomes, through the eyes of faith,
suddenly imaginable. The reflections of Habitat's Wisconsin state coordinator are representative of this faithfulness:

> Some might argue that building one, two, three or four new homes a year is
> but a drop out of the bucket of need. It's the doing that counts, and who
> knows where these little plantings of mustard seeds will lead? . . . If I start by
> helping one person, and my neighbor helps another and their neighbor
> another, we can make a difference; seed by seed we can turn a little woods
> into a mighty forest just by starting with one.[27]

Statements like this abound in the organizational literature. In fact,
whenever biblical stories are referenced to illustrate Habitat's work—
the stories of Noah, Joshua, Gideon, David, the prophets, Jesus' miracles, and many others—they invariably focus on the grand things that
God will accomplish through small acts performed by those least exalted

by an unbelieving world. "The crazy idea that works" or "Habitat for Insanity" are only two of the numerous phrases one hears bandied about that are meant to signal that the organization runs according to a divine logic deemed illogical on the world's terms. Even when people outside of Habitat are invoked to illustrate its sense of mission, it is usually to emphasize the sort of alternative logic represented by the mustard seed parable. Printed on a Habitat brochure, the following quote from Dorothy Day, the founder of the Catholic Worker movement, is a typical example: "What can one person do? What is the sense of our small effort? They cannot see that we must lay one brick at a time, take one step at a time. We can be responsible only for the one action of the present moment. But we can beg for an increase of love in our hearts that will vitalize and transform all our individual actions and know that God will take them and multiply them as Jesus multiplied the loaves and fishes."[28] "What can one person do?" is a perennial question even for those who are most socially conscious. The persistent answer at Habitat seems to be that one can at least do something and have faith that one's actions will produce boundless effects.

Notwithstanding Habitat's faith in a partnership with God, there is no denying that its work, as widespread as it is, remains "but a drop out of the bucket of need." As with the parabolic mustard seed, its ministry may one day expand to even grander proportions, but in the meantime there are other, more immediate and verifiable ways of understanding this partnership. Summed up by Fuller as "the conscience of the world concerning shelter," this second theme suggests that, in addition to building houses, Habitat remains faithful to its mission simply by witnessing to the problem of substandard housing.[29] The organization does not have to approach its bold, not-yet-achieved goal in order to be successful, according to this argument. It can succeed by faithfully stirring public awareness regarding poverty housing and inciting people to take action, even when that action is performed independently of Habitat. Former President Carter expresses this reasoning well:

> There is no way that Habitat can build all the homes that are necessary in the world.... What I'm talking about is—do a limited number of Habitat projects in a particular region and then try to encourage private investors and government officials and others to emulate what we're doing. This is what Habitat wants to do. Plant projects all over the world; sow seeds of hope, encouraging the poor to do all they can to help themselves; and cultivate

consciences among the affluent, urging them, privately or corporately, to join less fortunate folks in a spirit of partnership, to solve the problem together.[30]

Like the biblical prophets, Habitat attempts to critique the present insufficiency of affordable housing by speaking out on behalf of justice and, at the same time, energizing others to pursue the cause of justice by modeling it through its own work.[31] It is an institution that *denounces* the current state of affairs and *announces* a new, alternative possibility. By consciously assuming this prophetic role, the organization reaffirms and enacts its self-understanding of working in partnership with God and can claim a level of success even when it has not met its ultimate goal of eliminating all the shacks from the face of the earth.

As with its partnership with God, Habitat's partnering with other people is taken seriously enough to shape some of its most novel organizational features. One of these is its partnership with the homeowner families who eventually move into Habitat houses. They are not customers who buy their new homes on the market or clients who, as with HUD beneficiaries, are able to rent dwellings for reduced cost if they can abide living in public housing. They are partners who, along with paying for their homes, help to build them by working with people in the community who volunteer to give them, as it is often pithily put, "a hand up, not a handout." Depending on the practices of each affiliate, homeowner families are expected to perform between 300 and 600 hours of "sweat equity" (the national average is 430 hours), which can be directed toward anything from doing administrative work at the affiliate office to working on the construction site. Extended family, friends, and fellow employees or church members may assist them as well. Although Habitat does not mention it, the sweat-equity requirement is probably a factor in the organization's extensive popularity, since it tends to mark the homeowners as "deserving poor" who are not just trying to, as some people say, get something for nothing.

Other benefits of the sweat-equity requirement, which are heralded unreservedly, include: lowering the costs of construction; providing homeowners with transferable skills and greater self-esteem; giving homeowners an "ownership stake" in their communities that renters supposedly do not have; and increasing a sense of partnership with other members of the community in which they will eventually reside. This last benefit is especially significant. Habitat harbors high expectations, bordering on the miraculous, of the social integration and partnership that will result from people working together. Partnership arises when people, often those who would not ordinarily associate with one another, are brought together and afforded the opportunity for meaningful interaction. Barriers break down, stereotypes are cast aside, understanding and compassion are nurtured. And nothing, according to this view, facilitates this transformation better than sweat-equity hours. "Sweat equity is an excellent way for people in a new neighborhood to get acquainted," we are informed in Habitat's organizational literature. "Working side-by-side earning sweat equity leads to camaraderie. Often homeowners with completed requirements contribute hours for those having a hard time—truly families helping families."[32] Construction companies and government agencies can build dwellings for people to live in, but Habitat insists that only a spirit of partnership can ensure that these houses exist within strong communities.

Such communities, of course, cannot emerge when only the organization's homeowners are willing to become partners. Habitat is no less adamant that local people with adequate economic means must also be brought into partnership. Each local affiliate's Fund for Humanity exists as an economic partnership between the more affluent, who enrich it with their contributions, and the less privileged homeowners, who make mortgage payments into it each month. New houses could never be financed if people from either group shirked their financial responsibility. Nor could they be constructed affordably if volunteers—who in other house-building nonprofits serve principally on boards of directors and various committees—and homeowners alike did not perform the requisite labor together. These pragmatic concerns are still not the primary reasons why Habitat partners with predominantly middle-class people from local communities. Building houses with volunteer labor, after all, is not the fastest or most efficient way of getting the job done. Rather, volunteering holds such a prominent place within the organization because, reminiscent of Jordan's desire to create a "ministry to the affluent," Habitat believes strongly in challenging better-off citizens and inculcating in them a religiously inspired concern for the public good. The hope is that, through volunteering, they may come to feel more fulfilled and integrated into their communities. "As volunteers work side-by-side with partner families and other Habitat workers," reads one organizational publication, "Habitat becomes a ministry not only to those receiving houses, but also to the volunteers. Many volunteers gain a new insight about justice, Christian living, simplicity, service, and Christian responsibility."[33] In this respect, the ministry is intended to extend beyond the actual homeowners.

It is also a ministry that reaches beyond the local affiliate to encompass an even wider understanding of partnership, a "worldwide partnership." That this is a worldwide *organization* is obvious. Headquartered in Americus, Georgia, Habitat International is the organizational hub for hundreds of separately incorporated local affiliates scattered throughout the United States and abroad. By signing an Affiliate Covenant (see Appendix A), each one agrees to adhere to Habitat's main principles. Beyond that, Habitat also attempts to be a worldwide *partnership*, a goal that has led to another of the more distinctive aspects of the organization. Each local affiliate is expected, though not required, to tithe 10 percent of its undesignated cash donations to Habitat International to be used for building projects in developing nations.

This is a powerful innovation for a number of reasons. First, it symbolizes global interdependence and the attendant need to establish bonds of solidarity with others outside of the local purview. Some affiliates send their tithes to Americus to be allocated as needed; others designate a particular global region or even a "sister project" in hopes of establishing a more meaningful connection to another part of the world. Second, even though affiliates in all countries contribute tithes, this practice is regarded as particularly important for U.S. affiliates. American economic strength is seen as related to the severe poverty in underdeveloped nations, and tithing is a way of partly remedying the inequitable distribution of the world's wealth. It also provides shelter for greater numbers of people since housing costs in the developing world are a fraction of those in the United States.

Encouraging compliance with this aspect of partnership is an ongoing, and at times frustrating, task of the international organization. In 1995, for example, U.S. affiliates raised an estimated $200 million in donations but only tithed $3.7 million back to Americus.[34] The efforts Habitat has made toward increasing these numbers suggest that tithing is significant for a third reason. To quote a Habitat International board member on the subject, "Tithing is a fundamental act of faith in a giving spirit of partnership."[35] In other words, the practice of tithing— in contrast to the calculative, bottom-line attitude fostered by capitalist markets—demonstrates a willingness to privilege global partnership over local self-interests. It is also said to reflect a faithful partnership with God since an affiliate's generosity with its own financial resources is frequently interpreted as an unwavering trust that God will provide and that, like the mustard seed, even depleted resources will once again grow to a substantial size and bear unexpected fruits.

By now it should be clear that the concept of partnership is the cornerstone of Habitat's religious vision. Inadequate shelter is a tremendous problem throughout the world, to be sure. Yet the housing crisis is, according to this vision, only a symptom of a more encompassing spiritual crisis. The fallen, sinful condition of humankind is depicted as a loss of partnership with God and with one another. Thus Habitat's emphasis on reestablishing both aspects of that broken partnership serves as a utopian symbol capable of stimulating and orientating social action.[36] Or, to put it in the overtly Christian terms most familiar to the organizational leadership, partnership is a kind of shorthand for the kingdom of God, allusions to which are everywhere in Habitat promotional literature. "We always say in Habitat for Humanity® that we are doing a lot more than just building houses," writes Fuller. "We are building and seeking to be a part of building God's kingdom on earth. We are seeking to build relationships and we are challenging people to reach out and help others as others have reached out to help them."[37]

Habitat's work, then, amounts to house building in a sacral mode. It is set within the larger, indeed cosmic, context of an entire created order groaning to realize the wholeness and the fulfillment that God has intended for it. Its work, in this interpretation, participates in and cooperates with the work of the Creator, the activity of the prophets, and the saving ministry of Jesus because creating partnership is also generative of the coming Kingdom. Christian theologians who have attended to the symbol of God's kingdom have noted that it seems to carry with it two contradictory components: a present "already" side, and a future "not yet" side. This double-sided quality reflects an understanding that humanity, through present-day works of justice and compassion, may contribute to the coming of the Kingdom, but its final consummation can only be accomplished by God in the eschatological future.[38] Such is the mystery of the Christian conception of "salvation history."

This paradigm, which is deeply embedded within the Christian tradition, is mimicked by Habitat's understanding of partnership. Its self-proclaimed partnership with God—illustrated by its efforts to sway people's consciences and its mustard seed faith in the unlimited possibilities of small acts—is oriented toward the "not yet." It focuses on bringing people to believe and participate in what God is perceived to be doing through this housing ministry and will bring to fruition in a brighter future. At the same time, Habitat offers glimpses of this promised future, of the Kingdom as it is "already" present, through its partnership with other people. Sweat equity, volunteering, and tithing are structured components of the organization because, along with their practical importance, they function as enacted manifestations of partnership—of the Kingdom—as it already exists. They are deeply symbolic practices. As such, they are not only symbols *of* the cooperation and caring and interdependence that constitute authentic partnership, they are symbols *for* it as well.[39] They make it real.

These symbolic practices are enacted by people who work side by side, tithe liberally, and, in the process, create precisely the kind of partnership that Habitat envisions reigning in the as-yet-unattained future. The tremendous emphasis the organization places upon these practices indicates its awareness that they possess real power to shape the imaginations of the people whose actions they pattern. This is important since transforming people's visions of what is possible is essential if the quality of justice associated with the kingdom of God is ever to become a social reality. How well or how often Habitat actually brings about such personal transformations is difficult to say. The main point for now is simply to point out that Habitat's distinctive vision of partnership, representative as it is of the twofold understanding of the Kingdom, is a deeply religious one.

True Faith Requires Action

Although partnership is the single most prominent theme, Habitat's religious vision includes other noteworthy elements as well. Chief among these is the insistence that authentic religious faith must manifest itself in actions directed toward alleviating the want and distress of others. As long-time organizational leader Bob Stevens expressed it, "We at Habitat would not say that one should not preach the Gospel. We would say, though, that one should not merely preach the Gospel, but that the preaching of the Gospel must be accompanied by the doing of the Gospel."[40] No other single concept produces as immediate and as universal a consensus among Habitat supporters as this one. Moreover, no other vice is as roundly disdained as some people's tendency to focus on the letter of religious doctrine and ceremonialism at the expense of a more sublime spirit of service.

Jesus, "mighty in deed and word in the sight of God and all the people" (Luke 24:19), is overwhelmingly understood and portrayed within
the organization as a man of action, the paradigmatic volunteer helping and healing wherever he went. Biblical references used to describe
Habitat's work almost invariably include the final judgment scene in the
twenty-fifth chapter of Matthew's gospel, where, after separating the
righteous from the damned on the basis on their willingness to care for
others on earth, Jesus declares, "I tell you the truth, whatever you did
for one of the least of these brothers of mine, you did for me" (Matt.
25:40). If the early Christian theologians were now available for comment, they would certainly find the organization guilty of Pelagianism,
a third-century heresy depicting salvation to be more a matter of human
effort and good works than of the saving grace of Christ's redemption.
The famous New Testament passage from the Letter of James is quoted
practically everywhere: "So faith by itself, if it has no works, is dead"
(James 2:17). And, judging by its appearance on Habitat brochures,
bumper stickers, T-shirts, and other paraphernalia, the unofficial motto
of the organization would be a fragment from the First Letter of John,
"Our love should not be just words and talk; it must be true love, which
shows itself in action" (1 John 3:18).

Works and action—these are the signs of true religion, and hammering this message home is a major part of the organization's ministry.
Consider, for instance, the conclusion of a speech given by David Rowe,
the first president of Habitat's international board, on the occasion of
its tenth-year anniversary:

> The miserable, disease-ridden, dispiriting, life-threatening hellholes in which
> one-quarter of the world is living are a scar upon the face of the earth, but
> worse, they are a challenge to the gospel and an insult to the Easter story. . . .
> We need people who will start out to walk, but won't mind stopping to stoop
> down. We need people who will stoop down, but then won't mind cleaning
> up. And we need people, who after cleaning up, won't mind straightening up
> again and keep moving. We need people who realize that spiritual ain't worth
> spit without sweat.[41]

That faith requires action is a basic enough concept, and clearly it
can be articulated with a certain emotive force. Two important themes
emerge from this conviction. First, at Habitat, the corollary to the
necessity of living out one's faith is the generally accepted taboo against
overly intellectualizing it. Complicating the Gospel with labyrinthine
theological distinctions and interpretations consistently raised the ire

of Clarence Jordan, whose ideas, it should by now be apparent, remain influential within the organization. He often spoke of "incarnational evangelism," which for him meant that the best way to articulate religious ideas was to embody them in action. Theological erudition that detracted from that central premise warranted only sarcasm from him. "The Word became a sermon and was later expanded into a book, and the book sold well and inspired other books until of the making of books there was no end. And," Jordan concluded in disgust, "the Word died in darkness and was buried in the theological library."[42] Variations on this theme are common at Habitat. Downplaying the cognitive dimension of religious faith functions to highlight the active, ethical dimension.[43]

Another example of the same tendency is found in a promotional video, in which a youth minister is unfavorably comparing the lessons learned from studying religion with those gleaned by putting it into action. "I spent six years chipping away at a Masters in New Testament Studies," he explains looking intently into the camera, "and all the hours preparing my mind and writing papers, and even now writing sermons, doesn't compare to all I'm learning and teaching the young people about theology. And that's what they're learning. They are understanding what it means to put compassion into their hands and produce results."[44] The doing of faith, this young man seems to indicate, must take priority over the knowing of faith and, in the end, may be the best way to experience a meaningful knowing. Putting this in terms familiar to liberation theologians, true faith is best conceived of as right actions ("orthopraxy") rather than right beliefs ("orthodoxy"). Religious beliefs, these scholars unequivocally contend, cannot make sense outside of a context in which people are actively striving to make life more humane for others.[45]

A second consequence of the conviction that faith requires action is the religious significance typically attributed to Habitat houses. Since house-building is a premier example of helping to lift people out of sub-human conditions, houses become emblems of the power of faithfulness. The message seems to be that if social action is religiously significant, so too must be the product of that action. Understanding this requires reconsidering Jordan's emphasis on "incarnational evangelism." In Jesus, he argued, God's word and deed were united; Jesus embodies the in-breaking of the divine in the unlikely guise of a poor Jewish peasant. This is nothing new to those acquainted with Christian theology, but it is still startling to discover how frequently Habitat houses are described in similarly incarnational terms. They too are perceived as another unlikely sign of the continuing in-breaking of God. Explaining the sacred character of the apparently profane work in which Habitat is engaged, a member of the first international board put it this way:

> The Incarnation of the eternal Word in Jesus (John 1:14) also means that all of human life is to be regarded as holy, that is, dedicated to God's service and acceptable to Him. No longer is there the distinction between the sacred and profane, the religious and the secular. To build a temple for the worship of God is no more holy than to build a home for a needy person. A house is no less sacred than a sanctuary—perhaps it is even more sacred.... To build homes for God's people in need is to build a habitat for God.[46]

Fuller, who is fond of referring to Habitat houses as "sermons of pure truth," could not agree more. During one house dedication ceremony held on the day before Easter Sunday, he compared the new Habitat house with the old shack that was still standing directly behind it. "You want to know what the resurrection is all about?" he asked the onlookers in attendance. "When this service is over here, you go around back and see the empty tomb. And then you come in here and see the resurrected Lord, this is as symbolic of the resurrection as anything I know.... This is the evidence of the resurrected Christ," he exclaimed, displaying his conviction that authentic religion is about results, not doctrinal propositions.[47] Jesus, the man of action, proved himself to be the incarnation of God by virtue of the results of his life. In like manner, Habitat houses are depicted as incarnations of God's will for humanity because they too are the results of faithfulness and obedience to an irresistible call to service. The organization, in essence, describes them sacramentally, as ostensibly profane objects that actually make the sacred present to those with eyes to see.

The Inclusive "Theology of the Hammer"

Given Habitat's emphasis on practical action and its willingness to partner with anyone interested in doing so, the third major theme of its overall religious vision seems to follow naturally. This is its profound inclusivity, which is justified in various ways. First, it is consistent with the organization's sense that cooperating with God's will for the eradication of substandard housing is too bold and urgent an undertaking to exclude anyone from contributing to it. Furthermore, Habitat's profoundly holistic view of the human person keeps it from going the way of so many other paradenominational groups that cull support from religious constituencies interested in attending either to people's spiritual needs or to their material needs, but not both. Habitat, in contrast, wants to include people from across the religious spectrum and endeavors to do so by reminding them that its ministry is directed to both the body and spirit. Representative of this view are the comments made by religion professor and former international board member Clyde Tilley: "Too many conservatives or evangelicals have opted for the proclamation of the personal gospel. Too many liberals or mainliners have emphasized primarily the application of the social gospel," he wrote, calling for greater partnership among conservative and liberal faith communities. "There is no social gospel and no personal gospel. There is only the Good News of and about Jesus Christ. It is the Good News of deliverance to the total person—physical, economic, social, spiritual."[48]

Habitat's most innovative approach by far to making its ministry more inclusive is its staunch refusal to fixate on theological and ecclesiological minutiae. While an openly Christian organization, Habitat goes to great lengths to emphasize a nondogmatic character that makes it a suitable partner for an enormous diversity of people, including non-Christians for whom a more confessional stance would likely have little appeal. So committed is the organization to doctrinal minimalism that it unabashedly advocates its own "theology of the hammer." According to Fuller, who originated the term, "This simply means that as Christians we will agree on the use of the hammer as an instrument to manifest God's love. We may disagree," he continues, "on all sorts of things—baptism, communion, what night to have a prayer meeting, and how the preacher should dress—but we can agree on the imperative of the gospel to serve others in the name of the Lord. We can agree on the idea of building houses for God's people in need."[49] There is plenty of room for consensus here. What is more, Fuller and many others would be quick to add, the theology of the hammer does not water down Habitat's religious vision since its very centerpiece is a widespread and divinely ordained partnership of diverse people putting their faiths—whatever that might mean to each of them—into action.

A Religious Critique of the State and Market

Partnership, action, and inclusivity—these are religious values that together make up the organization's religious self-understanding. As compelling as it is, consideration of this self-understanding would be incomplete without mention of a fourth way that Habitat asserts itself as a religious enterprise. This is in its conscious resistance to the instrumental values of the state and market. Even though most people involved with the organization are unlikely to put it in these terms, there is a shared sense that Habitat's success comes, as Fuller puts it, "from operating within God's perspective, which usually sees situations just about reversed from the way the world sees them."[50]

In direct resistance to the profit-maximizing logic of the market, Habitat endeavors to conduct its financial affairs according to what it calls the "economics of Jesus" or, less often, "biblical economics." This is a set of six principles Fuller developed early in the organization's history, and they have been influential ever since. Although the first three have already been discussed, it is worth listing all of these principles together. The first, the inspiration for each affiliate's Fund for Humanity and the main reason for the affordability of Habitat homes, is the mandate to charge no interest and seek no profit when dealing with those in need. The second is the necessity of possessing a mustard seed faith, which, in operational terms, means that affiliates must be willing to show a trust in God by undertaking ambitious projects even when financial resources are sparse. Third, the notion that "the poverty of the 'have-nots' is directly related to the riches of the 'haves'" means that, especially within developed nations, the affluent must be willing to sacrifice their excess in order to meet the needs of the poor. Fourth, rather than increasing their funds through endowments or investments, affiliates should avoid such "hoarding" and spend immediately and liberally to build new houses without interruption. Fifth, the ministry to house the poor should be guided by the conviction that—regardless of such factors as race or social status or class background—"each human life, no matter how insignificant it may seem, is priceless." Finally, and closely connected to the previous principle, is the insistence that nothing except the reality of human need ought to be considered when providing assistance to others.[51]

With the exception of the unnegotiable first principle, to which all Habitat affiliates must abide if they are to retain their affiliate status, a faithful adherence to the "economics of Jesus" is, in all probability, as difficult and uneven in practice as is enactment of most other lofty ideals. As obvious as that may seem, it is just as evident that these principles have guided the organization throughout its history and are still taken quite seriously at all its levels. Habitat has consistently tried to remedy the ill effects of capitalism's market logic and, as evidenced by the "economics of Jesus," it does so by relying upon a countervailing logic based in the Christian faith.

This logic also accounts for the organization's cautious attitude toward the state. Although Habitat, as one might expect, is eager to enter into partnerships with government, these must remain within carefully delineated limits. Longstanding organizational policy dictates that public monies can only be used to "set the stage" for house-building. This stipulation allows Habitat to accept land and run-down houses and apartment buildings, either as grants or at a reduced price; infrastructural necessities including streets, sidewalks, and utilities; and the waiver of various permit fees. The only emendation to this policy was approved by the international board in 1994—and then only after much debate within the organization. It allows affiliates to accept government grants to hire staff and cover other administrative expenses.[52] For all of these purposes, though, funds can be accepted only if they come without "strings attached" that could compromise any of Habitat's basic principles and, interestingly, as long as they are not allocated for materials and labor used in actual housing construction. Government resources may set the stage for building, but they cannot be used to build.

The reasons given for this distinction are numerous, but they seem to fall into two main categories. The first is a set of pragmatic reasons. Government, in Habitat's estimation, is an unstable source of funds that, if relied upon too heavily, can create dependency; serious disruption inevitably follows if that support ceases to be available. Also, the bureaucratic red tape that usually accompanies state funding is viewed as potentially undermining to the affiliates' "person-to-person" organizational ethos and as almost certainly distracting from their main focus of "building homes and building community." Finally, Habitat is very clear that it does not want to compete for scarce public resources with other low-income housing organizations that may be in greater need of them. Filling a service niche and tapping into private sources of funding unavailable to other organizations is seen as the best way of not replicating the efforts of other groups and thus meeting more housing needs.

As valid and perhaps as sufficient as these reasons are, there are others. The second category of reasons has to do with protecting Habitat's religious vision; not surprisingly, these center upon the important theme of partnership. For example, Habitat is careful to prevent even the slightest infringement upon its ability to express—whether in song or prayer or in its promotional literature—its partnership with God. Its embrace of inclusivity is not the same thing as the state's universalist mandate. Habitat does not want to be so inclusive as to attenuate the very particular religious roots from which it grew. Fuller's is an exemplary, but definitely not singular, voice on this issue: "This firm foundation in Christ is so important that Habitat has resisted the ever-present temptation to accept government funds, which carry with them the very likelihood of changing that focus. Habitat for Humanity® wants to be a good partner with government; yet our roots, our motivation, and solid rock foundation in Jesus Christ must never be compromised for financial support from any source."[53]

Jealously guarding its Christian heritage is the most obvious way the organization demonstrates its preference for its religious vision over government funding. There are two additional, less obvious, ways that also suggest why state monies are effectively barred from the Habitat houses themselves. First, using government grants to purchase building materials could diminish the organization's partnership with the wider community. Monetary and in-kind donations for building materials are expected to come from the grassroots, from individuals and businesses wherever affiliates operate. If these partnerships were not nurtured, the argument proceeds, Habitat would construct homes like any other low-income builder, abandoning its further goal of strengthening communities by the wayside. Similarly, if drawing the line at building *materials* is not an arbitrary designation, neither is keeping state funding from the building *process*. Again, Habitat wants to protect its partnership with the community by mobilizing volunteers to build houses, and this reasoning includes its partnership with homeowners as well. Community members would just be "throwing money at the problem" if government grants were used to hire professional contractors, while homeowners would always remain clients and never themselves come to feel like full-fledged members of their communities.

It is in the building process that these two populations come together as partners in a common endeavor and not, as Habitat fears most, as wealthy patrons and the patronized poor. The materials and labor required for building bring people together, making Habitat houses the privileged locale for the emergence of partnership. Because of the religious nature of this partnership, embodying as it does the kingdom of God, protecting it from state involvement is a means by which Habitat displays its deeply religious organizational logic. Since they incarnate God's kingdom, Habitat policy seems to declare, these houses must not be desecrated, even for benign purposes, by the hands of the temporal kingdom, the state. Therefore, just as the "economics of Jesus" is essentially a form of resistance against the pathologies attendant to the market sector, Habitat's government funds policy is an attempt to protect its religious vision of partnership from the state.

It is unlikely that most Habitat staff and supporters would state the case in precisely these terms. The foregoing interpretation, after all, has been just that: an interpretation. Its aim has been to demonstrate that the overall ministry and many of its most defining operational features and policies cannot be fully understood without an appreciation of the distinctly religious vision that has guided Habitat for more than two decades. It remains to be seen how this vision is implemented, an issue, addressed in the following chapter, that pertains to Habitat's unique organizational structure.

3

Habitat's Organizational Structure and Growth

There is no such thing as a "good person" as such. There is only the good father or the good mother, the good physician or the good plumber, the good churchperson, the good citizen. The good person of the subjective virtues, to be sure, provides the personal integrity of the individual; without it the viable society is not possible. But from the point of view of the institutional commonwealth the merely good individual is good for nothing. Moreover, the narrow range of responsibility of the man or woman who confines attention merely to family and job serves to dehumanize the self.

James Luther Adams, *The Prophethood of All Believers*

Celebrating an Organization on the Move

If you had been in Los Angeles during that first week in August and happened past the pristine campus of Loyola Marymount University, you probably would not have noticed anything out of the ordinary. The central quad area was alive with students—a few hundred of them—some scurrying to class, some lounging on the grass and conversing with peers, the more energetic among them tossing a Frisbee into a faintly salted summer breeze. "Nothing new here," you might say to yourself, strolling onward.

Closer inspection would have produced a different conclusion. Had you canvassed the scene more intently, you would have noted the "students" were predominantly older than the average collegian. You might have heard fragments of conversation about everything from safety and liability issues on construction sites in Nashua, New Hampshire, to honing grant-writing skills in San Antonio, Texas. If nothing else, you certainly would have noticed everyone wearing Habitat for Humanity® nametags and carrying organization-logoed literature describing the latest in housing designs or explaining how to form a corporate adopt-a-home program or produce a better affiliate newsletter. You would come to see that this was not a typical day on campus. It was "Celebration '94," Habitat's eighteenth-anniversary gathering.

Among those in attendance were concerned members of churches or civic groups seeking to become more familiar with the organization in anticipation of one day founding a local affiliate. From affiliates already in operation were staff and volunteers intent upon improving their work and networking with others doing the same. Representing Habitat projects dispersed within five other continents were organizational leaders invited to give updates of house-building projects undertaken abroad. Coordinating the event and conducting most of the workshops were Habitat International staff brought in from the organization's headquarters in Americus, Georgia, or from its numerous offices scattered throughout the country.

This latter group was responsible for the many details this three-day occasion entailed. They held devotions each morning on a sloping campus lawn. They served meals each morning, noon, and evening in the college gymnasium. They organized well-attended and inspirational meetings each night in the mission-style Sacred Heart Chapel, where gospel choirs, musicians, guest speakers, and, of course, Millard Fuller reminded the gathered faithful and curious of the many reasons why Habitat's ministry should indeed be celebrated. Perhaps the international staff's most significant contribution was their offering a full sixty-five different workshops in classrooms throughout the campus. To get a sense of the disparate issues covered, consider a sampling of titles: "Conducting Evaluative Research for Your Affiliate," "Forming a Board of Directors," "Establishing and Maintaining Effective Church Relations," "Partnering with Commercial Builders," "The Affiliate Insurance Program," and "The Future of Government and Institutional Partnerships with Habitat." Workshops focused on improving communication within the organization—like the one explaining how to log onto Habitat's electronic bulletin board system—and with people outside of the organization, such as the workshop on producing flashy Habitat infomercials. Some workshops gave tips on how to attract a broad array of middle-income volunteers, and others discussed how to narrow low-income homeowner applicants to a select few. One workshop offered by Linda Fuller reminded people of "The Early Years" of Habitat, and another, led by a former executive vice-president of the organization, asked them to consider "The Future of Habitat for Humanity®."

Events like this one, and others similar to it, are revealing. They demonstrate, as James Luther Adams put it, that people are willing to resist confining their "attention merely to family and job" through participating with paradenominational groups like Habitat. They suggest that Habitat has come to recognize that individuals may prove "good for nothing" if they are not organized and provided institutional vehicles by which their goodness can be steered in effective directions. The meticulous planning that made "Celebration '94" such a success and the complex issues addressed during it are a testament to the purposeful and expansive organization Habitat has created within a very short time.

This is not to say that the organization has become a palatial abode for bureaucratic ostentation. It has simply, as they say in the construction trades, "added on" to its original structure in a number of ways worth exploring. The first thing to notice about the organization is that it consists of three basic administrative layers: the international organization, the local affiliates, and the various area offices and regional centers that serve as organizational liaisons between them. Discussing each of these should suggest how far Habitat has come since its founding at Koinonia Farm in the autumn of 1976.

A Complex Organization for Simple, Decent Houses

Level One: The International Organization

Despite some people's protestations that Habitat's international headquarters ought to be located closer to the political and economic decision makers in cosmopolitan Atlanta, it remains within a few miles of Koinonia, situated in the central square of quaint Americus, Georgia. Actually, Habitat permeates the town. Its numerous volunteer houses

are scattered seemingly everywhere. The three-story Rylander building in the town center provides work space for approximately 200 people while other employees work in a twenty-eight-unit apartment complex that has been converted into offices. A $121 million organization
in 1999, Habitat is one of the largest employers in Americus. It is managed by about 25 senior salaried personnel, who direct the activities of
roughly 325 paid employees (another 600 work abroad and in the area
offices and regional centers in the United States) and more than 150
long-term volunteers who typically serve for at least a year. The latter
are reimbursed with housing, health insurance, and a modest weekly
stipend. Many more short-term volunteers are also integrally involved,
and they contribute significantly to the organization's enormous presence within the town. The throngs of people, especially young ones,
walking down the street wearing tool belts and blue jeans, the many
Habitat-sponsored community events, and, of course, the abundance of
"simple, decent houses" scattered within and just outside of town are
constant reminders of what a fixture the organization has become within
Americus.

Habitat's success internationally has come from its ability to fashion
an organizational vessel able to contain its religiously informed vision
while also respecting its natural fluidity. Edgar Stoesz, former chairman
of the international board, appreciates this balance very well. "Habitat
is an organization. Millard [Fuller] doesn't buy that. He thinks it's a
movement, and I hope it is. But we're also an organization." He then
avers, "The Habitat paradigm is the most powerful paradigm I know.
We need to make our organization worthy of our paradigm."[1] This difficult task is one Habitat takes seriously. The very structure of the organization reflects a conscious effort to remain true to its original charism.
Its board of directors consists of Fuller plus twenty-seven church, community, and (particularly recently) business leaders, the same number
that came to that first Habitat conference in 1976. Fuller, the president
and chief executive officer, remains the charismatic and titular leader of
the organization, although the day-to-day operations are now in the
hands of David Williams, the executive vice president and chief operations officer. On the next rung of the administrative ladder are the
heads of the three main branches of organizational operations. The first
of these is Habitat Support Services, which entails such functions as
human resource administration, personnel training, and institutional
development and communications. This branch also has responsibility

for raising money and managing other resources, functions so basic (and critical) to any organization that further comment seems unnecessary. The other two branches implementing programs do warrant fuller discussion because they reflect Habitat's foundational religious vision. They are the means by which Habitat pursues its dual goal of eliminating poverty housing from the face of the earth and, in the meantime, informing people's consciences about the problem of inadequate shelter.

Charged with advancing the consciousness-raising part of this goal is the second main organizational branch, Public Awareness and Education. The means by which it does this are diverse enough to defy easy summation. They include such things as marketing the seven books Fuller has written about the organization, selling Habitat merchandise, distributing the latest informational literature and stylish promotional packets, establishing a Habitat Web site on the Internet (which regularly logs a million "hits" per month)—the list could go on nearly interminably. None of these efforts, however, receive as much public attention and praise as the so-called special events. The Jimmy Carter Work Projects are good examples. So are the annual Collegiate Challenges, during which, in 1999, 7,500 college students spent their spring breaks building houses and raising a combined $650,000 at 158 participating U.S. affiliates.[2] Another example is the annual Building on Faith week, during which faith communities are asked to partner with local Habitat affiliates by providing the money and volunteers for a week-long blitz build. In 1999 churches and synagogues came together at 200 locations in North America and built 300 houses.[3] Here too the list could go on. One way to get a sense of the disparate ventures undertaken by this branch of the organization is to describe briefly the different departments that exist within it.

Among the more important is the Church Relations Department, located in Murfreesboro, Tennessee. It assists affiliates in developing solid church partnerships by providing them with training sessions and various resources for church outreach, establishing working relationships with denominational leaders, and developing church events designed to generate interest in low-income housing. Topping the list of these events would be the International Day of Prayer and Action. Held on the third Sunday of September, its purpose is to encourage churches to incorporate the issue of inadequate housing into their worship services that day. To accompany their offerings of prayer, Habitat suggests four other ways for churches to assist their work. Joining the "Carpenter's Club" means that they have agreed to make a regular financial contribution to their local affiliate. Churches involved with the "Nehemiah Program" provide the funds and perhaps the volunteers to build a specific portion of a single house (the framing, roof, or the like). The "Covenant Church" and "Adopt-a-Home" programs are more extensive forms of congregational involvement. Participating in the first requires churches to sign a covenant with the local affiliate, agreeing to provide it with prayer as well as financial and volunteer support. Adopting a home means basically that: Churches, either individually or in partnership with others, take responsibility for all the funding and labor needed for the construction of an entire house. Of course, any church, or any individual for that matter, can assist Habitat in any way they desire. The Church Relations Department tries to make this easier by packaging involvement opportunities in clearly defined and doable ways and then assisting local affiliates in making them known to different religious bodies.

Also deserving comment is Campus Chapters. Since Baylor University became the first in 1987, this department has created more than six hundred chapters and now has its sights on having Habitat present on all of the nation's approximately three thousand college campuses. Some high school chapters are forming as well. The purpose is to raise awareness about housing issues among students and to generate their support for nearby affiliates. Expanding this program is, similar to church outreach, considered a priority at Habitat. Like the churches, schools have been targeted as critical socialization institutions within which Habitat's consciousness-raising message must resound if the organization is to strike a chord with active citizens in the future.

Another way of spreading that message is facilitated by Habitat's Global Village department. Begun in 1989, this program organizes work groups and sends them to Habitat affiliates in more than forty developing countries for two- and three-week stints. The affiliates hosting these "work camps" provide leadership and try to make the experience a meaningful one for participants. They, in turn, are expected to raise the money for the houses they build; pay for their own travel, food, and accommodations; and recount their experiences through public speaking and writing when they return home. By all accounts, these experiences are as physically and emotionally challenging for participants as they are eye-opening, and, perhaps partly because of this, they are growing in popularity. Just over one hundred of these work camps were sent out in 1999, each consisting of between ten and twenty volunteers.

Habitat's international scope does not preclude it from modeling a concern for local communities. That is why, in 1992, it began the Sumter County Initiative, an ambitious effort to partner with government, businesses, and other community groups to repair or replace the approximately five hundred substandard houses standing (some barely) within its home county. By 1999 roughly three hundred houses had been completed, and, given the program's increasing momentum, it is likely its goal will be attained before long. The larger aim of demonstrating that major changes can take place in a single community if resources are pooled and imaginations are captured has, according to Habitat leaders, already been largely accomplished.

Not all of this work is based in Americus. As with the Church Relations Department in Tennessee, Habitat has recently begun establishing offices in other parts of the country with mandates to deal creatively with new issues facing the organization. Located in Sioux Falls, South Dakota, the American Indian Initiative is a good example. Its work has focused on bringing the Habitat paradigm to reservations in the hope of furthering the success of the Eagle Butte affiliate in the aftermath of the 1994 Jimmy Carter Work Project. Another example is the Urban Initiative, which is Habitat's attempt to have a greater impact within inner cities by working more extensively with other community-based groups. In addition to building or renovating multiple homes within single neighborhoods, it represents a first foray into a more complicated approach to housing, which includes trying to enhance commercial development in selected areas and address problems like crime, drugs, and unemployment. To date the initiative's office has been established in Chicago, and pilot projects are underway at four selected affiliates, each receiving technical support and fundraising assistance from the international headquarters.[4] A comparable approach has been pursued by the La Frontera Initiative. Its work has centered upon the poor, unincorporated rural subdivisions ("colonias") that dot the Mexican-American border, more than twelve hundred of them in Texas alone. Working out of its office in McAllen, Texas, Habitat intends to form affiliates in as many colonias as possible and thus draw public attention and funding to the poor who reside in them. Next, the Diversity Department was set up in Chicago with the aim of establishing new partnerships with minority groups; the intention is to alter the predominantly white makeup of Habitat's organizational leadership.[5] Finally, Habitat opened a Washington, D.C., office in 1993 for the purpose of serving as a liaison between it and other national and international organizations that might assist with its ministry. Overall, these initiatives and others attest to the seriousness with which Habitat pursues its goal of informing people's consciences about housing needs.[6]

Getting houses built, needless to say, is the other part of Habitat's dual goal. Making sure this is done as quickly, cheaply, and as well as possible is the function of the third organizational branch. Referred to as Habitat Affiliates Worldwide, this branch is further divided into U.S. Affiliates (numbering approximately 1,500) and International Affiliates (numbering more than 300). Their efforts in 1999 alone led to the construction of 13,682 houses: 4,906 in the United States and a full 8,776 elsewhere, particularly in the developing world.

Besides providing much-needed start-up capital (which in 1999 included $7 million from U.S. affiliates' tithes), Habitat International supplements most international affiliates' fundraising programs with money for land, construction materials, transportation, and the expenses of training and supporting local staff, including the nearly 200 "international partners" who volunteer for three-year commitments at overseas affiliates. U.S. affiliates, on the other hand, are expected to do their own fundraising. Even here, though, the international organization covers the expenses of such things as the land and construction materials for special projects (in which affiliates participate), training seminars and informational materials for affiliates, and Habitat International's area offices and regional centers throughout the United States. Both the International Affiliates and U.S. Affiliates departments are extremely important. Helping to coordinate the activities of all those local initiatives, assisting in the formation of new ones, handling unforeseen problems, and networking with other like-minded organizations are ongoing responsibilities indispensable to the organization. Habitat International's commitment to assuming those responsibilities as the number of affiliates grows dramatically is evidenced by the large staff employed at its headquarters and elsewhere.

Level Two: The Area Offices and Regional Centers

Under International Affiliates are, along with nearly fifty national offices, four main areas with directors working out of the Americus headquarters: Africa/Middle East; Asia/Pacific; Europe/New Independent

States/Canada; and Latin America/Caribbean. The organization of the U.S. Affiliates program, to which all further comments will refer, is more elaborate. Habitat has divided the United States into five areas, with a staffed office located within each. The areas are each further divided into three regions (also with fully staffed offices) representing between two to seven states, depending upon the size of the states and number of local affiliates within them. Area offices and regional centers work to coordinate the U.S. Affiliate program and provide guidance and other resources as needed. Both are also part of Habitat International; they are not separately incorporated, as the local affiliates are. They are essentially responsible for ensuring that the fifteen hundred local affiliates under their care are well acquainted with Habitat's founding vision and methods of operation. Hosting annual regional conferences, numerous training sessions, and perhaps state meetings are ways in which they perform this crucial role.[7] Additional responsibilities include assisting with special events held by Habitat International and, when necessary, augmenting local affiliates' efforts in fundraising, building material procurement, and volunteer recruitment.

Level Three: The Local Affiliates

Habitat's most multifarious administrative layer consists of the many grassroots affiliates formed by concerned citizens in their local communities. About one-third of all affiliates have paid staff; others have not yet reached that stage of growth, and still others may remain "kitchen table" initiatives without ever possessing the administrative accoutrements that one normally associates with a nonprofit organization. Some build scores of houses every year, while others look forward to building one house as an annual accomplishment. The newest and smallest of affiliates may be content to rehab a house or two, or perhaps undertake such projects as painting the inside of the local homeless shelter or clearing some overgrown public land that has become an eyesore. Almost any project, these groups explain, can be useful for creating interest, making a difference, and establishing momentum for a nascent Habitat affiliate. In some (particularly rural) areas, land for building is purchased relatively cheaply, whereas in more densely populated communities land is often so expensive that affiliates must rely on local governments to make unused or foreclosed properties available to them at low cost. Some affiliates scatter their houses throughout a given area, while others cluster them together, hoping to revive an entire neighborhood. These are only a few of the myriad variations one encounters, and they serve as a reminder that Habitat is at once a single international organization and a loose collection of hundreds of local entities. Fortunately, even a loose organizational embrace creates a certain degree of commonality among affiliates, from which more general observations can be made. This is true because each local affiliate must, first, undergo a uniform affiliation process and, second, possess a single organizational structure shared by all Habitat affiliates. A brief description of this twofold commonality should provide an adequate description of this third administrative layer.

From start to finish, the affiliation process usually takes between nine and twelve months. The intentionality, comprehensiveness, and sheer length of this process is a function of Habitat International's deep concern that its affiliates be formed as full-fledged incarnations of the Habitat ethos, not simply as well-intentioned house-building initiatives. To understand what is involved, it is instructive to consider the two-volume orientation handbook distributed to prospective affiliates. It explains the entire process, consisting of no fewer than seventy-seven steps. (See Appendix B for an abbreviated listing.) For the sake of simplicity, these steps can be placed within seven major categories that, for the most part, must be accomplished serially. Explaining each of these should illustrate how common ground can be created between otherwise diverse local affiliates.

The first twelve steps taken by people interested in starting an affiliate are designed to "lay the foundation" for the organization. This is done primarily through education. These groups or individuals must contact the nearest regional center for information about Habitat, attend regional meetings and training sessions, and visit an established affiliate to get a sense of how the organization works. Reading some of Fuller's books and subscribing to the organization's publications, *Habitat World* and *The Affiliate Update*, are also strongly recommended.[8] Being educated about Habitat's ministry is not enough, though. Would-be affiliates must also take time to learn about other nonprofit and government housing initiatives, speak to as many churches, civic groups, and community organizations as possible, and make contact with the targeted "community of need" to learn about the concerns of low-income people in their area. Particularly important is conducting a thorough "housing needs assessment" to determine if there is a sizable population, earning between 30 to 50 percent of the area's median income, who are without suitable housing and who are unserved by existing community programs.

After this is done, a second set of steps, focusing on "becoming a prospective affiliate," are taken. First, a steering committee of at least twelve people must be formed. Their names and addresses are sent to the nearest regional center so they can begin receiving Habitat's informational literature. The committee will need plenty of enthusiasm and a wide variety of skills, which is why attorneys, social workers, contractors, and neighborhood residents are typically members. Particular emphasis is placed upon forming steering committees representative of the cultural diversity existing within actual communities, although that does not always occur. Once the steering committee has defined the geographic area to be served and decided upon an affiliate name that reflects it, they request permission to use the Habitat name from Americus and, if approved, acquire the status of "prospective affiliate."

This is important because it gives the fledgling affiliate access to additional informational resources, such as Habitat's five-volume *Affiliate Operations Manual,* and to an abundance of promotional materials permitting it to commence upon a third category of steps, "enlarging the base of support." This entails fundraising, giving presentations to churches and community organizations, making contacts with the media, businesses, and local government, and essentially spreading the word about the ministry. Affiliates are directed to hold at least one well-advertised public meeting within the target community for the purposes of nurturing partnerships with people living in their local area. They are also expected to develop a database of potential volunteers, listing their interests and skills, who can be contacted when the affiliate is ready to form operating committees or begin a building project.

The fourth and fifth categories can be mentioned briefly. The steps under the rubric "legal considerations" guide the affiliate through the complicated process of gaining tax-exempt 501(c)(3) status, which includes drafting articles of incorporation (to be approved by Habitat as well as the requisite state agencies), voting on the affiliate's bylaws, and developing various fiscal policies and procedures. These steps are painstaking, but they differ little from those necessary to form any nonprofit organization. The next category, "committee formation," on the other hand, involves getting sufficiently trained volunteers to serve on the five mandatory operating committees for Habitat affiliates: Development, Family Selection, Family Nurture, Site Selection, and Building

Committee. These make up the invariable organizational structure of local affiliates, and, because of their centrality for understanding how affiliates work, they are explained more fully below.

There are two final sets of steps in the affiliation process. Nominating and then electing a twelve- to twenty-person board of directors is the beginning of the next category. The board is then guided by Habitat in addressing such issues as how to structure titles to Habitat homes, the possible hiring of staff, the number of "sweat equity" hours to require, and the affiliate's tithing goals. The board's responsibility includes signing the affiliate covenant with Habitat International as well. After that is submitted, a final category of steps, "application for affiliation and approval," begins. Mostly this involves producing paperwork attesting that the many steps in the affiliation process have been followed and demonstrating that the mandatory organizational structure is firmly in place. If the application is approved by the regional director, the area director, and, finally, Habitat's international board of directors, a new local affiliate is founded.

This process, as challenging as it usually proves to be, is intended to mold well-meaning, but often inchoate, grassroots interest in doing something about substandard housing into Habitat's demonstrably effective organizational form. Local affiliates, one could say, undergo a common gestation period. Importantly, their subsequent maturation also proceeds in a uniform direction by virtue of every affiliate possessing a similar structure. (See Appendix C.) Habitat International mandates that they carry out their work through five operating committees.*

The first of these is the Development Committee responsible for fundraising and public relations. These tasks, often performed by separate committees in some larger affiliates, must be undertaken by any nonprofit aspiring to success over the long term. Perhaps the only way Habitat distinguishes itself here is by its emphasis on spreading its message as widely as possible within a given community. Affiliates are expected to research their community's housing needs and make them well known through the media and their own publications. Special priority is given to making public presentations at churches, schools, civic groups, and community organizations. The point is to inform people about housing issues and to make Habitat's work, as much as possible, the work of the entire community rather than a few "true believers." Generating that sort of widespread involvement is part of Habitat's approach to fundraising as well. Even before submitting their application for affiliation, affiliates are required by Americus to raise a minimum of three thousand dollars from at least fifteen different sources in their communities to demonstrate a sufficiently broad range of local support. Affiliates, in short, must be in partnership with their local communities in order to live up to Habitat's founding vision. Further, given the capital-intensive nature of housing construction, they are unlikely to be successful without this broad approach to fundraising. Thus, individuals, churches, foundations, corporations, government agencies (within the previously mentioned limits), banks capable of providing low-interest loans, contractors, and building suppliers willing to give in-kind donations are all part of an extremely eclectic array with something to offer Habitat. By putting their resources to good use, affiliates are able to build houses and, in accordance with organizational ideology, build a sense of responsibility to the community among a broad selection of groups within it. Aside from its emphasis on fostering extensive partnerships, however, the Development Committee at a Habitat affiliate is probably similar to those of other nonprofits. This cannot be said of the other operating committees, two of which focus on the homeowners and two on the houses; they reflect more of the uniqueness of Habitat's ministry.

The Family Selection Committee, one of the two that deal most directly with the homeowners, is responsible for devising fair application procedures for Habitat homes, screening applications, interviewing potential homeowner families, and recommending those selected to the affiliate board for approval. Although the specifics may vary from one locale to another, all Habitat affiliates must base their family-selection decisions upon three basic criteria. The first, generally considered the most important of these, is the applicant family's need for adequate shelter, although the criteria used for determining need are quite variable. For some affiliates, it might mean that family members live in a house that lacks proper plumbing or wiring or shows signs of severe structural damage. Often overcrowding is taken to be grounds for approval. Some affiliates, especially in urban areas, maintain that living in certain deteriorated, crime-ridden housing projects—even public housing projects—is enough to qualify. So varied are the potentially acceptable indicators of inadequate living conditions that every applicant family receives a home visit and is interviewed by (usually two) members of the Family Selection Committee. Once need is established, the committee then makes sure the family does not meet the income requirements for any conventional or government-assisted loan programs for low-income groups. People usually qualify for these if they make between 50 and 75 percent of the median income for a given geographic area; consequently, for many affiliates, that percentage serves as a maximum income guideline for assessing financial need among applicants.

A family's need, defined as inadequate shelter and insufficient resources, cannot be so extreme that they are unprepared for the financial burdens of home ownership, which include paying the costs of the mortgage, taxes, insurance, and utilities. Many affiliates require applicants to have a combined monthly income that is at least three times their expected monthly house payments but no more than six times that amount. The second criterion for family selection, then, is the applicant family's ability to afford a Habitat house. Their combined resources can come from wages, alimony payments, child support, and public assistance. All of these income sources, as well as any outstanding debts, are meticulously confirmed through employment records and other forms of verification: credit reports, landlord and personal references, and so forth. While some might see the qualifying process as excessively intrusive, Habitat sees it as the only realistic means of identifying suitable applicants.

The third family-selection criterion is "willingness to partner" with the affiliate. Applicants, in other words, should understand and accept that they are not simply going to become home buyers or passive beneficiaries. They should be willing to become partners, a role that includes completing the requisite sweat equity hours, making a down payment and monthly mortgage payments in a timely fashion, conscientiously maintaining their home, and faithfully attending family-nurture sessions. Checking references, home visits, and interviews with the applicants are the means Habitat uses to determine their willingness to partner. While clearly an inexact category, it is taken quite seriously since the partnership, even if one considers only the time between ground breaking and move-in days, can last more than a year. Therefore, accepting only those families who buy into Habitat's vision and are prepared to commit themselves to it—with all its ups and downs, delays, and sometimes headaches—is important if the organization is to function smoothly.

Following the selection of the homeowner families, making certain that the relationship between them and the affiliate is one of authentic (not patronizing) partnership is the goal of the third operating committee: the Family Nurture Committee. From the time they are selected until six months or more after the homeowners move in, this committee functions as the primary liaison between the families and the affiliate. Recognizing that Habitat homeowners not only lack experience with home ownership but also frequently face such problems as a lack of education, low self-esteem, debts, and improper nutrition and health care, the committee usually designates one member to be a family's "sponsor" and to help them through whatever difficulties may arise. Most fundamentally, this person is supposed to be sensitive to the family members' needs and provide them with guidance as they fulfill Habitat's expectations while, just as importantly, being receptive to whatever feedback or complaints they might have concerning the affiliate. Sponsors assist in all kinds of ways. They help the homeowners get involved in affiliate-run meetings and special events and make them feel welcome. They assist with new experiences that run the gamut from coping with media attention (homeowners, after all, are likely to make the evening news) to choosing a floor plan or color scheme for their houses.

Two areas of involvement are particularly important. First, they help acclimate the families to the responsibilities of home ownership by giving advice about property taxes, insurance, home maintenance, and mortgage payments. Also, should those monthly payments become delinquent, the sponsor takes on the additional role of mediator between the family and affiliate in order to help them come to a mutually fair solution, which could mean granting an extension or even restructuring the payment schedule. Second, the sponsor is responsible for keeping track of the family's sweat equity hours and, when necessary, encouraging their completion. They frequently suggest creative, non-Habitat-related activities to which some of those hours (usually no more than 20 percent) can be applied, such as enrolling in a literacy or GED program or participating in a local Neighborhood Watch group.

Finally, the Family Nurture Committee as a whole takes the initiative in empowering the homeowners. Many affiliates, for example, offer classes for prospective and current homeowners on practical topics like do-it-yourself home repairs, budgeting, home insurance policies, or almost anything else its homeowners request. Others provide education on those same topics by developing a homeowner's manual. It is also not uncommon for the Family Nurture Committee to serve as a catalyst for the development of homeowners' associations, through which Habitat families themselves take on the responsibility of nurturing one another. In Jacksonville, Florida, for example, the homeowners' association plans all the house-dedication ceremonies for new Habitat homeowners. The one in Americus is even more active. It established an emergency fund to dispense loans to families trying to cope with financial difficulties. Habitat encourages such efforts because they reinforce its conviction that homeowners should not simply be housed and then left to fend for themselves, but rather should receive the person-to-person nurturance that defines caring communities.

Although its commitment to partnering with homeowners means that Habitat is about more than just building houses, houses too need careful attention if the organization is to be successful. This is the concern of the remaining two operating committees. The Site Selection Committee is typically composed of members who have real estate and construction experience. Its duties are basically twofold. First, it identifies target areas in which—conditional on there being both a clear need and an expressed desire for Habitat's involvement—the affiliate should operate. Then the committee takes on the task of trying to obtain property for building. Decisions have to be made as to whether the affiliate should build many homes on subdivided tracts of land or on scattered isolated sites, whether it should rehabilitate old homes or build new ones, and, if the latter is the case, whether it should undertake single-family or multifamily construction. Sometimes these decisions are made for the affiliate, as on those fortuitous, though rare, occasions when it receives a building or piece of land as a donation. At other times, affiliates simply buy whatever land they can afford or whatever tax-delinquent properties government agencies make available to them. In any case, real estate is seldom obtained without laborious investigation. Even when a particular property seems feasible, the committee would be remiss if it approved the purchase without researching zoning laws to confirm that the lot size is appropriate for a Habitat house, ensuring that the property is free of environmental liabilities, such as improper drainage or toxic waste, and seeking competent legal advice to determine if the property is burdened with back taxes, liens, or title defects.

As involved as these issues are, they do not compare to the avalanche of details and near-limitless chores that come with building houses, especially with minimal capital and the labor of unskilled homeowners and volunteers. Probably only those with contracting experience can understand the assiduous planning and endless technicalities that go into heavy construction projects. It would be futile to attempt to delineate all the steps necessary to construct even "simple, decent houses"; suffice to say that they are all trod by the local affiliate's Building Committee. In smaller affiliates its duties include coordinating and overseeing every aspect of the building process, scheduling and directing (and often teaching) volunteers and homeowners at the construction site, hiring and directing paid subcontractors when they are needed, arranging for the necessary permits and inspections—essentially making sure the work gets done. With larger affiliates, these hands-on jobs are typically delegated to affiliate staff. In fact, after the executive director, the next person a growing affiliate inevitably hires is a construction supervisor, who is usually pivotal to its success. In these larger affiliates, the Building Committee attends to other, though no less important, matters. Among these are coming up with design criteria for the houses, procuring building materials from suppliers, and, since members are very likely to be part of the professional construction community, providing the affiliate with whatever free services they can and making contacts with other professionals to persuade them to do likewise.

As with the affiliation process, then, the five mandatory operating committees give Habitat some degree of uniformity at the grassroots level. Other committees, though not required, are sometimes added to this general structure. Trying to increase involvement among faith communities, some affiliates form Church Relations Committees. Concerned to maintain or accentuate the religious character of their work, some add a Worship and Celebration Committee, which will arrange brief devotional services at the building site and assist in groundbreaking and house-dedication ceremonies. Many affiliates find Volunteer Coordination Committees to be virtually indispensable as they increase in size; and, as these volunteers keep hammering, an accompanying Safety Committee is sometimes established to improve their chances of doing do so without injury. These committees and others may added at the discretion of each local affiliate. Apart from Habitat's requirement that they establish the main operating committees and undergo a common affiliation process, they are free to function as they choose without interference from the international headquarters or its regional centers. In truth, without such local autonomy, Habitat might never have achieved the impressive levels of success it now enjoys.

Habitat's Growth and Its Limitations

Faith in a Nationwide Outbreak of "Habititus"

From the very beginning, Habitat's religious vision has shaped its ideology, its unique practices, and, as this chapter has discussed, much of its effective organizational structure. Because it was so entwined with his own religious sensibilities, Fuller took it as a matter of course—even a matter of faith—that the organization would grow. Ever brimming with confidence, he soon started referring to it as a "movement," a term that came with unmistakable connotations of massive grassroots mobilization and increasing vigor. Everywhere he detected symptoms of what he still calls "Habititus." This is his word for the contagious effect Habitat volunteers, putting their religious faiths into action, have upon others, who are certain to succumb to that same feverish impulse. Yet, despite Fuller's optimistic prognosis, it was not clear just how widespread "Habititus" would become during the early years of the ministry.

The organization, though expanding, appeared rather modest at the outset. In 1983, for example, fewer than fifty volunteers and only seven salaried staff worked out of a few houses in Americus. By the end of that year, only eighteen international affiliates and thirty-nine U.S. affiliates were in operation. Only 523 houses had been built or renovated at that point, the vast majority of them outside of the United States. Most of the work done out of Americus was geared toward making the organization more popularly known. The most notable of those efforts was the seven-hundred-mile walk from Americus to Indianapolis completed by the Fullers and a small group of Habitat faithful in celebration of the organization's seventh anniversary. The hundred thousand dollars they raised from pledges was, to date, an unparalleled success.[9] Clearly, the organization was slowly expanding under Fuller's leadership. His creative ideas and irrepressible pep gave it needed momentum, and his "riches to rags" life story served as a badge of credibility to anyone, especially potential supporters, with questions about his abilities or convictions. But as Habitat struggled to broaden its scope and reputation, Fuller's considerable talents were not enough to give the organization the infectious quality he always claimed it possessed. If anything like that has occurred, it is probably attributable to the boost former President Jimmy Carter has given the organization. The public attention he musters has spread its message here and abroad. As a political figure, he has probably also appealed to more secular individuals who might otherwise have been cautious about Habitat's overtly religious tenor. Whatever the case, he has made Habitat a household name among both religious and secular people, a fact that accounts for much of the organization's current success.

The turning point came in 1984, when Fuller took the nine-mile drive from Americus to Plains to inquire whether Carter, who had already donated money to Habitat and spoken at a couple of its local functions, would be willing to become even more involved.[10] As Fuller recounts it, his meeting with President and Mrs. Carter at their home was a brief one, and it ended with him asking, in his usual unreserved manner, "Are you interested in Habitat for Humanity®, or are you very interested?" Prefacing his response with his trademark grin, Carter replied, "We're very interested." To prove it, he proposed that Fuller make out a list of ways the two of them could be of assistance. Within two weeks, a letter was in Carter's hands. In it Fuller included a set of fifteen suggestions, which included: serving on Habitat's board; making contacts with the media and key individuals; helping with fundraising; endorsing a direct-mail campaign; promoting the organization through speaking engagements, public service announcements, and a thirty-minute video; personally volunteering and contributing money; and, lastly, praying for the success of the ministry. Much to everyone's surprise, the Carters agreed to do everything outlined in the letter. The consequences were nearly as immediate as they were catalytic for Habitat. Its total revenues for 1984 amounted to approximately $3.5 million, a respectable increase from the $2.4 million for the previous year. With Carter's involvement, however, things took off. He chaired a two-year, $10 Million Campaign Committee that, by the time of Habitat's tenth-year anniversary in 1986, had exceeded its goal by raising over $12 million. By 1995 Habitat International's total annual revenues approached $60 million, an amount that does not include the fundraising efforts of local affiliates. The latter, if added, would have brought the total to well over $100 million.

Although Habitat has been very deliberate about how best to capitalize on the former president's renown, arguably his most significant contribution to the ministry began serendipitously or, as Carter himself insists, by "an act of God."[11] Jogging through lower Manhattan one spring morning in 1984, he happened upon a six-story tenement building that, having recently been acquired by Habitat, was being gutted in preparation for renovation by a cadre of local volunteers. Carter stopped

and was given an unofficial tour of the site by the director of the bud-
ding New York affiliate, to whom he offered whatever assistance he
could give. Word of that casual overture got back to Fuller, who was
not one to dismiss such offers. With Carter's consent, he chartered a
bus to take the former president and his wife, a group of volunteers from
Maranatha Baptist Church, where they were members, and several others picked up along the way—fifty people in total—back to Manhattan
the following September to work on that building for five days. So
began the first Jimmy Carter Work Project.

Compared to later projects, this one was much less ambitious. But
like each of the subsequent ones, it was a media magnet, and it put
Habitat on the American nonprofit map almost overnight. It began as
the former president got off the bus in New York. He was accosted by
about seventy-five news reporters, photographers, and TV camera oper-
ators, all drawn to the story of a powerful man humbling himself before
the strength of his own convictions. The media coverage lasted throughout, and Carter was forthcoming as always. "I don't know of another
project anywhere that has such a combination of inspiration, enjoyment, excitement, potential growth and direct tangible benefits to the
poor," he told the cameras. "It's compatible with the things I tried to
do as President in support of human rights, justice, caring for people
who are poor but want to do something about their situation."[12]
Explained in such terms, Habitat could make sense to many types of
people, but Carter could also speak in explicitly religious language. At
an evening worship service following a twelve-hour day of manual labor,
he read a Gospel passage about the need for humility when giving to
others, and then confided to those assembled, "I think what we have
been doing this week is part of serving Christ's kingdom; it's been one
of the most notable steps in my Christian life."[13] Statements such as
these are very effective for spreading the word about Habitat. In much
the same way as Carter's 1976 presidential victory had opened the eyes
of many to the political power of evangelical Christians, he was beginning to awaken Americans to the importance and benefits of voluntarism. At the same time he did wonders for Habitat's public image.

Also noteworthy was Carter's part in resolving what has easily been
Habitat's most significant internal crisis. In 1990 Fuller was accused of
sexual harassment by five female employees in Americus. Although he
apologized and insisted that it was all a misunderstanding, the event
sowed enough divisiveness within the organization that it was nearly

cracked to its foundations. Some people in Americus, whether siding with Fuller or not, simply wanted to forget the ugliness of the situation and move on. Others, convinced his behavior toward the women was neither proper nor isolated, confronted him. They seem to have been supported by people wanting to get rid of Fuller, who, in addition to many laudable qualities, possessed a well-earned reputation for micromanagement and insensitivity to others and, at times, a leadership style that bordered on the autocratic. This inability to loosen the reins of control, often referred to as "founder's syndrome," is understandable given the amount of work and commitment that are necessary to bring an organization like Habitat into existence. According to many, however, it was just plain exasperating to work with Fuller. The atmosphere at Habitat grew toxic, and for the first time the ministry was receiving negative, and at times embarrassing, publicity.

Under much pressure and seeing no other alternative, the board stripped Fuller of his decision-making power and reconfigured his role within the organization to be a more ceremonial one, limited to public speaking, raising money, and writing books. He tried to come to terms with this arrangement but eventually found it so intolerable that he tendered his resignation to the board. At this point, Carter's influence became pivotal. He chided the board for its internal squabbling and threatened to leave in support of Fuller, a move that cost Habitat substantial financial support, including a $2 million line of credit from First Atlanta Bank.

Carter's expression of support for Fuller put the ministry into fiscal turmoil and, almost inadvertently, brought an end to the crisis. First, in an effort to cut costs, forty-three employees were fired, including the organization's three chaplains and David Rowe, the widely respected director of international affiliates who had served as Habitat's board chairman for an unsurpassed nine years. This caused nothing short of an uproar because those four people, as well as many of the others, were among those who had confronted Fuller about his improper conduct. Although it is not clear that this was the case, many felt that the fired staff members had been targeted as malcontents. It is clear that the firings rid Habitat of many of its dissident voices and effectively quieted any that still remained in Americus.

The financial difficulties ensuing from Carter's warning had a second effect as well: They forced the board to act decisively and creatively. They did this by making Fuller Habitat's CEO while instituting a subordinate chief-of-operations position to handle the day-to-day management of the ministry. This resolution was acceptable to Fuller because it permitted him to retain his administrative powers and still left plenty of time to travel and promote Habitat as he saw fit. It also served Habitat since it wrested some power from Fuller and made room for a new administrator with precisely the managerial skills he lacked. Thus, in addition to making Habitat more attractive to the American public, Carter, less intentionally, also had a part in making it a more effective organization, better able to direct its accelerating growth.

Growing is one of the things Habitat seems to do best. A key indicator of growth is its data on house construction. It took fifteen years for the first ten thousand houses to be built worldwide, an achievement worthy of some boasting. Yet the next ten thousand took only two years, the following ten thousand came in just fourteen months, and the organization expects in the near future to begin building twenty thousand homes a year worldwide. It is practically impossible to keep up with this expansion. Focusing on the American context simplifies matters, but here too the numbers are striking. In 1996 the nearly 1,300 U.S. affiliates located in all fifty states were about double the number (661) existing just five years earlier; in 1999 there were approximately 1,500 affiliates. An impressive twenty-nine thousand houses had been built in the United States, and, given that this number is nearly double the total of only four years earlier, it seems that Habitat's domestic construction is accelerating as dramatically as it is globally. As long as the nation's rising housing costs far outpace wage increases, Habitat houses will remain in demand. With their average cost of $42,500 in 1999 dollars, it is small wonder that so many of their owners declare them to be true godsends.[14]

Looking at these homeowner families, of which one-third are headed by single mothers, is another way of calculating the ministry's increasing impact in the United States. In 1999, roughly one hundred thousand Americans resided in Habitat homes, slightly more than half of whom were under the age of eighteen. Without Habitat, their prospects of finding suitable housing would have been severely limited, particularly since about 80 percent of adult Habitat homeowners have only high school educations or less. According to a 1998 HUD-sponsored evaluation of Habitat, a full 43 percent of homeowners earn less than half of the national median income, and another 34 percent earn between 50 and 80 percent of that figure. Only one in five of all homeowners surveyed believe they could have afforded their own home without Habitat.[15] Their need for housing priced below conventional market rates, therefore, is very pronounced—so much so that most are conscientious about making their house payments in a timely fashion. A recent organizational self-study revealed that 90 percent of homeowners were current on their mortgage payments, and fewer than 1 percent had defaulted on their loans to the extent that foreclosure became necessary.[16] In the main, people who move into Habitat houses stay in them and, by most accounts, are happy to do so.

Because of its proven effectiveness, the organization attracts huge numbers of supporters who, like the homeowners, are happy to be a part of Habitat. In 1993, for instance, approximately 250,000 people volunteered at U.S. affiliates and, in doing so, performed over five million hours of service to their local communities. Since the number of Habitat affiliates has increased more than 50 percent since then and its annual house production has more than doubled, there is good reason to believe that volunteering with the organization has experienced a similarly precipitous increase. As imprecise as this statement may be, it is important to keep in mind that Habitat is growing so rapidly that hard numbers fail to tell the story and, at least at this point in its history, become outdated extremely quickly. For now, it is enough to reiterate that Habitat's ability to draw more and more people to its work—along with its remarkable increase in affiliates, building projects, and homeowners— indicate that its ministry is both spreading and deserving of the closer attention it will receive in subsequent chapters.

A Cautionary Note

Habitat's enviable growth can be attributed to the stimulating and gratifying nature of its work, its appealing religious vision derived from the thought of Jordan and Fuller, an organizational structure that is at once well defined and flexible enough to conform to local contexts, and its positive public image. In the previous chapter and this one, these points have been addressed in turn. Now a simple cautionary note must be struck. When Fuller, even the promotional zealot, uses the term "Habititus" and other enthusiastic language to describe the organization's impact and momentum, he can sound overly optimistic about the capacity of Habitat and other nonprofit housing agencies to address the problem of inadequate shelter in the United States. Such enthusiasm can lull people into believing that voluntary efforts, without a commitment from the federal government, are enough to provide homes for people.

This belief is demonstrably false. As beneficent as nonprofits like Habitat are for mobilizing what might otherwise be "good for nothing" individual goodness, their proportions are indisputably not sufficient to meet America's housing needs.

Even a cursory glance at the data is quite bracing. About 14.5 million American households qualify for government housing assistance but, because of funding restrictions, only about 4.1 million households actually receive any.[17] Among those 10.4 million households not being helped, HUD researchers classify 5.3 million as facing "worst case housing needs." These are families earning less than 50 percent of their area's median income who either spend more than 50 percent of their earnings on rent and utilities or live in housing with severe physical deficiencies, such as a lack of electricity or indoor plumbing.[18] Helping even these families—a mere subset of the total number in need—is beyond the capability of the approximately two thousand nonprofit housing groups currently working within the United States. To do so would take more than a century since these groups altogether now build about fifty thousand units each year, a number that, while sizable, is still insufficient to meet the existing need.[19]

Many people who financially support, volunteer with, or are employed at Habitat tend to overlook this. At times they can be so busy with the work at hand and so focused on Habitat's lush, though isolated, islands of success, they forget these islands are located in a vast ocean of need. Many others, however, are well aware of the gap between what Habitat can do and the extent of the need. They typically respond by saying the organization is still successful in the sense that it continues to plug away at its dual goal of building houses and informing consciences. Interestingly, in addition to these more manifest goals, they are also apt to argue that Habitat performs the latent function of making its participants better citizens through the very process of joining together to improve their communities.[20] This citizenship theme is significant because an active citizenry is essential for the well-being of democratic societies such as ours. And since this theme is so prevalent at Habitat, it is also an important key for unlocking some of the deeper meanings and subtle tensions embedded within its organizational culture. The next two chapters will attempt to unravel those meanings and tensions.

4

Citizenship and Its Class-Based Distortions

In the modern democratic state, citizens are bound to certain sorts of obedience, but not to eternal vigilance or to the hard work of "ruling." Pluralist participation is not a duty, but only a means to realize values that ought, perhaps, to be realized, values that are carried, as it were, by the word "citizenship" and that many of us want to uphold, but to which individual citizens are not necessarily committed. But we should be clear about our alternatives. If we are not willing to rule in our turn, other men . . . will rule out of theirs. They will call us citizens, but we will be something less.

Michael Walzer, *Obligations: Essays on Disobedience, War, and Citizenship*

Family Selection and Citizenship in St. Paul

One way to assess the claim that involvement with Habitat performs the latent function of making people into better citizens—the intent of this chapter and the next—is to watch some of them in action. Plenty of action is precisely what one sees at the ten-year-old Twin Cities Habitat for Humanity®. By the autumn of 1994, it had proven itself to be one of the most successful and fastest-growing local affiliates in the United States. Even in a climate that brings most construction, with the exception of some interior work, to a snowy, shivering freeze during its long winter months, the affiliate was planning to complete an estimable twenty-eight homes in that year alone. Put in more human terms, this meant that twenty-eight families, whose average annual gross income was $15,756, would spend that winter in a warm house, payments for which averaged only $263 per month.

Helping to make that dream a reality were Habitat supporters throughout the seven-county metro area. They included an excess of 6,000 volunteers, 5,000 individual and business donors, and the approximately 250 local congregations that, alone, were responsible for raising nearly one-quarter of the affiliate's annual revenue. The affiliate, in turn, proved itself to be a shrewd steward of these funds. Its extensive use of dedicated volunteers and modest administrative overhead enabled it to direct a full 86 percent of its total budget toward ongoing construction efforts. If these numbers are any indication, Twin Cities Habitat appeared to be a voluntary-sector success story. That they only tell part of the story becomes evident when one inquires a bit more closely and discovers that the organization is also capable of mobilizing concerned citizens willing to participate in the life of their own communities.

One such community is St. Paul, Minnesota. Along with four nearby geographic locales, it has a Habitat "chapter" incorporated into the larger Twin Cities affiliate.[1] About a mile from the red brick buildings and neatly trimmed trees that distinguish St. Paul's downtown area is a predominantly working-class neighborhood. Here things are quieter. Cars course slowly through a gridlike arrangement of streets lined with two-story wooden houses. These would all appear uniformly rectangular were it not for their variety of front porches, protruding chimneys, and occasional gables. As darkness fell one evening in late September, these houses looked even more indistinguishable—that is, except for one. Outside were parked an unusually large number of cars and inside every light was turned on, which, given that there were no curtains or shades in the windows, emblazoned the structure in a white glow and revealed the house to be empty of furniture but nearly filled with people.

This was not just any house, nor were these typical guests. The house had been purchased by the Minneapolis Community Development Agency (MCDA) with funds provided by the federal government's HOPE III (Housing Opportunities for People Everywhere) program, which is designed to underwrite the purchase of publicly held properties for low-income families. The MCDA then sold it to Habitat for a dollar, as it had done with about forty other houses since 1987, with the expectation that the affiliate would rehabilitate it with resources and voluntary labor from the community and, of course, from the selected homeowner family as well. That explains the guests. About a dozen of them were employees from the Minnegasco utility company, which periodically sends groups to work on Habitat homes throughout the Twin Cities area. Most had worked all that day in lieu of going to their jobs, while a few had gotten into the habit of volunteering at this particular house a few nights each month after work hours.

The scent of fresh pizza in the air suggested that the crew had recently eaten a dinner of sorts and were planning to work a while longer before calling it a day. A few of them squatted on the unswept plywood floor next to the refrigerator and, sharing socket wrenches and a tattered set of instructions, were trying to piece the kitchen cabinets together and affix them to the wall above. "You call yourself an engineer?" one voice exclaimed, followed by peals of laughter and then a half-hearted, flabbergasted riposte. Other volunteers were applying paint to the walls and ceilings of two small bedrooms, or were using turpentine to remove it from the windowpanes and mahogany baseboards of the third, nearly completed, master bedroom. Such work is typically slow and tedious; the difference between it and what happens during promotional events like blitz builds is glaring. Indeed, just rehabbing this old house had already taken more than three months, and a date for moving in had still not been set.

Raymond Espinoza—husband, father of four, supermarket clerk, part-time business student, and future Habitat homeowner—was also working in the master bedroom with one of the Minnegasco volunteers installing two sliding doors for the walk-in closet. Beside him, with one hand clutching a soft-drink can and the other readied to hand the men whatever tools they requested, was his six-year-old son, Felipe, who made little effort to hide his enthusiasm about the evening. "This is going to be my parents' room," he announced to all who would listen. "Before we all stayed in one room, but now there's tons of space to move around. Me and my brother might even get bunk beds in our room." The volunteers smiled at this and seemed eager to hear more until Espinoza, in a somewhat hushed tone, asked his son to retrieve a dustpan and broom from the kitchen.

That was not going to be easy. By that time, the kitchen was overflowing with more people, who were chatting with the Minnegasco group and complimenting them on their day's progress. "Done yet?" a couple of them queried jokingly. Then they gave exaggerated shrugs as if to denote their awareness of the myriad tasks needing to be accomplished before such a question could be posed seriously. Some had filtered into the adjoining living room and taken seats on milk crates, unopened boxes of linoleum tile, five-gallon tubs of plastering compound, and a few paint-speckled stools and chairs. All were arranged in something approximating a circle and illuminated by bare light bulbs dangling from the cracked ceiling above. A few of the visitors were dressed casually while others, noticeably more cautious about where they sat, were still wearing office attire. Shortly after 7:30, a total of eighteen men and women—all white and ranging in age from their early thirties to their sixties—had assembled and called to order the monthly board meeting of Habitat's St. Paul chapter.

Predictably, the agenda proceeded with the chair of each operating committee taking a turn describing the work it had accomplished that month and then answering questions and leading further discussion as needed. The Development Committee outlined its plans for two upcoming house-dedication ceremonies and then reported on the progress of the affiliate's capital campaign. To date it had amassed close to $1.2 million; and along with the $350,000 expected from the local Wilder Foundation and another $430,000 from the perennially magnanimous Lutheran Brotherhood, it hoped to raise at least another $50,000 from the board and committee members representing each of the five local chapters. The latter remark appeared to surprise no one and was met with the concurring nods of people who understand that they are expected to give more than an occasional evening to the organization.

Eventually, people's attention was directed toward the houses. The chair of the Building Committee, an architect, presented a number of innovative construction designs and discussed the relative merits of each based on their ability to maximize space, conserve energy, cut costs, and meet the families' needs as articulated by the chapter's active homeowner's association. All of them were deemed acceptable by the larger group as long as they met with the approval of the homeowners and could be built within the ever-present financial constraints. Then, in light of a recent episode of vandalism at a near-finished Habitat house, the issue of purchasing security alarms for construction sites was raised but ultimately tabled until further information, especially about costs, could be acquired. The group agreed to the tentative solution of informing people associated with the organization of the need to regularly drive by Habitat houses to ensure that things were in order. That brought the meeting's focus to site selection. The committee chair spoke of difficulties related to the governmental "red tape" accompanying HOPE III houses. He reported that the state requires agencies rehabbing these structures to install sprinkler systems costing approximately three thousand dollars and, for those houses built prior to 1970, mandates the professional removal of lead paint from the premises, which typically costs about fifteen thousand dollars. It was obvious to everyone that, while such fees raise the cost of Habitat homes, nothing could be done apart from continuing to work with the government in the hope of modifying those requirements.

As the meeting wore on, it was impossible not to be impressed by these knowledgeable and reflective board members. The Minnegasco volunteers tried to work quietly, but even when they did not, the eighteen people seated around the circle leaned toward one another, listened intently, took notes, and shared their insights, which often came from many years of experience in the construction trades, real estate, social services, and, perhaps just as frequently, community activism. They were resolute in navigating a flood of details. From drafting effective press releases to leveraging government funds to comparing long-term costs of electric and gas water heaters—seemingly nothing escaped the breadth of their concern. Yet, it was when the meeting turned toward the homeowner families that the depth of their concern became most evident. Since Family Nurture is an affiliate-level committee at Twin Cities Habitat, rather than part of each chapter structure,[2] family selection was the next agenda item.

Of the 125 homeowner applications the affiliate planned to process by the end of the year, about one-quarter of those families lived in St. Paul, so it was up to these board members to decide if these applicants would make acceptable partners with the organization. The lengthy and often emotional deliberations that precede such decisions indicate they are not taken lightly. This meeting was no exception. Pertinent information about each prospective family was presented by two committee members who had been assigned to them. These members had visited them at home and were aware of their present housing conditions; they had also inquired into each family's personal references, financial situations, credit histories, and various other aspects of their personal lives. As is usually the procedure, the committee members gave a brief assessment of their assigned family's background, explained why they seemed to meet Habitat's three selection criteria (need, ability to pay, and willingness to be responsible partners) and, finally, they indicated how strongly they recommended the family to the board. Six of these presentations were made by different committee members, followed by group discussion and then a final vote. Two of the discussions were brief, and the votes were immediate affirmations of the families' suitability. The other four, however, were not so simple. Furrowed brows and, at times, impatient tones were signs of the strains that accompany heavy responsibility. Still, however falteringly, this was a weight the board members endeavored to bear with as much integrity as they together could muster.

Shannon Hunter's homeowner application, for instance, presented them with something of a conundrum. For nearly a year, she had been separated from her husband and the father of her five children, the youngest of whom was only eight weeks old. On her application, she claimed that they were planning to divorce, but there were rumors that the separation was actually a ploy to ensure that her family would continue to receive welfare checks from the government. At first, interestingly, the questions posed by board members were of a more practical nature. The committee members who interviewed her highlighted the fact that she was active in her local church and was trying to get off welfare, but they admitted that, since her husband had been the family's sole provider, she had no employment experience. "How do we know that she'll be able to hold down a job and make her mortgage payments?" one man asked. Another mentioned that if she did get a decent job and then eventually reunited with her husband, their combined incomes might exceed the upper limit for Habitat homeowners. "If we tell her that," he continued, "does that mean we'd be, in effect, encouraging her to get a divorce so that she continues to qualify?" About half of those who spoke felt such questions were serious enough to compromise her application, while others insisted that it was not their place to try to "predict the future" and, thus, any judgment should be based on the actual situation of a mother and five children in need.

This debate continued unresolved until an older woman raised the "moral issue" of Hunter's possible dishonesty in order to receive welfare benefits. "I have a real problem with someone who's willing to cheat the system to get ahead," she said. Although some agreed with this line of argument, it raised still more debate about the dangers of evaluating applicants on the basis of character. "Just because we're not HUD doesn't mean we're God!" asserted one board member, who also suggested that they all might find themselves homeless if access to affordable housing were contingent upon one's moral rectitude. Who could disagree? Certainly not the older woman who, nevertheless, reminded everyone that, even if Hunter did lie to the welfare office, that was actually less important than the potential negative consequences for the affiliate if they partnered with a person who could not be more forthcoming about her relationship with her husband. That opinion, after almost a half-hour of discussion, won the day. They simply could not make a responsible decision without more information, and so her application was tabled until the next board meeting. In the meantime, the Family Selection Committee was asked to inquire "respectfully" and "nonjudgmentally" about her personal situation so that a clearer assessment could be made.

Neil Castell's application was another one that stymied the board. After the death of his wife, he and his seven-year-old daughter, Lauren, had moved from a small town about a hundred miles away to St. Paul, where they resided in a small, poorly insulated apartment. He was a handyman who had most recently worked as a roofer, but now, instead of finding greater employment opportunity in the Twin Cities as he anticipated, he was trying to make ends meet as a lower-paid general laborer. None of the board members doubted Castell's "work ethic," a term they used liberally in referring to his application. However, because he was a single parent with no family in the area to assist him, a few people voiced concerns about his having enough free time to complete his sweat-equity hours. In response the committee member who was recommending his approval assured everyone of his determination to fulfill that obligation. She even seemed surprised when a consensus emerged regarding the feasibility of crediting Castell with more hours than he would actually spend at the building site because he was an exceptionally skilled worker. The board was willing to be flexible and their approval seemed certain until one member noticed that Lauren was being sent to a Catholic elementary school in order, as Castell put it on his application, "to get a better moral education." As with Shannon Hunter, this information precipitated some questions about how candid he was being with the affiliate.

"When I hear private school," one man said, "I tend to think he's probably doing some side jobs and getting paid under the table." The previously mentioned committee member responded abruptly to that comment: "How can you jump right to that conclusion? Who's to say he isn't telling the truth and is just willing to scrimp and save to put his daughter through Catholic schools? You know, maybe it's worth the sacrifice to him!" That remark ignited another discussion of the dangers of intruding too far into the personal affairs of the homeowner applicants. But, again, the issue came down to their responsibility to the affiliate. Because of Castell's on-again–off-again employment pattern, his declared earnings were considered to be enough of an issue to warrant further scrutiny. His past employers would be contacted, and he would be asked some follow-up questions.

Before moving on, one of the professional contractors in the group proffered what he considered to be a more strategic reason for rejecting this particular application. Noting that the cost of building a two-bedroom house was not significantly less than that of three- or even four-bedroom homes, he concluded that, "as crass as this might sound, the affiliate isn't getting as much bang for the buck when we build for just two people." If Habitat was sincere about its goal of eradicating poverty housing, he continued with some support from others, then it should make some effort to maximize the number of people it helps. Seconding this point, the man beside him added that, even when two-bedroom houses are constructed, they can frequently accommodate an entire family of four rather than just an unmarried man and his daughter. No one argued with these points, yet there were clearly values, other than cost efficiency, worth considering.

Someone mentioned that increasing the occupancy of the houses would put a population strain on certain neighborhoods, especially those having many Habitat homes clustered together. A diversity of family structures was also an asset to neighborhoods, said another. Several people insisted that a cost-benefit approach to family selection was sufficiently discriminatory to be rejected for ethical reasons as well as on the grounds that it would expose the affiliate to lawsuits, particularly as Habitat became better known and was perceived as a huge nonprofit with plenty of money to spend on court settlements. Finally, a passionate case was made by a few people, some of whom had not spoken prior to that point, about the need to remain true to Habitat's three selection criteria, individuals' needs being foremost. "People need houses, that has to be our bottom line" was the most emblematic and memorable phrase volleyed during the ensuing verbal skirmish.

Eventually, a truce was called. Policy guidelines would clearly have to be drafted and discussed, but this was not the time. The Castell application had already been set aside until the next month's meeting, and there were more to evaluate.

On the basis of need alone, Julius and Lillian Huggins and their four children would easily qualify as new Habitat homeowners. For twenty years the family had lived in Julius's parents' basement, which they had converted into a one-bedroom apartment. The children all slept in the living room, which, due to persistent water problems, was often crowded with mosquitoes as well. The committee member presenting their application accented the positive: the Hugginses appeared to be a loving couple; she worked part-time in order to be more available for the children; for the past four years, he had worked for a company that distributes telephone directories, and he also volunteered as a pastor at the store-front Pentecostal church he helped start. No problems there. But, the presenter admitted, there was a bit of a downside. The couple was experiencing significant disciplinary problems with their two sons, the oldest of whom had been arrested on separate occasions for vandalism and burglary. Also, Julius Huggins had been on disability leave from his job because of an as-yet-unidentified illness that drained him of much of his energy and, at times, afflicted him with severe headaches. "I know they have problems," the committee member declared in summary, "but I just have a feeling that they'll make it as homeowners."

The group appreciated her candor, and one man even took the opportunity to remind those gathered that intuition is an important asset in the difficult family-selection process. Yet some people expressed apprehension about putting two arguably troubled boys into the "tough part of town" in which Habitat had been building. Julius Huggins's health was also a topic of conversation. But these were brief exchanges. Indeed, no discernible objection was raised when the chapter president commented, "If we're working with families that don't have any problems, we're working with the wrong families." A willingness to take risks to help people get on their feet, in other words, was an accepted part of the group's modus operandi. But there did seem to be limits.

These manifested themselves when the parents' motivation came into question. The twenty-plus years that they had spent in that depressing basement apartment left some to wonder if they were adequately motivated to do their sweat-equity hours, attend homeowner classes and affiliate functions, and, ultimately, assume the responsibilities attendant to financing and maintaining their own home. Everyone seemed to acknowledge the importance of this issue. It suggested an unavoidable tension that was captured succinctly by the chair of the Public Relations Committee. "Taking risks is what ministry is all about," he explained, "but we're also in the business of setting people up to succeed and not to fail as partners." Intuition, then, had a place, but so did a sense of responsibility to the affiliate, which meant choosing families who were likely to do their part in fashioning Habitat's ideal of partnership into a reality. So, again, some delicate questions would have to be posed. There would be no decision about the Huggins family until someone had a chance to inquire as to exactly how serious they were about home ownership and, for good measure, determine if they would be willing to volunteer with the affiliate on a provisional basis before their application was finalized.

Motivation was the least of the group's worries when it began to address the application submitted by Denar and Kaila Haileselassie. They were prepared to do whatever was necessary to get them and their three children out of their one-bedroom apartment located in a neighborhood with more than its share of crime as well as, they insisted, inadequate schools. Education was important to them, they were described as "an incredibly close family," and they wanted nothing more than to be contributing members of a real community. They sounded perfect and had already demonstrated their perseverance by restarting their lives after emigrating from Ethiopia. There, because of sporadic religious persecution by the Marxist government, Denar had been imprisoned for over a year before he was released and granted political asylum in the United States. Working as a travel agent and part-time dishwasher, he was eventually able to bring his family into the country after three years' separation. Everyone on the board seemed impressed with this story—so much so that they, quite uncharacteristically, evinced few misgivings upon learning that Denar had declared bankruptcy during the previous year, after losing money investing in an unsuccessful travel agency conglomerate. The woman who presented the family's application explained that had Denar fully understood the bankruptcy process at the time, he never would have filed and, furthermore, his earning capacity has consistently improved since then. The board concurred unanimously but was still unable to approve the Haileselassies as a homeowner family.

The sticking point was their citizenship status. No one was quite sure whether they were U.S. citizens, legal residents, or "illegal aliens," or even how much those distinctions mattered. One man suggested that priority ought to be given to people who are actually citizens, but this view received little sympathy. "Should they sign loyalty oaths too?" was the sarcastic question posed by one member, who soon apologized. "Habitat builds for Ethiopians in Ethiopia; why can't we do the same in this country?" asked another. This was the perspective of the majority. During the conversation that followed, Habitat was variously labeled an "international organization," "an idea that transcends nationalities and race," and "as inclusive as the kingdom of God." It, in short, was largely perceived as no respecter of national boundaries.

Most of the board members seemed to appreciate such statements, which reminded them that their efforts had to be as nondiscriminatory as poverty itself. Group solidarity, after all, is typically molded by the force of such discussions. That does not mean that the problem was solved, though. While many people were adamant that concern about the applicants' citizenship status was irrelevant, and possibly even xenophobic, others were not so certain. One woman reasoned that, given that the ability to pay for a house was one of the family-selection criteria, the possibility that an illegal family could be deported and thus default on their mortgage had to be considered. The man who had previously complained about the bureaucratic difficulties associated with the HOPE III program mentioned that, despite all the headaches, government had served as a tremendous ally for the affiliate. "If we start putting people without green cards into houses," he warned, "I don't think the state will keep supplying us with money and property—we need to think about the political consequences of our actions." This remark stirred further dissent. That Habitat was not required to ask applicants if they were legal residents was quickly brought to the group's attention. Even if it were, some continued, it would be preferable to offer a witness against such a mandate by resisting it publicly. Round and round the discussion went until the board president, noticing that the meeting had gone on for two and a half hours, suggested that a policy regarding citizenship status would have to be ironed out—but not that night. A fourth family would have to wait at least another month until an important decision regarding their lives could be made.

The chair of the Site Selection Committee let out a loud, adjourning sigh. "I second that," declared a woman seated next to him, stretching her arms upward and then slapping him on the back, perhaps a bit harder than she intended. Then everyone stood, stretched, and broke into small groups to chat briefly before making their way into the crisp night air. A few stragglers stayed behind to turn off lights and, with light hammer taps, reseal some paint cans left open by the long-departed Minnegasco volunteers.

Without nights like this one, the daily dawning of the altruism and civic participation that animate the American voluntary sector would be unthinkable. Inevitably, many of the most sublime expressive values to which our associative endeavors are dedicated would also, in time, be eclipsed. Hence, it was fitting that the board meeting should close with a consideration of citizenship. Actually, the members attended to only half of the broader issue. Their concern, although important, was limited to determining the citizenship rights and status of a family of Ethiopian immigrants. Not questioned was the quality of their own citizenship. Citizenship also entails an obligation to participate actively in promoting the good of the community, a duty that surely was not lost on the board members who had gathered in that circle for so long. They, in a sense, were willing to do "the hard work of 'ruling,'" which, in the quotation prefacing this chapter, is how political philosopher Michael Walzer describes the supererogatory, participatory aspect of citizenship.[3]

As citizens, we are all ruled; as active citizens, we are ruled and all also take a turn in ruling. Since Aristotle this has been the pluralist ideal of democracy.[4] In the Athens of his time, this paradigm referred to the sharing of public offices among citizens who, given the small scale of the polis, were likely to "know one another's characters" and thus trust one another to rule responsibly.[5] The vast scale of modern nations now makes this solution impossible and has necessitated the representative form of democracy, as exists in the United States.[6] Casting ballots and contributing money are accepted means by which individual citizens acquire a voice in such a political system. But, as attested by perennially high levels of voter apathy and the periodic clamoring for campaign-finance reform, these means tend to be more alienating than empowering for an increasing proportion of the American public.[7]

Today the voice of an empowered citizenry is heard most clearly within "civil society," the politically nuanced term for what has heretofore been identified as the voluntary sector. It is within its "free spaces" of community responsibility, self-organization, and decision making that active citizens are taught and then expected to rule their fellows at the appropriate junctures.[8] What values should be emphasized? Where should funds be allocated? How can we engage the wider public? Which family can be raised from its inadequate living conditions? These are the questions that are asked from within the associations and organizations of the voluntary sector, and when they receive the hard answers wrought of civic participation and deliberation, there one discovers a rule "by the people."

The circle of Habitat board members who grappled with the complexities of the family selection process were, as Walzer suggests, willing to rule in their turn. No doubt they continued to do so at the following month's meeting, when they perhaps resolved the four disputed cases and presumably confronted difficult new issues.[9] The same, moreover, could be said for volunteers such as the Minnegasco group and, to an extent, Raymond and Felipe Espinoza. By volunteering, even in a hands-on and less adjudicating manner, they also contribute to an organization that promotes certain expressive values according to which the hard work of ruling fellow citizens proceeds. Habitat, then, provides the institutional space in which people can live out their commitment to active citizenship.

Yet even extremely sophisticated pluralists like Walzer sometimes lead one to believe that the mere existence of benign structures mediating between the individual citizen and the state is enough to warrant placing the laurels of citizenship on everyone associated with them.[10] Less noticed is the important reality that, even within deservedly touted organizations like Habitat, citizenship is an ongoing challenge. It is just as capable of devolving into, as Walzer puts it, "something less" when these organizations actually thrive as when they do not. To illustrate this reality in both this chapter and the next, let us address four ways in which, according to the organization's prevalent ideology, Habitat serves to make people better citizens within their own communities. These latent civic benefits of Habitat—empowerment, social integration, edification, and freedom—are also the long-acclaimed characteristics of a strong citizenry. But while precious to any democratic society, they are also quite fragile and, as we shall see, ever vulnerable to degenerating into "something less" than the ideal.

Empowerment: Of Those With or Without Power?

The Disempowering Effects of the State and Market

Among the benefits of active participation for a democratic citizenry, few have been highlighted as consistently as the theme of empowerment. This was a theme that preoccupied James Madison in his famed contributions to what are now known as *The Federalist Papers,* which argued for a federal system of governance for the newly independent American states. As is well known, he favored a separation of powers by which the federal government was to be partitioned into the executive, legislative (further divided bicamerally), and judicial functions. Its prerogatives would be additionally curtailed by the power given to (similarly partitioned) state governments. Moreover, just as individual state governments were intended to mediate between the federal government and society, he prescribed a wide array of voluntary associations, or "factions," existing within society itself and functioning to divide political power further still. He envisioned that "society itself will be broken into so many parts, interests and classes of citizens, that the rights of individuals or of the minority will be in little danger from interested combinations of the majority."[11] A plethora of minority interests and values, he argued, must be represented by voluntary associations, which in turn should be formed and run by citizens empowered enough to keep political power sufficiently dispersed throughout the new nation.

This particular benefit of association is mentioned or implied frequently by people involved with Habitat. As if by some mysterious act of associational alchemy, participating with the organization is perceived to transform individuals into shiningly empowered citizens. One reason for this widespread conviction is their equal certainty regarding the *disempowering* effects of the state and market sectors.

That Habitat should harbor a suspicion of the market is hardly front-page news. The seeds of the organization, after all, grew from the same ground in rural Georgia that served as floors for many of the dilapidated cold-water shacks littering the surrounding countryside. The most prominent biblical values voiced by its evangelical founders were essentially admonitions against profit-making at the expense of justice and against competitiveness rather than partnership. The values associated with the "economics of Jesus" are hardly guiding stars for venture capitalists. From its beginnings Habitat has parried the logic of the rationalized capitalist economy by asserting its own countervailing religious values and by addressing the needs of those lower-income people left behind when housing is dispensed as inequitably as any other commodity on the market.

When volunteers and paid staff at Americus and various local affiliates discuss economic matters, they demonstrate an acute awareness of how disempowering the market is for low-income people. Being unable to afford a decent home, they maintain, can mire poor families in substandard living situations that are nearly inescapable, and that are particularly harmful for children. Some of the fourteen staff members at the East Bay Habitat office, located in the basement of an old Presbyterian church in downtown Oakland, California, were among the most thoughtful commentators on this issue I encountered. The affiliate is currently building a forty-house development in an East Oakland neighborhood that has become synonymous with the crime, drugs, and violence so often residing in pockets of urban poverty that are surrounded by other areas of greater, sometimes glaring, affluence. Working in this neighborhood affords a first-hand glimpse at the disempowering effects of the market. Describing why he became so interested in housing issues, Donald Smith, one of the staff members, explained:

> Housing is sort of at that level where, if they have it sufficiently, it allows people to really begin to focus their energy on other areas of their life and in the life of the community. But, if you don't have it, then those other areas suffer and I think we're seeing that in our society today. When you have to put so much energy into the basics, then so many other things suffer—taking care of your kids, for instance. And if you can't take care of your kids, then they grow up essentially having to raise themselves. What are the consequences of having to raise yourself as a kid? Well, maybe you haven't learned how to deal with conflict appropriately, so now the only way you can deal with it is to bop somebody over the head or shoot them with a gun. If you can't clothe yourself and house yourself and feed yourself, then maybe you can't educate yourself because you don't have the energy to invest in that. It's all connected and I think we need to look at it from that perspective.

Housing, in short, is seen as such a fundamental need that, if unmet, it will deprive people of the power to rise from their plight and perpetuate poverty through successive generations.

Denise Kraybill, another staff member, agrees. She had been a successful manager at a posh hotel in San Francisco, where she came face to face with the financial struggles of the mostly immigrant maids whose work she supervised. She instituted an English as a Second Language (ESL) program for them at the hotel, but, realizing that she wanted to dedicate herself more fully to social service work, she eventually quit her job and came to Habitat. "Housing spreads to everything," she insists, "to the families, the kids, education and, ultimately, has an effect on the adults that the community produces. Because of my privileged background, I had a great head start. I think Habitat houses can be one step toward nurturing that same feeling in other people too." Notice the optimism. The implied argument seems to be: Inadequate housing disempowers people; adequate housing, alternatively, empowers them; ergo, enabling people to own their own homes empowers them to be better citizens, and they will be willing, as a matter of course, to assume that responsibility. Variants of this general attitude, and optimists like Kraybill who embody it, are rife within Habitat. It is neatly summed up in one of Habitat's more frequently repeated slogans, "Building houses, building community." Providing houses for people means that the people residing within them will necessarily build solid communities.

One must then ask why so many financially secure and properly housed Americans do not do their share in "building community" by contributing time and money to organizations like Habitat. When that question was posed in interviews, respondents almost without exception argued that middle- and upper-class people are also disempowered by the market. Not material deprivation but an addiction to materialism and a paralyzing spiritual emptiness are usually identified as the culprits. Well-off individuals are not miserly sinners, bourgeois exploiters, or incorrigible misanthropists; they have simply bought into a consumer culture that equates being more with having more. They become so preoccupied with their careers and material possessions, and with attaining the "good life," that they have little time or energy left to contribute to the good of their communities. Emblematic of this state of affairs is the notion of the American Dream. As it is commonly understood, this ideal refers to a single family acquiring enough material wealth to buy their own home and sustain themselves in reasonable comfort. At Habitat, however, this ideal undergoes an interesting transvaluation. It becomes an ignominious representation of the cultural poverty of a society that extols selfishness and leaves people too spiritually impotent to care about much beyond their own selves. Denise

Kraybill is prone to using the term with these negative connotations, and she provides some elaboration:

> It's so isolating. You drive into your garage, walk into your house, have dinner—but, what about your neighbors? They become phased out as a priority because we become our own priority. But does it buy happiness? I don't think so. There's still a void. I struggle with all that myself, but maybe I shouldn't even be struggling. Maybe I should just give up on that American Dream voice in the back of my head and just trust God completely. But it's so hard to be countercultural.

> *But isn't Habitat promoting that American Dream in a sense?*

> Yes, that's a struggle too. But the situations of most of our homeowners are so much worse, so we're just keeping them from getting into debt. And it's really just a step up toward decency rather than the total American Dream. Also, it's not an isolating thing because they're expected to work on their homes with other people and get involved in their community after that.

Kraybill struggles against giving in to the cultural Sirens singing the allures of the American Dream. She also takes consolation that they remain out of earshot of most Habitat homeowners, for whom Habitat is "just a step up toward decency rather than the total American Dream." Her struggle seems sincere, and she is extremely dedicated to her work. But her remarks, and Donald Smith's, reflect an ideological tendency that is quite common in Habitat. According to him, some people are disempowered because they have too little, while she suggests that others are disempowered because they have too much. He rightly asserts that housing is "connected" to such basic needs as nutrition and education, while she equates the individualism symbolized by the American Dream with much that is wrong with our society.

The tendency in discussions like these, however, is for topics like housing and the American Dream to serve as proxies for the larger economic forces undergirding and ultimately dividing social classes within the United States. Getting a house or rejecting the prevailing cultural ethos of individualism are taken to be penultimate solutions to a systemic problem that is left unaddressed. Inadequate housing and American individualism may well be disempowering to different segments of the population, and they are astutely identified as such among Habitat supporters; but less attention tends to be given to the fact that they are the effects of a larger cause best understood as the rationalized capitalist market.

If suspicion of the capitalist market does not go deep enough among Habitat supporters, the opposite is true of their attitude toward the state. As one might expect, Habitat enjoys a broad base of support from across the political spectrum. Its prevailing political temper, however, tends toward a collective wariness of the state. Among the ranks of Habitat volunteers and staff, one often hears from political conservatives who want to limit "big government," especially in the area of welfare provision. Those who situate themselves closer to the political left usually advocate a greater social role for government. That seldom keeps them from being outspoken critics of ineffectual and impersonal government policies, and they are apt to defend their position with exasperated tales of HUD's extreme bureaucratization or of the intolerable conditions in nearby public housing projects. Many would like to see all levels of government increase their financial assistance to Habitat, as long as its own funding guidelines are respected. Their basic attitude usually concurs with that of the executive staff member at Americus who asserted that Habitat should announce to the state, "You have an obligation to help us to do this because we do it without screwing the taxpayer." They also do it, most would add, without disempowering the American citizen.

As divergent as conservatives and liberals are in American politics, within Habitat they usually seem to be singing from the same sheet—the refrain being that Habitat empowers people while the state is likely to burden them with the yoke of dependency and passivity. No attitude permeates the organization as thoroughly as this one. Larry Grierson, a professional contractor with a degree in social work who is currently employed as a regional director for Habitat International, provides a representative summation:

> Traditionally, helping those living in substandard housing means handing out a check, but Habitat is about building relationships between people. The homeowners are able to do things for themselves because homeownership—and the work that gets them there—provides them with a source of real empowerment. I don't think you can get that through subsidized housing, which is only provided on a rental basis and allows people to stay passive.

Being empowered means being able to do for oneself and being a contributing member of society, things denied those who are mere beneficiaries of the contributions of others. Indeed, so chary is Grierson about fostering dependency among Habitat families that he resolutely opposed a proposal, advocated by well-intentioned local community leaders, to exempt homeowners from paying property taxes for their first ten years of homeownership. "That sort of policy would distinguish them from the community rather than inviting them into full participation in society," he insisted with the approval of the international organization. Mention of this participatory ideal raises a corollary assumption prevalent at Habitat. Disempowerment is not only a function of government trying to do too much for low-income people. There is also a strong consensus that it can just as easily be experienced by higher-income people when government assumes responsibilities that are properly theirs. As with the market, the state can disempower even more affluent citizens—in this case, by relieving them of their obligations to others and of the feeling that they are making a difference in their communities.

The Empowerment Ideal for Homeowner Families

So what exactly is meant by empowerment at Habitat? While this question elicits a host of different responses, the organization differs in its understanding of empowerment for homeowner families and for its middle-class volunteers. Homeowners are usually said to be empowered when they have an "ownership stake" in their communities. The literal ownership of a home, in other words, is typically thought to provide people with a concern for the goings-on in their local communities, as well as the self-esteem necessary to become actively contributing members. A central tenet of Habitat ideology is the expectation that homeowners will become upstanding neighbors and assume their civic responsibilities (and there is an underlying assumption that they are not already doing these things). This expectation can even serve as a factor in evaluating an applicant's "willingness to partner" during the family selection process. For instance, discussing a single mother who had applied for a Habitat home but was apprehensive about the neighborhood into which she would be moving, Denise Kraybill explained:

> She was a potential homeowner, but she wasn't going to any of the meetings. She said she didn't feel comfortable or safe walking around the neighborhood where the meetings were held. But that was going to be *her* neighborhood. So I finally had to say, "That isn't what Habitat is about. You're supposed to be willing to help make that neighborhood a strong one where nobody's afraid to walk around at night." Well, that message got through to her and she withdrew from the program because she decided that it just wasn't for her.

And who could blame her? The often-heard message that "got through to her" was that homeowners are expected to move boldly into neighborhoods that are often located in reputedly dangerous (and thus relatively inexpensive) urban areas and transform them, simply by behaving as empowered and law-abiding citizens. This does not seem a realistic expectation, especially when many affiliates build only one isolated home in such areas at a time.

Additional reservations are supported by a 1996 study of homeowners at the Twin Cities affiliate.[12] Forty percent of those interviewed reported feeling less safe in their new neighborhoods, and, given their new responsibilities as homeowners, nearly half claimed to have less free time than they did before partnering with Habitat. One should be careful about expecting people who feel less secure and more harried to be exceptionally empowered, particularly when no comparable expectations are directed at anyone else associated within the organization. For example, while Habitat aspires to make volunteers into better citizens, no one expects them to put themselves on the line to this extent. They are free to return to their safe, perhaps upscale, neighborhoods after their weekly, monthly, annual, or one-time volunteer stint. They come and go as they please and are not expected, as are the homeowners, to be so radically changed by their involvement with Habitat.

Regardless of its problems, this vision of the empowered homeowner who becomes an active contributor to the community has remained the organization's ideal. Back issues of the organization's major promotional publication, *Habitat World*, provide countless expressions of it. Fifteen years ago homeowner Cecelia Dukuly fled the political unrest in her Liberian homeland; now she owns her own restaurant specializing in African cuisine, and she even catered the Milwaukee affiliate's tenth-anniversary celebration.[13] Two years after moving her family into their new Habitat house in Raleigh, North Carolina, Imelda Jackson began her own nonprofit day-care center with an enrollment of sixty-five children and a tuition kept low enough to assist struggling families.[14] After partnering with the affiliate in Lafayette, Indiana, Mary Stone wrote a book providing financial advice and encouragement to low-income families—this in addition to holding down a full-time job and serving as president of a writers' club and as treasurer of her church.[15] Sharon McPherson-Mullins and her four children were homeless before they moved into their Habitat home, an event so transformative for her that she went on to found a new affiliate in Hamilton County, Indiana.[16] The assistant director of Habitat International's Rocky Mountain area, Rosalinda Armenta, is also a homeowner; she and her six children had been migrant farm workers and then occupants of public housing before their lives were similarly changed by the organization.[17] Members of the homeowners' association in Kingsport, Tennessee—working mostly on nights and weekends for four solid months—single-handedly built a Habitat house as a token of their gratitude and obligation to their community.[18]

This litany could go on and on, and it is a reminder that this sort of homeowner empowerment, although an ideal, has its basis in truth. The previously cited homeowner survey discovered that a staggering 82 percent felt that, since partnering with the organization, their fundamental outlook on life had become more positive. Another study of the same affiliate found that 35 percent of homeowner families saw improvement in their children's grades, 58 percent reported less family conflict, and 68 percent experienced an overall improvement in their financial condition since moving into their homes.[19] With such favorable changes occurring within these families, it makes sense that many of them would be able to reach outside of themselves and recognize their embeddedness or ownership stake in their communities.

Few people have recognized this as clearly as Leslie Reems. The death of her husband and escalating hospital bills for her chronically ill son were tremendous burdens for her, but since moving into her Habitat home she has begun to do more than just get by. "I just couldn't believe that complete strangers would come to work on my house," she mused. She then described how the experience of being helped convinced her to help others through her involvement with the local PTA, her volunteer work as an organizer of an annual sidewalk arts festival, and as a member of the Family Nurture Committee at the Sioux Falls affiliate. Soon after being part of a successful community effort to prevent the closing of a local middle school, she described this newfound sense of responsibility:

> I've been living in this house with the kids and just came to the realization that this is my house, my town, and that's my kids' school. I realized I had to help take responsibility for the community, and I can expect something from others in return. I think a single Habitat family that can stand on its own can touch so many other people. My kids touch the lives of their teachers. And the teachers can say, "Those are the Reems kids who live at 329 South Moreland." And that's who they'll be. And they can count on them being there year after year, and they'll always be known as those same kids at 329 South Moreland.

Igniting this kind of community responsibility is what homeowner empowerment is all about. For many, living in a Habitat house can, as one affiliate staff member put it, "result in nothing more than a simple change of address." The move ignites no spark of concern for the public good. Such people may have too many economic and perhaps personal problems for their lives to be completely turned around by moving into a simple, decent home. Yet for other people like Leslie Reems, the experience of homeownership can prove to be transformative. Those are the people upheld as exemplars by the organization.

The Empowerment Ideal for Habitat Volunteers

The possibility of transformation exists for volunteers as well. The experience of hammering away at a weekend blitz build or serving on an affiliate operating committee could provide them with a sense of their own efficacy and an accompanying desire to contribute even more to their communities. As a result, they may volunteer more frequently, contribute money more liberally, and consider the needs of others more seriously. Or, on the other hand, none of these things may occur. The experience of volunteering may yield little more than vague feelings of self-congratulation, perhaps a mention on one's résumé under "community service," but few, if any, repeat performances. As with the homeowners, the likelihood that the people who volunteer (or are staff members) at Habitat will be transformed into anything approaching model citizens varies from individual to individual.

Unlike the homeowners, though, empowerment for the largely middle-class volunteers is not generally conceived of as requiring such a thoroughgoing personal change. Instead, it assumes a much more modest guise. The empowered volunteer is understood not necessarily as someone who does remarkable things but rather as a person who does at least *some*thing. The individualism symbolized by the notion of the American Dream is seen as so pervasive that many people cannot see through it to discern their connectedness to their fellow citizens. Recall Denise Kraybill's succinct observation, "it's so hard to be countercultural." Who could disagree? What is more, many Habitat respondents acknowledge another, perhaps harder, obstacle. Even those who recognize the importance of contributing to their communities must still overcome the lurking sense of despair that can paralyze people when facing the gaping enormity of social problems such as inadequate housing.

World hunger, environmental devastation, the population explosion, urban poverty, the AIDS epidemic, chilling scenes of violence both at home and abroad—these are some of the other daunting causes that Habitat volunteers and staff mention when discussing their feelings of despair and, ultimately, their decisions to do their part in the face of it all. Society's problems are vast, individual contributions toward their solution are relatively minuscule, but empowerment amounts to people's willingness to make that contribution regardless and trust that some good will come from it. Rebecca McNab, a staff member at the Redwood City affiliate, summed it up this way: "Especially in this day and age, we are so overwhelmed by social problems that it's hard to know what to do. Habitat is only one little piece. There are many, many things that need doing but it's hard to know where to start and sometimes you feel helpless and hopeless. But this [Habitat] gives us a chance to at least start. And it's only a start, you know? But that's how to get things done."

Many volunteers and staff confide that they too have confronted feelings of helplessness and hopelessness and—true to the mustard seed vision of the organization—have resolved that their small efforts can help to "get things done." They are not self-styled social crusaders; their estimations of their work are usually humble. One volunteer described his as helping to "chisel the corner off the problem" and another as "placing one piece in a gigantic puzzle." One man, a cofounder of a local affiliate, suggested that voluntarism was nothing more than "leaning your weight on the side of the answer." Grandiose action, therefore, is not required of the empowered volunteer. What is required are small acts, preferably linked to expectations they will bear much fruit.

One of the implications of this ideology is that, since small acts are possible for anyone, they are obligatory for everyone. The culture of individualism and the malaise of despair may be disempowering, this argument suggests, but they are not exonerating. Three corollary points are typically presented to support this claim. First, everyone has something to offer their communities, so they should offer it. "We're not going to survive unless people start to give a shit," declares Josh Berryman, a computer consultant who estimates that he has spent about twenty of the previous month's evenings volunteering with Habitat, his church, and the town soccer league. "Imagine how much more can happen if everybody got involved. Everybody's got a skill of some sort they can contribute." Second, everyone has sufficient opportunity to help their communities, so they should take it. The social justice program director at a Catholic covenant church with the Twin Cities affiliate, Michelle Prelinger, states this case strongly. "Whether it's with the church or the Boy Scouts or some other community group, you need to allow yourself to become part of the fabric of your community. You need to get involved, and there are plenty of organizations that are there to make it easy to do just that." Third, given the potentially dramatic results that could come from everyone setting aside their misgivings and contributing to their communities, no citizen is exempt from the duty to do so. No one summarized this attitude, and the stark optimism it reveals, better than Rachel Whetten, the executive director of an affiliate in New Jersey:

> As far as the country is concerned, I know we can be better than we are, but that means we have to take better care of each other. We have so many resources available to us to make things better, we should use them to pull people out of need. That's why I get bitter about people who don't do anything—because there are plenty of opportunities out there to plug into and do something. I know because I went through that transition myself. I was feeling despair because the problems in our society were so large. But when I discovered Habitat, I found I could do one small thing and that was enough since now I don't feel so powerless anymore. What if everyone felt that way?
>
> *What if everyone felt that way?*
>
> This country would be an amazing place to live. And it could all take off if people could just take a chance and do whatever small thing that's in front of them and trust that it'll make a difference.
>
> *What then?*
>
> When people's basic needs are met then I think we could go back to when there was a real sense of community in this country.

"If everyone felt that way," she is convinced, then a more just society would be within reach. That most people possess the capacity and opportunity to contribute to that end means that they *ought* to feel that way and are thus obligated to respond accordingly.

This sense of general obligation is one of the positive consequences of an organizational ethos that equates empowerment with the ability of volunteers to overcome individualism and despair by performing even modest acts of altruism. Another interesting quality of Habitat is that the hands-on character of its work is ideal for sustaining that very sort of empowerment. People who contribute to Habitat's ministry may renounce some of the enticements of an individualistic culture, and they may trust that their relatively minor efforts will somehow make a difference in solving major problems. But this does not mean that they are willing to meld into a self-renunciatory and undifferentiated mass of their fellow citizens, leaving no traces of their own presence behind. On the contrary, they are nearly unanimous not only in wanting their own *individual* efforts to make a difference but also in needing assurance that they have done so. It was the rare interview in which the respondent did not recount several incidents when he or she experienced the satisfaction of making a distinct, individual contribution to the organization. Whether it was the successful solicitation of funds or building materials from a local business, a presentation about Habitat given at one's church, an important point argued at a committee meeting, or the rows of shingles nailed in straight on a precariously pitched roof—everyone had something to be individually proud of. The phrase "I'm getting more out of this than the homeowners" was uttered often enough during interviews to dissuade anyone from thinking that theirs was an altruism devoid of any self-interest.

The individual self, therefore, does not disappear when it is empowered to do for others. Moreover, the physical reality of Habitat houses makes them tangible markers of people's efforts, evidence that their volunteering has made a real difference. Without exception, volunteers and staff answered affirmatively when asked if they occasionally drive by Habitat homes and proudly inspect their work. Most went on to describe, often in exuberant detail, the feelings of fulfillment they experience at such times. Memories of personal interactions at the construction site or on operating committees and the existence of a solid structure standing for a job well done (or simply *done*, as some of the more skilled workers are prone to complain) serve as reminders that their volunteer work is worthwhile, that despair is not warranted. Victoria Gillespie, a regional director with Habitat International, seems to agree. Reflecting on the many volunteers she has met during her six years with the organization, she concludes:

> They really have a commitment to making the world a better place. And the reason that they're drawn to Habitat particularly is because it's very concrete. This is a pragmatist's heaven. It's like you get up in the morning, you get out on the site, and by the end of the day there's a roof up or

there's something to put your hand on. You can come back ten years later
and say to your kids, "I put that window in there." And people do that.
They come through when you move in and they say, "I did that closet."

Habitat's work is pragmatic enough to engage individuals, and its completed houses are palpable markers that their work is efficacious and
hence worthwhile. Small acts make a difference, the basic message reads.
That this message is so palatable to many busy Americans no doubt
accounts for much of the organization's popularity in the United States.

Social Class and the Distortion of Habitat's Empowerment Ideal

Although volunteer empowerment at Habitat is usually deemed both
obligatory and worthwhile, it also has a darker side that reflects the
asymmetry of expectations for homeowners and volunteers. As discussed, homeowners are supposed to live up to an empowerment ideal
that anticipates their metamorphosis into model citizens, but volunteers are considered empowered when they simply break the bonds of
their own stasis. Only a portion of all homeowners could realistically
be empowered on those terms, and, due to their high visibility within
affiliates, those who are not so empowered remain under the judgmental
eye of the organization. Volunteers, on the other hand, all successfully
achieve the level of empowerment expected of them just by virtue of
being volunteers. They are all viewed as civic success stories. Other
people who do not volunteer, because they are supposedly too lazy or
apathetic or too disempowered by American individualism are, unlike
the homeowners, simply not part of the Habitat schema and not available for moralistic scrutiny.

The end result is the establishment of a kind of status hierarchy: The
putatively always-empowered volunteers tend to be perceived as superior to the merely sometimes-empowered homeowners, simply on the
basis of their success in realizing Habitat's civic ideal. Their accrual of
greater status within the organization legitimates the volunteers' greater
influence within local affiliates, which is actually based on their superior class status. Because of their lower class status, in other words,
homeowners need Habitat. At the same time, because the organization
relies on the cost-effectiveness of unpaid labor, Habitat needs its middle-class volunteers. Volunteering is born of a commingling of suffi-
ciency and insufficiency. The need for volunteers and the comparative
neediness of homeowners creates a power differential between them
based on social class.

This may be obvious to the outside observer, but the key point is that it is rendered less obvious within the organization by its own language of empowerment. Habitat's presumed success in empowering volunteers not only obscures the fact that they are empowered mostly because of their economic privilege but frequently allows volunteers to take center stage within affiliates. "Sadly," observes Victoria Gillespie, "what happens too often is that the needs of the volunteers become primary so that they become the main constituent rather than the homeowners, who become second-class citizens in an organization that tells them they're supposed to be the centerpiece." When this occurs, Habitat's ideal of civic empowerment for all can become distorted by social class and devolve into "something less" than originally intended by the organization. Highlighting three common dynamics within affiliates should be sufficient to demonstrate this critical tension.

First, despite sincere efforts by many volunteers and staff members to abide by Habitat's partnership vision, an appreciable strand of paternalism winds through the organization. It is apparent at every stage of homeowner involvement with the local affiliate. Diane Martinez, an assistant regional director who was raised in a poor Hispanic family in San Diego, is very sensitive to such manifestations of paternalism. She is aware that, as long as affiliates conform to the organization's basic principles, Habitat International possesses only the "power of persuasion" to ensure they do their work in the spirit of partnership. It angers her, she admits, when an occasional affiliate tries to make homeowners do more than their specified sweat-equity hours because "they feel the families are getting a great deal and aren't grateful enough." So far she has dissuaded them from passing such policies, but the paternalistic attitude remains. During the family-selection process, for example, it is commonplace for committee members doing home visits to note how clean the family's house is in their reports. Some affiliates have even pushed for compulsory home inspections after the homeowners have moved in. Both of these practices are unacceptable to her. "I can't see where that comes from other than a sort of judgment that people have to be like us," she says. "I think about my family and think they'd kick someone out if they ever came and, later on, rated their house on how clean or dirty is was. I'm telling you, they wouldn't be Habitat homeowners, they'd rather not have a house. Their pride would be too injured."

Even after homeowner families have been selected, a paternalistic attitude toward them can persist. Arthur Bensman has witnessed this firsthand. After his family lost their home during an earthquake in 1989, they became homeowners, and he eventually proved himself more than worthy of the Habitat ideal by becoming a VISTA volunteer at his local affiliate. He was happy to "give something back to the community" but, through his extensive experience with Habitat, came to realize that "there's a real stigma that comes with being a homeowner and it's tough to shake it even within the organization." Rules such as the one that prohibits homeowners from serving on affiliates' Family Selection Committees bother Bensman. "If the volunteers have enough integrity to respect the privacy of applicants," he asks, "then why shouldn't the homeowners?" Actually, this is a rhetorical question. As he later reveals, he is well aware that the answer has something to do with a widespread deprecation of their abilities:

> People often think that homeowners aren't capable of doing some things. I've listened to many of the volunteers talk about homeowners and they say things like, "Oh, they were so articulate" and this and that—as if they shouldn't have been. But I never hear that when a volunteer comes in and says he wants to work. They don't say, "Wow, how articulate." They put him to work. People hand off the biggest tasks to volunteers that just come walking through the door. But a homeowner comes through the door and people say, "We have to find something easy for him to do."

Many respondents, especially among the homeowners, confirmed Arthur's observations. Just as many indicated that this kind of treatment extends past the sweat-equity stage and continues even after homeowners move into their houses. One disgruntled homeowner with a long-term "visitor" was angered when his affiliate tried to prevent people other than the original occupants from living in Habitat homes. Exasperated, he asked, "How would you like it if someone said, 'Hey, your mother-in-law has been visiting too long, get her butt out?'" The scrutiny of homeowners by people working at the affiliates has become a pattern. Examples include the board member who wanted an explanation for a Jaguar parked in front of a Habitat house occupied for more than a year; the affiliate that called a meeting so a homeowner could prove his new boat was a gift from his brother; another affiliate that considered evicting a homeowner family for installing a satellite dish in their yard. Such stories are easy to come by, and they reveal the tendency of many Habitat volunteers to presume that people with basic needs are necessarily inferior and cannot possibly live respectable middle-class lives as they do. One affiliate executive director, Gary Andrusz, discusses this tendency insightfully:

You know, to get people to contribute money you have to build this defini-tion of need. Well, when you build this definition of need, you open your-self up to questions of whether they really have a need. Is their need their own problem? Did they cause their own problem? You create those ques-tions among your donors and in people's minds. And we get into terrible debates. I mean, as soon as our families move into their house we seem to have people—naturally so—watching them. The one I find to be a hoot is the number of people—and I mean board members, volunteers, and so forth—who criticize our families if they have cable TV put in. They just think that's terrible. Well, that just comes from a very puritanical view that says, "Television is bad!" For all those people know, those families are sit-ting down with their children watching *Arts and Entertainment*. So our families are put under the microscope much too much.

It is frequently only the families who are unmistakably empowered according to Habitat's high homeowner standards who can escape this sort of paternalism. Those not so clearly empowered can be treated as permanent beneficiaries, a role permitting volunteers to see themselves as permanent benefactors. It is also a role that minimizes the power of homeowners within the organization, especially since many become disaffected and, as a result, do not even try to voice their opinions and concerns. As prevalent as this tendency is, however, Andrusz's disclo-sure that the volunteers and staff at the affiliate "get into terrible debates" over it suggests that he and like-minded others try to confront the paternalism within the organization. Displays of paternalism rather than authentic partnership compromise Habitat's expectations of empowerment, but it is important to note that, to the extent that it is recognized and resisted, paternalism remains more of an organiza-tional tension than an inevitable and unchallenged characteristic of all affiliates.

The same is true of a second dynamic reinforcing the power differ-ential within affiliates: the tendency of affiliates to focus more on mak-ing volunteers and contributors feel empowered than on empowering homeowners. If Habitat wants to continue appealing to its supporters, it must ensure that they feel good about the organization and about themselves. But this can be especially frustrating for the homeowners, who frequently come to feel like second-class citizens as a result. Once again, Arthur Bensman provides some critical insight:

The toughest part of it is dealing with people who are doing it for a good experience while the reality is that I have to live it everyday. That's tough. A lot of people sign up and, to their credit, they plunge right in, but they know they're after an experience for whatever length of time. They're going to indulge themselves in this experience and then they're going to remove themselves. But I'm here. I'm invested in this community and I'm going to be here after they're gone. So the question is how much do I buy into making sure they have a good experience? The affiliate has to be concerned with providing a good experience for the volunteers so they come back. But nobody thinks that homeowner should have a good experience.

Expressed here are not merely feelings of being left out. Deeper consequences emerge when the organization privileges the volunteer experience over that of homeowners: The emphasis on making the volunteers feel empowered can actually interfere with homeowner empowerment. For instance, even though most homeowners hold down jobs and many would prefer to do their sweat equity at the affiliate office or in night school, affiliates are apt to pressure them to work at the construction site, where volunteers can meet them and, thus, have more of a personally fulfilling experience. It may be more empowering for the homeowners to have a choice in determining how they partner with the organization. But, as one affiliate board member explained, many think the homeowners should be made to work alongside the volunteers, who, without a chance to interact with the homeowners, would be "robbed of the feeling of helping the needy."

Other displays of homeowner empowerment can meet with similar resistance. The homeowner couple who organized their many friends and relatives to assist them with their sweat equity hours—which, together, they completed in only a few days—were considered "cheaters" rather than acknowledged for their initiative. The woman who got a building supply company to donate fourteen thousand dollars' worth of lumber to the affiliate and some beautiful marble tile for the walkway to her own Habitat house was castigated as a "control freak." "If she's that organized, then she doesn't need Habitat," said one volunteer, one of several who felt that marble tile, although cost-free, was not "simple enough" for a homeowner walkway. Finally, given Leslie Reems's dream of keeping her family at 329 South Moreland "year after year," it is small wonder that she would be one of the more popular homeowners among the volunteers and staff at the Sioux Falls affiliate. Yet residing in a Habitat house within a mile of her is another single mother, Marilyn Driggers, whose own dream of paying off her mortgage early, selling her house for a profit, and then moving to a location of her choice receives a cooler reception from volunteers. Those goals may define real empowerment for Driggers, but one gets the impression that some volunteers would be disappointed if, when driving by her house to glean a sense of fulfillment from their efforts, they did not see her and her children still there. Nevertheless, homeowners like Driggers and these others—to use a term sometimes heard among staff members—"get the program." They take their status as partners seriously and try to act autonomously. Unfortunately, although their actual empowerment is valued by many people within the organization, it can meet with resistance when it threatens to minimize the mere feelings of empowerment that are seemingly the inviolable right of every volunteer.

In addition to the organization's paternalism and its fixation on volunteers, another reason for the homeowners' relative subordination is their characteristic reticence to exert whatever power they might have within affiliates. For them, the class and often racial differences between themselves and most of the volunteers and staff mean that, in the words of one homeowner, Habitat seems like "somebody else's program." The best efforts of Family Nurture Committees and of countless others who are respectful and sensitive to the homeowners are frequently not enough to keep them from feeling like outsiders. This and the fact that, unlike volunteers and staff, they have much at stake in their partnership with Habitat explains what another homeowner described as a widespread "fear of rocking the boat."

Sociologist Amitai Etzioni distinguished between utilitarian organizations, which obtain commitment from their members through material rewards, and normative organizations (including most voluntary associations), from which members derive such symbolic rewards as self-esteem, acceptance, or feelings of moral integrity.[20] These categories collide at Habitat. The commitment of volunteers and most staff members is principally normative, which means there are few restrictions against, and maybe even commendable reasons for, rocking the boat if something is unacceptable to them. On the other hand, regardless of how thoroughly homeowners "get it" and buy into the norms of the organization, they are still tied to Habitat for utilitarian reasons. They may be alienated by middle-class volunteers who see them simply as "poor people." They may experience some discomfort when—perhaps during a family-selection interview or when the media is present at the building site—they feel what one homeowner identified as "pressure to say something Christian to make people happy." And, finally, they may get angry when a legion of college students, regardless of their good intentions, descends upon their Habitat house seeking a community-service "experience" as an alternative spring break. Despite these discomforts and more, the homeowners are getting a house at a significantly reduced price, and for them that usually has to be the bottom line. The empowerment they experience from Habitat is usually devoted mostly to following the organization's rules, doing their sweat equity, and making their mortgage payments.

That might not seem like much to many at Habitat who hold homeowners up to an ideal that, while not impossible, is also not one that volunteers are expected or necessarily encouraged to attain. Volunteers are the ones who are made to feel most empowered by the organization, and they often see the homeowners more as needy clients than as partners. Meanwhile, the homeowners are confronted with the organization's paternalism and fixation on the meaningfulness of the volunteer experience while they, due to their perceived outsider status and unwillingness to compromise their utilitarian interests, avoid confronting the organization on these and other matters. The perception of them as clients, then, becomes something of a self-fulfilling prophecy. When they are treated that way, homeowners are likely to get the message and seek no more involvement with their affiliate than they would with any other housing program or corporation. They get their homes, but they do not always get to feel at home in an organization that, ironically, prides itself on its partnership with low-income families.

There are no iron laws here. For every Leslie Reems delighted with Habitat and intending to remain an active participant in its ministry, there is likely to be a Marilyn Driggers content to use the organization as a stepping-stone to some other goal. No doubt there are other homeowners who do not want much to do with the organization at all. The degree to which different affiliates are able to empower both volunteers and homeowners also varies. Therefore, even though Habitat's organizational culture places a premium on constructing empowered citizens, one should be cautious in generalizing about its success in doing so. What is possible to conclude is that the three tendencies distorting the possibility of equal empowerment among volunteers and homeowners are a function of social class.

Habitat supporters typically rail against substandard housing but seldom attend to its root causes, which include such trends as declining real wages, rampant corporate downsizing and relocations, regressive tax policies, and drastically reduced welfare spending.[21] Even when a few people raised such issues in their interviews with me, social class was presented as something "out there" rather than something that is continually reproduced within the organization itself. Yet it is. People's empowerment within affiliates tends to be distorted into "something less" than intended when it is constrained by class power. When the emphasis shifts to fulfilling, rather than challenging, middle- and upperclass volunteers and to subordinating the homeowners, the class hierarchy operative within the social world becomes operative at Habitat and legitimated by it as well. The Habitat "have nots" aspiring to purchase their own homes, the Habitat "haves" giving them a hand up, the adoring media capturing it all–these convey that ours is a caring society in which we can all make it if we work hard enough. The system receives little criticism. If, as Henry David Thoreau once scornfully declared, "There are a thousand hacking at the branches of evil to one who is striking at the root," it seems many at Habitat are doing a good deal of hacking at the expense of more carefully aimed blows at the class structure.[22]

Habitat has been wary of state intrusion, as its government funds policy indicates. Yet the effects of the market—epitomized by the persistence of class inequality—appear within its own walls like a Trojan horse, allowed through its gates but bearing an undetected challenge. The organization's vision of empowerment for volunteers and homeowners alike succumbs to this challenge when empowerment within affiliates accrues to people according to their social class, as if it were a market commodity. A parallel challenge stands before its vision of social integration, which, at times, can likewise be occluded by the difference in class power between homeowners and volunteers.

Social Integration: Who Integrates with Whom?

Habitat's Integrative Ideal and Breaking Down Social Barriers

Another classical political theorist convinced of the latent benefits of civic participation was Jean-Jacques Rousseau. In his renowned text *The Social Contract*, he envisioned an ideal society in which citizens would participate extensively (particularly in making laws) and in the process learn to let go of their own particular wills (*volonté particulière*) and think in terms of what is best for all, the general will (*volonté générale*).[23] Civic participation and mutual cooperation with others, he suggested, instill in people a deeper sense of belonging to their own society. Seemingly insurmountable divisions between individuals and groups are transcended, private interests become less paramount, and citizens become integrated into their larger communities, the good of which they come to perceive and then desire.

This has long been a major theme among theorists of participatory democracy, and it is also a prominent theme within Habitat's organizational culture. Throughout its promotional literature, one discovers stories of people who, despite their differences, come to a fuller recognition of their commonalities as a result of working together. Catholics and Protestants work side by side in Northern Ireland, Contra and Sandinista sympathizers build together in Nicaragua, blacks and whites partner to address South Africa's housing shortage, and affluent Americans at home and abroad—work with lower-income families. Testimonies to the reconciliation and understanding that such cross-over experiences generate are standard fare at Habitat. It is as if the sound of hammers pounding nails has an effect similar to that of Gideon's storied trumpet blast—the walls of discord, ignorance, and self-interest come tumbling down. And rising from the rubble, according to Habitat ideology, are solid citizens capable of seeing similarities between themselves and others and of acknowledging their common interests in improving their communities.

As an international organization, Habitat gives its American constituents a sense of connectedness to the rest of the world through innovations such as the Global Village program and by dint of affiliate tithes that go to construction projects overseas. It seems an organization well suited to accommodate people with a Stoic "citizen of the world" understanding of civic obligation not confined by political boundaries. No doubt, that is exactly why some are attracted to the organization. Focusing primarily on Habitat's international scope, however, can mean underestimating its extreme sense of localism. Few motifs are more recurring at Habitat than the need to be involved in one's own local community and to interact with as wide a diversity of people within it as possible. Facilitating this sort of integration, its advocates usually continue, is exactly what participating in Habitat does.

One by-product of this localism is Habitat supporters' characteristic skepticism about philanthropic efforts that do not encourage people to become integrated into their communities. They disdain agencies and programs that simply "throw money at problems" or display more concern for poverty and injustice halfway around the world than for the needs most proximate to them. This kind of approach is generally considered a cop-out, a way for people to keep a safe distance from the complexities of real social problems and to keep their presuppositions about the poor from being challenged by real people. Such agencies and programs are suspect because they leave standing the walls of misunderstanding and fear between people. A social worker and board member of Habitat's St. Paul chapter, Maureen McClellan, made this point astutely:

> This country has ascribed a great deal of shame to being poor and there's a sense that poor people deserve their situation somehow. People become afraid of poverty and, since they're afraid of it, they don't want to see it. So they never go into the inner cities where it can be seen. It's particularly tragic because it sets up barriers between people in our communities. So it becomes easier to send money to Rwanda or Tanzania and people don't have the guts anymore to even look at the poverty on their own street. That's why Habitat is a good program. It makes poverty real to people and allows them to be open to the other people in their community.

Directing one's gaze toward the problems in Rwanda or Tanzania is devalued to the extent that it means turning away from entering into relationships with the people nearest us. Real relationships require time and often some courage, but they allow fear to be overcome. According to most respondents, they are also more effective than simply sending money abroad. Deirdre Schorske, board president at another Twin Cities chapter, discusses in memorable terms the ineffectiveness of sending money to a relief operation in Haiti. "I don't think it's very helpful for us to drop our largesse on other countries and then leave, which is what we do because we don't have the resources to really solve anything for them." She continues, "We're like a seagull that flies over those countries, craps on them and then turns around and heads home. What good is that?" To this question, most people at Habitat would likely reply, "None." What Charles Dickens once referred to as "telescopic philanthropy"—the propensity to care about a distant abstraction of humanity rather than the actual people in one's community—has no place within a person-to-person ministry intent on bringing citizens together.[24]

Schorske's further comments are helpful for articulating another by-product of Habitat's localism. When a diversity of people work and interact with one another at Habitat, they are said to engender greater mutual understanding. To the question of whether the organization should rely less on the work of volunteers, she responds, "No, if you did that then Habitat's basic precept of people helping people would be ruined. There's no sense of community if people just write checks and let someone else do the work for them. You also can't forget," she elaborates, "that there's more going on than just hammering nails. Working in a hands-on way allows people to meet other people, to learn about other cultures, and to basically get out of their comfort zone. You can't understand people's problems if you don't see them. You have to be there."

Statements like this one are prevalent within the organization. "Habitat tries to involve as many people as possible and be totally diverse," concurs Russell Bailyn, a long-time volunteer at the Sioux Falls affiliate. "It brings a real, not just fake, sense of community. It allows different types of people to connect with one another so that they can understand each other. That way, maybe they can get more things done besides building houses." Both he and Deirdre Schorske uphold the importance of establishing greater understanding between diverse groups of people, and they equate this with what each refers to as a "sense of community." She mentions that "there's more going on than just hammering nails," and he hopes that disparate people interacting with one another is a harbinger that "they can get more things done besides building houses." Both of them, true to the organization's dominant ideology, anticipate "more" from Habitat than just simple, decent houses. They expect that community will be built as well. They expect that, by relating to one another while doing the basic and beneficial work of sheltering families in need, people will come to a greater appreciation of how much they have in common. As a consequence, individual differences will seem relatively petty; feelings of being part of an encompassing, inclusive whole will loom larger.

Specific visions of what this "more," this community, will look like are rare among respondents. Even those who accept the organization's religious imagery of building the kingdom of God are nearly universally agnostic about its particularities. They claim to have no exact blueprints for how it ought to be constructed on earth. Instead, they represent the eagerly anticipated "sense of community" with such slogans as "a society where people look out for one another," "a caring society," or "a society knit more tightly." With no definitive notions of how the good society ought to look, most people are content to assert what it ought *not* to be. They overwhelmingly agree that it ought not be marred by various forms of divisiveness that threaten the establishment of community.

One example of this divisiveness is the polarization of political opinion in the United States, especially with regard to social justice issues. These are solvable, say conservative ideologues, if greater stress is placed upon personal responsibility and on traditional, supposedly waning, family values. Not so, argue their liberal counterparts, insisting on new social programs to aid the victims strewn in the wake of the juggernaut of capitalism.[25] American public discourse seems beset with diatribes exchanged between these two camps. And, particularly as covered in the mass media, they are prone to talk past one another (usually in distinctly uncivil terms), leaving the more moderate views of what political journalist E. J. Dionne refers to as the "restive majority" with less of a public hearing.[26]

However, because Habitat is such an intuitively sensible organization, with a Horatio Alger-like "pull yourself up by the bootstraps" quality, it has been widely embraced by both political liberals and conservatives. Many supporters optimistically see this as an indication that Habitat can help transcend political ideologies on still other matters of public concern. According to this view, its incontestably positive work provides a firm foundation for building consensus between liberals and conservatives. As affiliate executive director, Scott Quinley, comments, "One of Habitat's unique qualities is that it's attracted people from the entire political spectrum. This is crucial because, if you look around, our society, in general, seems to be becoming more and more Balkanized all the time." But, he adds with visible conviction, "Habitat is a way of cooperating together on the basis of some common values." These comments are representative of a popular sentiment at Habitat: The polarization endemic to America's civic culture can only be alleviated if there are social spaces in which people from along the entire political spectrum can meet, converse, and inevitably discover the important values that they hold in common. Habitat committees and building sites are generally considered to be such spaces.

They are also believed to be social spaces in which a second contributor of social fragmentation—racial divisions—can be overcome. Studies indicate that these are currently being exacerbated by an increasing geographic and institutional separation among racial groups in the

United States. For instance, the glaring separation between black and white communities is captured by the title of Douglas Massey and Nancy Denton's analysis of the nation's continuing pattern of residential segregation: *American Apartheid.* Epitomized by the urban ghetto, segregated housing produces concentrations of black (and, to a lesser extent, Hispanic) poverty, leading in turn to the evisceration of minority social institutions, reinforcement of racial prejudice, and the perpetuation of race-based social tensions well into the future. "Until policymakers, social scientists, and private citizens recognize the crucial role of America's own apartheid in perpetuating urban poverty and racial injustice," the authors contend, "the United States will remain a deeply divided and troubled society."[27]

Bringing people to recognize this troubling racial chasm and bridge it is another facet of Habitat's integrative ideal. The organization's mainly white volunteers express appreciation for the opportunity, as some put it, to move beyond their "comfort zone" and interact with homeowners, about two-thirds of whom are black or Hispanic. Such interaction is said to make clear how much we all have in common, and this, in Diane Hackett's view, is an important lesson. She is the pastor of a United Methodist church in Sioux Falls that has been a covenant church with the local affiliate for a few years. Thankful that Habitat serves as a means for her congregation to become more of a "neighbor to our neighbors," Hackett credits the organization with forcing many of her congregants to come to terms with their covert racist attitudes. "Why are we giving a house to them?" was the initial reaction of some upon discovering that the house they were financing and building had been designated for a family of Nigerian refugees living in a dilapidated apartment complex right next to their church. These attitudes, she explains, changed as time wore on:

> I mean you sign on the line [to become a Covenant Church] and people
> all interpret that the way they need to. But you're giving them some really
> profound faith stances. You know, you see a family you didn't choose—a
> Nigerian family. We would never have chosen them and we're like, "We're
> building so they get to buy this house? I'll be damned." You know? And
> that's pretty profound. And eventually people were digging the foundation
> of the house—digging in the dirt with these little black kids. And church
> members were saying, "Boy, these kids are really cute and they like digging
> in dirt just like our kids." I mean, that seems like something we should all
> know by now. But those kinds of experiences and having to live out those
> faith stances—that's a pretty nice mix.

An appreciation of our common humanity, irrespective of racial differences is, as Hackett states, "something we should all know by now." For those who do not know it or need reminding, the expectation at Habitat is that working alongside people of other races will inculcate that valuable lesson.

A third important division among Americans today comes from the lack of interaction between different social classes. According to former Labor Secretary Robert Reich, this situation is particularly problematic in light of certain economic changes, particularly the rise of those professionals he calls "symbolic analysts," who make up approximately one-fifth of the American workforce. These are professionals whose work is essentially conceptual, whose interests are geared more to the global economy than to their local communities, and who can afford such luxuries as separate schools, separate forms of entertainment, and separate, often gated, residential communities. Concerned about their potential detriment to the common good, he writes, "Distinguished from the rest of the population by their global linkages, good schools, comfortable lifestyles, excellent health care, and abundance of security guards, symbolic analysts will complete their secession from the union."[28] This "secession of the successful," in other words, refers to their increasing separation from the larger, less affluent community and from an attendant sense of civic responsibility. Their withdrawal into comfortable residential and institutional enclaves, unlike the segregation of the urban underclass, is of their own choosing and is designed to maximize their own private interests.

Not surprisingly, volunteers and staff at Habitat, many of whom fill the ranks of the symbolic analysts, credit the organization for dismantling class boundaries and fostering greater social integration in the process. By providing them with direct contact with low-income people, in other words, Habitat affords them the understanding and empathy that are the hallmarks of real community. Francine Bromley is insistent about this. Long active in her Presbyterian Church, she became one of the founders of her local affiliate and, for the first three years, spent between twenty and thirty hours each week getting it off the ground. Like many other volunteers, she confides that she was first attracted to Habitat because affordable housing seemed such an unambiguously worthy commitment. "Maybe I should be, but I'm never sure of which public policy routes to take," she admitted. "I've always been able to see the different sides of most political issues and have never felt sufficiently informed to decide strongly for one side or the other." From afar, most political issues appeared confusing, but they became less so when she began to interact with people outside of her upper-middle-class enclave:

> I think it's important that, when people work together, they get to know each other, especially the rich and poor. Both tend to live such separate lives. The rich don't know people on welfare or why a mother doesn't get her child inoculated—perhaps she doesn't have a car. But when they have to interact, say with a project like Habitat, the two—rich and poor—get to know each other. I'm not sure, but I think that kind of contact would influence our voting. We'd be more informed of the whole picture. How can you know if people are being hurt unless you have opportunities to talk to one another?

Bringing different people together and flouting class distinctions, then, is the way to establish a sense of community and to become well informed about the common good. In the words of Victor Millman, an executive staff member at the Americus headquarters, this is a "radical vision." He grumbles about being "trapped in the office," but takes some consolation in having occasional opportunities to participate in local building projects (especially with the Sumter County Initiative) and to meet the homeowners. "So now I walk through town and I run into Silas Wilcox and we stop and talk to one another," he explains. "This is great because we never would have known one another before—and my kids know his kids. There's something radical and transformative that took place there."

Agreeing with Francine Bromley, Millman is convinced that the barriers between rich and poor must come down before mutual understanding and even an approximation of justice can exist in our society. So convinced is he, in fact, that he recommends comparable experiences for policy makers as well. "I would love to see an unemployed welfare mother sitting at the same table as Newt Gingrich," he smirks. "And before Newt goes too far to limit welfare, that he really personally gets to know a woman who has three children, is supporting them on her own and might pay 90 percent of her income on child care if she has no welfare. For them to know one another on a personal one-to-one basis is, for me, a radical vision." For him, as for many other respondents, this is a vision based upon his understanding of what he calls the "radically inclusive ministry of Jesus." Millman elaborates by alluding to the gospel accounts of Jesus' habit of sharing meals with the poor and other marginalized people, and he explains that this was Jesus' way of denouncing the oppressive social hierarchies of his day. Indeed, it is precisely this sort of prophetic table fellowship that he desires for the former Speaker of the House and the unemployed welfare mother, and he implies that such a table is set on a daily basis at Habitat.

Interpreting Jesus' ministry as being more concerned about the wholeness of the community than the holiness of an elite few is typical among Habitat supporters. Just as typical is their awareness that political, racial, and class differences do more than keep people apart; they breed distrust and ignorance as well. At their best, Habitat's volunteers and staff perceive, with exceptional keenness, that ours is a fractured, separated society, and they are concerned with healing those fractures. They demonstrate an innate optimism about the good that can come when different people, however briefly, are brought together by their organization. Each of the respondents cited has offered glimpses of such optimism, but no one epitomizes it better than Gordon Knebel, a former real estate executive who, since 1990, has held one of the top executive staff positions at Habitat International's headquarters in Americus.

Knebel first became attracted to Habitat when, during one of its regional conferences, he witnessed a commissioning ceremony for two International Partners—one white and one black—who were being sent to build houses in their native South Africa, which was then at the peak of its racial conflict. He mentions how moved he was by that experience and then gives a nutshell summary of what social integration means at Habitat:

Is Habitat a good citizenship organization?

Yes, it is, and I'll tell you why. The greatest by-product of any Habitat project—affiliate, special event, you name it—is the bridging between rich and poor, black and white, Catholic and Baptist, or Christian and Jew. You take, for example, one thousand white, middle-class or rich suburbanites and dump them in Ward 7 of southeast Washington, D.C., for a week [as was done during the 1992 Jimmy Carter Work Project] and something happens.

What happens?

Fear is overcome. There is a realization that, "Wait a minute, these folks are just like we are." That happens. You get with these homeowner families and you realize they're worried about their grandkids, they're worried about their future, taxes are onerous to them. You know, the whole litany is the same litany.

So what does that do? Is that just acquired information?

No, no, it's life-changing. Absolutely. You sit in Albuquerque [his former home] as I did and you watch *NYPD Blue* and you form an impression of what New York City is like. We all have an image of what's going on, on the reservation, in the inner city, in Guatemala—we form them. And they have impressions of what's going on here. The folks in the inner city have a very clear impression of what life in the suburbs is all about. And it's all false and it all creates fear and it creates envies and jealousies that are unfounded. It creates barriers. So you get these folks together and suddenly, for a few of them at least, these barriers start to break down.

What does that say about good citizenship?

I'll tell you what it says about bad citizenship. It's exemplified by what's going on in our inner cities. We have no enemy as great as the inner city situation. So, good citizenship is finding ways to fix it. Habitat is not *the* answer but it is *an* answer. It's a response. It's a way to bring people together. So it's throwing pebbles into the lake, but there are ripples that happen. More people get involved and more people get interested.

This is Habitat's ideal vision of social integration. To write it off as so naïve as to have no relation to reality would be to dismiss Knebel's experience, and those of countless others, of how Habitat has opened them up to a fuller understanding of community and to their own responsibilities as citizens. As with the issue of empowerment, however, there are organizational tensions at play. This integrative vision is a contested one, and it too is always at risk of becoming "something less" than what people like Knebel experience or earnestly hope it to be. Three qualities of the vision account for this tendency: It is presumptive, asymmetrical, and noninstitutionalized.

Social Class and the Distortion of Habitat's Integrative Ideal

Habitat's vision is presumptive because Knebel's widely shared conviction that "barriers start to break down" is simply taken at face value by many at Habitat, without any elaboration or explanation of why it would be so. Versions of this simple assertion are plentiful at Habitat. They seem to be based on the assumption that if the social divisions within the United States engender so many problems, then bringing people together must necessarily produce advantageous results. Closer consideration reveals the presumptive nature of this expectation. One wonders how present Habitat's mainly middle-class and white volunteers actually are to the poor, often nonwhite communities in which the affiliates work. Deirdre Schorske maintains that "you have to be there"; Francine Bromley says we need "opportunities to talk to one another"; and Victor Millman claims that "to know one another on a personal one-to-one basis" can be radical. Yet the extent to which volunteers can authentically be present to others—in other words, meaningfully be there, talk to, and get to know people who are different from them—when voluntarism is so intermittent remains an open question.

Even when people do volunteer regularly, they usually do so with others who are not so different from themselves. For the most part, Habitat volunteers show up with their friends, families, classmates, and fellow members of their civic organization, church, or their workplace's community service group. Habitat's Global Village work camps, as well as its corporate sponsor, Campus Chapter and Covenant Church programs, actually encourage people to volunteer with familiar others. The result is that their volunteer stints are experienced and interpreted from within their own reference groups. It is thus difficult for volunteers to be genuinely open to those who are different from them. Contrary to the Habitat ideal, volunteering is apt to be merely an "experience" available to people of certain lifestyle enclaves, instead of a means for stepping outside of those enclaves to risk authentic encounters with difference.

Failure to recognize this is the main reason that many Habitat advocates assume that barriers break down as much for homeowners as they purportedly do for volunteers. For instance, Gordon Knebel suggests that people's faulty perceptions of those who are different create fears that erect unnecessary barriers. This makes sense for select volunteers. It is perfectly conceivable that, to the degree that they actually can be open to "the other," their volunteering may disabuse them of whatever negative stereotypes they have of people living in poorer areas and allow their fears of such people to be overcome. That kind of experience would likely be considered a fulfilling one for most volunteers.

Opportunities for such self-actualizing experiences are, after all, available to most people with privilege. Yet the converse is not necessarily true. Those with less privilege may be similarly disabused of their stereotypes, but it is not the case that their perceptions about "life in the suburbs" are false and unfounded. On the contrary, they arise from the actual economic disparities between themselves and more affluent Americans, including Habitat's volunteers; these do not simply break down with the wandlike wave of a hammer. The volunteers gain an opportunity to learn "how the other half lives," but what do the homeowners learn? To suggest that they learn to overcome "envies and jealousies" of those enjoying a comfortable standard of living becomes absurd if one considers that the entire capitalist system is fueled by people desiring for themselves what others have. Most of the homeowner families' prior living conditions would tend to justify deep feelings of envy toward even the most well-meaning of volunteers. Habitat supporters rarely face these criticisms because they tend to presume the homeowners' experience to be the same as their own. This presumption is a function of their being less present and attentive to the unequivocal otherness of the homeowners than Habitat's integrative ideal would lead one to believe.

Even when people are attentive to the homeowners, this ideal can also be compromised by a second quality, its asymmetry. The ideal of integrating different people into a larger communal whole can become skewed when it represents only the integration of homeowners into the middle-class ethos of volunteers. That ethos is often interpreted and legitimated as normative, and homeowners are deemed to be properly integrated when they are willing to conform to it. This explains the language of sameness commonly expressed by Habitat supporters. With a remarkable frequency, volunteers indicate that what allows them to let their barriers down is not their newfound respect for the otherness and difference of homeowners and a dedication to find common ground regardless. Rather, it is their discovery of an essential sameness between themselves and the homeowners, which allows them to, in effect, side-step the challenge of grappling with their differences. Many of the Methodists in Diane Hackett's congregation became more receptive to their Nigerian partner family when they saw that their children were "just like our kids," and Gordon Knebel is certainly correct in his interpretation of the "Ah ha!" experience of so many volunteers braving beyond their comfort zones: "these folks are just like we are."

The problem is that these are typically not statements heard when barriers come tumbling down as much as they are indications that homeowners have ventured over to the supposedly more respectable side of those barriers. Only a few respondents recognized this and acknowledged that Habitat's organizational culture constructs this sense of sameness by tending to select homeowner families most like the volunteers themselves. This occurs when Family Selection Committee members, quite naturally, develop clear affinities for families who, like them, are polite, affectionate toward one another, work hard, care about education, and otherwise demonstrate a capacity or aspiration to live by middle-class values. Recognizing this, and somewhat disturbed by it, affiliate executive director Gary Andrusz comments:

> When you really get down to brass tacks, I tend to hear the members of the Family Selection Committee saying things like, "You just fall in love with some of these people when you meet them." And they'll say, regardless of the policy, "I really wanted to help such and such a family." Well, that such and such a family was "the lovely." I heard somebody once say, "It's easy to love the lovely, it's hard to love the unlovely." We have a family that's substantially dysfunctional and we're always dealing with gossip from volunteers about this family. They bring much comment regarding our decision to help them.

Beyond highlighting the inclination of volunteers to "love the lovely," Gary also explains that homeowners are under the close inspection of a wider public, which has a similar penchant for the lovely. Because this public includes the media and potential volunteers and funders, the construction of sameness occurs in another way. This is the more conscious bias, particularly among fledgling affiliates, for selecting homeowner families with fewer personal and financial problems so they are more likely to succeed and, at the same time, represent the organization in the best possible light. Nothing generates public support like successful Habitat families, and nothing is taken to be an intimation of success more than the resemblance of their habits and priorities to those of middle-class families.

Michael Quattrone, an assistant regional director for Habitat International, was one of the respondents who flagged this propensity. "We have a tendency to sell Habitat," he says regretfully, "by announcing that we have a family selection process by which we pick good people who are willing to work on their house for five hundred hours. So we tell people that these families deserve a break because they have what it takes to be like us and they're not going to screw up the neighborhood." Even though Quattrone is aware that such assurances help to stem the preclusive tide of NIMBYism ("Not in My Back Yard") that can rise within many communities, he has good reason to be concerned about affiliates judging the worthiness of homeowner applicants on the basis of middle-class values.

For instance, Rebecca McNab, the staff member at the Redwood City affiliate, had nothing but glowing things to say about the homeowners she knew, and she emphasized how much they could teach volunteers. When asked for specifics, she explained:

Well, especially now that the families are working at the site, the volunteers are getting to know the families. You know, one of the stereotypes is that poor people are not working. But what they find out when they talk to a lot of these families is that they're working like crazy. And they need to hear about what kind of jobs they're working at. They need to hear their dreams and their hopes for their children's educations and their eventual success in life. Just as an example, both of the Martinez girls I mentioned earlier are seriously talking about going to college when they graduate. So they [the volunteers] get to just talk to the families and hear their comments about what a house is going to mean to them in terms for their futures. So I think they learn a lot just by getting to know these people. They get to put human faces on social problems.

McNab's determination to avoid stereotyping the poor is an admirable one. Still, the question arises: How glowing would her remarks have been if the homeowners were not so hard-working, interested in their children's educations, and so willing to make "comments about what a house is going to mean to them" for the benefit of the volunteers? One is also left to ponder whether the volunteers would be as eager to hear from them if the "human faces" they encountered among homeowners did not, in certain respects, so resemble their own.

A third and final reason for being dubious about this integrative vision is that it has not been deliberately institutionalized within the organization itself. As discussed, Gordon Knebel, the executive staff member in Americus, matter-of-factly presumes that bringing people together means that "barriers start to break down," that the experience is "life-changing" for some people, and, even when it is not, "there are ripples that happen" that get still others involved with the ministry. He presumes that different people are engaging one another and lives are being changed as a result. In fact, linking diverse groups of people together, he maintains, is "the greatest byproduct of any Habitat project." But if social integration is such an important byproduct, why is it left to chance? Why are interactions with diverse others left to chance encounters at Habitat events between political conservatives and liberals, rich and poor, white and black and so forth, rather than being built into the organization itself? Such questions are important to Michael Quattrone. Reflecting on them, he explains:

We bring people from all over the place to build houses. Nobody really relates, everybody's soon gone, the house is built, so what? You have a house. It's great for the family that has the house, but it's not the bigger vision. To me, it has to be sustained. You have to break down the barriers, keep them broken down and then be in relationship. Habitat usually falls short of the ideal of doing all this great stuff, but it doesn't mean we shouldn't have it as a vision. It can happen. What I would like to see is for us to love our vision enough to focus on it more and try to make it happen more.

Providing opportunities for relationships and understanding to develop is the core of the vision, but in order to take this ideal seriously—to "be it," as Michael implores—Habitat has to make it an institutionalized feature of its ministry. The only problem is that, like any franchise operation, the structure of the local affiliates is so predetermined and standardized that it is resistant to innovations that could help forge closer, more intentional relationships with lower-income families and communities. According to Jenna Ketchin, one of the most active homeowners at the San Francisco affiliate, the likelihood of better incorporating homeowners and other people from low-income communities into Habitat's work is decreased if the organization continues functioning as usual:

> We talk about community, but people come out and discover that it's a huge wheel and it's rolling. It's not as grassroots as everybody thinks. You don't have as much input. And, because of that, people from poorer communities don't buy into it. Take the board of directors as an example. There's nobody from this community on it. And if you get some of our people on it, even if they're community leaders, they're sort of intimidated because you've got board members who are giving these big checks and all that. I look at Habitat as a big wheel with lots of spokes called committees and the boards and all that stuff. That's what we've invented to start rolling. But what happens is that when we're ready for a family, we just tell them to jump on.

There are other gadflies within Habitat who agree with Ketchin. They would like to see affiliates reinvent the wheel in certain respects so that volunteers and homeowners are given more opportunities to interact with one another. Some, for example, believe homeowners should do their sweat equity as volunteer coordinators for their affiliates so they would have to work with volunteers more closely. Other people think Habitat should adopt more of the strategies of community-development organizations (as is now being tried through the still-modest efforts of the Urban Initiative), which could include providing daycare, job training, and literacy programs and doing political advocacy work on housing-related issues. Sometimes people say Habitat should display a deeper solidarity with the poor by establishing community centers in poor neighborhoods or encouraging public demonstrations in protest of the inhuman living conditions that exist within the country.

At present there appears to be little support for such organizational changes at the affiliate level. If the organization is, as Ketchin describes it, a "huge wheel" that keeps rolling along, that is fine with most Habitat supporters, who are more comfortable with a known quantity and seldom have the time or energy to make innovations. Even when occasional changes are made to deepen affiliates' relationships with the low-income communities nearest to them, they do not always succeed in bringing people together in the manner desired. Typically, the central factor is Habitat's preference for encouraging individuals and communities to partner with its ministry, rather than being open to ways in which it can *itself* become a partner to whatever grassroots efforts are already at work within those same communities. As with the homeowners, Habitat often expects low-income communities to "jump on," but rarely inquires as to how it can help grease the wheels of the social activism and service that may currently be turning within poorer communities.

Area director Victoria Gillespie is one of the respondents who attributed this failure to the inability of many middle-class Habitat supporters to acknowledge, or even "see," the initiatives undertaken by those who are different from them. "We are like the European colonists," she explains, sighing. "We come into a neighborhood and we don't see anything there. We don't see culture, we don't see strengths, we don't see gifts—all we see is need. What I'm pushing for is for us to come into a community and say, 'What's already here?'" What is actually there, she indicates, is concerned citizens working in community organizations, neighborhood centers, social service programs, and the like, many of whom would be amenable to entering into flexible, creative partnerships with Habitat. "But, again, we don't see those people," she reiterates, "They look so much like the problem, we don't see them."

She and Michael Quattrone seem united in their view that unless Habitat is sincere enough about its integrative vision to institutionalize opportunities for diverse individuals to interact with one another, many middle-class volunteers will remain blind to the good that is being done in communities other than their own. The organizational wheel will roll along, but Habitat supporters will tend to volunteer primarily with people from their own middle-class enclaves and will be tempted to select homeowners who seem to share their own values. Some volunteers might consider their experiences life-changing, but how integrative will they really be? Will barriers be broken down and common interests perceived if people at Habitat are not forced to look beyond their class barriers or consider much beyond their own self-interest?

Volunteering is linked to people's self-interest. It allows them to live out the expressive values they believe in, and it makes them feel good about themselves for doing so. People have a real interest in these things. Yet, when voluntarism fails to reach across class barriers and integrate the (perhaps contrary) perspectives of those who are supposed to be helped, it can become just another feel-good leisure activity available to those better-off citizens with a taste, however fleeting, for benevolence.[29] The existing social order based on inequitable class relations, moreover, is left unchallenged. This is because voluntarism (like charity) is an essentially self-imposed activity that extends only as far as the people engaged in it deem appropriate rather than necessarily being stretched far enough to meet others' actual needs. As long as they fail to reach across barriers and truly understand lower-income people's everyday realities, volunteers' sense of obligation to them will likely always fall short of those needs.

Furthermore, since voluntarism is so often cloaked in self-righteousness, it can hide the tattered rags of its own inadequacy and thus leave individual privilege intact, instead of raising questions about the class system that allots privilege so arbitrarily. Achieving Habitat's integrative ideal of breaking down the barriers separating its middle-class volunteers from the poorer homeowners could challenge these tendencies. Yet, as with the issue of empowerment, this ideal—this latent benefit of participation—remains a point of organizational tension at Habitat. It too is no doubt realized at certain points. As I have described, however, it frequently betrays a presumptive, asymmetrical, and noninstitutionalized character that reflects the inequitable class positions of the organization's homeowners and its volunteers and, at times, staff. This critical tension, in other words, suggests that the active citizenship generated within Habitat can devolve into "something less" than the ideal when distorted by the barrier-maintaining power of social class.

5

Citizenship and the Instrumental Logic of the Market

> The salesman's world has now become everybody's world, and, in some part, everybody has become a salesman. The enlarged market has become at once more impersonal and more intimate. What is there that does not pass through the market? Science and love, virtue and conscience, friendliness, carefully nurtured skills and animosities? This is a time of venality. The market now reaches into every institution and every relation. The bargaining manner, the huckstering animus, the memorized theology of pep, the commercialized evaluation of personal traits—they are all around us; in public and in private there is the tang and feel of salesmanship.
>
> C. Wright Mills, *White Collar*

"What is there that does not pass through the market?" This unsettling question, which C. Wright Mills posed nearly half a century ago, is still relevant today. Indeed, the expressive values that are the very lifeblood of the voluntary sector frequently—and especially when they are institutionalized—congeal into instrumental concerns. Expressive values "pass through the market" when the people who promote them in public are required to keep a close eye on organizational costs, concentrate on efficiency, or strategize about how to sell their organization to the broader populace. Even voluntary sector initiatives, after all, have to concern themselves with such matters if they are to remain fiscally viable and thus survive over the long term. Those able to develop an organizational culture without the "tang and feel of salesmanship" still experience significant tensions as the market impinges upon their work.

Habitat has not been exempt from these tensions. While the organization institutionalizes certain expressive values that rouse a rich and active understanding of citizenship, these can, nevertheless, be compromised by the market. As we saw in the last chapter, the values associated with citizen empowerment and social integration are apt to become "something less" when the major *effect of the market*, discrepancies in class power, produce a rift between affiliate volunteers (and, to a lesser extent, staff) and homeowners. But there is another potential rift to consider: This is a rift between the supporters who expect Habitat to run according to its founding expressive values and the affiliate itself (or the international headquarters), which can become increasingly constrained to abide by the rationalized *logic of the market* as it frequently seeps into its organizational culture. Dubbed by Jurgen Habermas as the "colonization of the lifeworld," this process can result in expressive values being routed from voluntary sector organizations like Habitat, which eventually come to be more driven by instrumental, bottom-line concerns.[1] Although there is no single path by which this occurs, the dynamics of professionalization and commercialization are features of the general process. Both are evident within Habitat, and, to the extent that they threaten to undermine the latent benefits of civic education and organizational freedom respectively, these dynamics create still more tensions within this house-building ministry.

Civic Education and the Issue of Professionalization

Educating Citizens at Habitat

The well-known utilitarian philosopher John Stuart Mill expressed, along with his many contributions to political theory, a third latent benefit of voluntarism. Like Rousseau, he was aware that civic participation integrates individuals by forcing them to "weigh interests not their own,"[2] and, with Madison, he acknowledged the capacity of voluntary associations to disperse political power throughout the populace. An additional virtue of voluntarism, in his estimation, was its ability to inculcate important civic skills and better familiarize citizens with the social realities surrounding them. Elaborating on this educative role of voluntary associations in his groundbreaking essay, *On Liberty*, Mill contends:

> In many cases, though individuals may not do the particular thing so well, on the average, as the officers of government, it is nevertheless desirable that it should be done by them, rather than by the government, as a means to their own mental education—a mode of strengthening their active faculties, exercising their judgment, and giving them a familiar knowledge of the subjects with which they are thus left to deal. This is the principal, though not the sole, recommendation ... of the conduct of industrial and philanthropic enterprises by voluntary associations.[3]

Even though Mill proposed a representative form of government whereby elected elites would predominate (against which Rousseau warned most adamantly), it was at the local level that individuals could and must learn democracy by being attentive to their fellow citizens and finding solutions to common problems.

These expectations are similarly expressed at Habitat. Part of its mission as "the conscience of the world concerning shelter" is to educate people about the problem of substandard housing in the hopes of moving them to take action. That is not all. That the ensuing action is itself educative is a commonplace assumption within the organization. Long-time affiliate committee member Jill Grierson explains that being involved with Habitat is important for raising people's awareness of their communities' needs. "By empowering people, building community, and just making people more community conscious, this kind of work can inform people and lead them to believe that they can do even more, whether it be in their neighborhoods or their school district or even by deciding to get together to build a new playground for the kids," she says.

Along with people like Grierson who claim to be more "community conscious" are many others who value the skills they acquire through working with the organization. Ten years ago, Wendy Farganis was making ends meet by stringing together various "mind-numbing, dead-end jobs" when she volunteered on her first Habitat house. Since then, she has served on a number of operational committees and eventually became her local affiliate's board president. "I'm getting so much out of this" is a statement repeatedly expressed by Habitat supporters. Farganis elaborates upon it by indicating the kinds of skills she has actually gotten out of her volunteering. "When I started with Habitat, I was working as a secretary," she recalls. "I had a lot of skills that weren't being used. But Habitat allowed me to express my competence and use my skills at meetings and with giving presentations and planning events and whatever. That's why volunteers need to be used well so others can get that same sort of satisfaction too."

The previous chapter raised the issue of Habitat focusing too much on its volunteers. Jill Grierson's and Wendy Farganis's responses explain why many within the organization feel justified in doing this. When volunteers are "used well," the argument goes, they will gain the "sort of satisfaction" that impels them to do much more. Compared to Habitat homeowners, volunteers may have to do very little in order to be considered empowered according to Habitat's (double) standard, but there is a near-universal conviction that even the most minimal, when-I-get-around-to-it sort of involvement draws volunteers into an educational process by which they become increasingly dedicated citizens. This is said to occur in two ways. The simplest is that supporters learn more about the reality of substandard housing by working with Habitat. Because this incites their concern, volunteers decide to increase their efforts *within* the organization. Those who wield hammers will devote more time to the construction site, those who do committee work will perform their duties more responsibly, those who give money will give more generously, and so forth. In reality, sometimes this happens for certain individuals and sometimes it frankly does not.

There is also a second way in which participating with Habitat is supposed to be edifying for citizens. Sensitive about Habitat's being perceived as just another "charity" organization neglecting to address the root causes of social injustice, many claim that involvement with the organization actually does, over time, lead people toward more systemic approaches to social issues. These supporters perceive working with the organization to be a consciousness-raising experience that educates people and challenges them to move beyond offering charity to a more encompassing, justice-centered approach to poverty. They become, as some people like to say, "ruined for life" because they never see the world and their place in it quite the same again. Interestingly, and almost without exception, people who express confidence in this educative process are just as certain that the pursuit of a more radical social justice agenda should be undertaken *outside* of the organization. Those whose perspectives have been duly radicalized, they argue, have typically gone on to other things and are no longer with Habitat. The absence of such people makes this argument irrefutable and, along with the fact that Habitat has made no systematic effort to assess it, likely accounts for its persistence within the organization.

That participating in Habitat gives people a greater understanding of unjust social structures and piques them to undertake justice-centered approaches for addressing them is one of the most cherished beliefs among supporters. They profess this conviction faithfully, often adding reasons why Habitat itself should not take on a more radical agenda. One is the contention that Habitat's current approach to poverty housing already appeals to large numbers of people who might not be mobilized if its work were done differently. This is the opinion of Michelle Prelinger, the social justice program director at a Catholic Church covenanted with the Twin Cities affiliate. She mentions how different Habitat is from Loaves and Fishes, the homeless feeding program with which she is also involved, even though she describes it as a charity-based "band-aid program." Stressing that Habitat "goes beyond charity," she elaborates, "I see Habitat as sort of in the middle between charity and a fully justice-orientated program that seeks to get at the causes of poverty and injustice. But that's OK," she continues, "because it fills a niche and often people's involvement in this kind of work starts with charity work and then moves on. It's part of a continuing education process." Habitat's work, just as it is, successfully accommodates those people whose social commitments are best matched by an organization that pursues an agenda "between charity and a fully justice-orientated program." Habitat, Prelinger insists, functions as an important service niche dynamic enough to initiate its supporters into an ongoing "education process" that ultimately acquaints them with the root causes of poverty. As we have seen, this is also a niche that, given its appeal to conservatives and liberals alike, is broad enough to accommodate a vast constituency and thus ensure the organization's enviable effectiveness.

This suggests a second reason for not expanding the ministry. It is, as one volunteer stated it, "already running on all cylinders." By focusing on building houses, many supporters argue, Habitat is not only doing what it does best, it also has more than enough work to keep itself occupied well into the future. Expanding its focus would mean detracting from its proven effectiveness and venturing into areas better addressed by other, less hands-on organizations. Habitat International executive staff member Gordon Knebel states this case succinctly:

> We are in the business of building decent housing. Our success is in our focus, and when we lose that, we will lose effectiveness. Beyond that, we shouldn't be doing more political work. We don't need to because we're not at that point. At some distant point when there are only fifty families left to be housed and it's going to take a sit-down strike to do it, we've got to do it. But we certainly don't need to do a sit-down strike today because there is plenty of poverty to go around. You can aim in any direction and point and there will be a family that needs a decent house.

In sum, there is a strong consensus among supporters convinced that Habitat is sufficiently appealing, busy, and, most of all, sufficiently edifying to continue its work in the same way it has done since its very founding.

Professionalization at the International Headquarters

One can see why the issue of professionalism has become a pressing concern for many people at Habitat. They fear that if organizational decision making and the use of civic skills are monopolized by paid professionals, the result will be to reduce the opportunities for hands-on participation within their communities by which the average volunteer learns to be a better citizen.[4] The organization may still *use* volunteers and *serve* homeowners, but that is perceived as a far cry from its founding vision of *partnering* with a diversity of people who are growing together in their understanding of what constitutes their common good.[5] Such distinctions, it is further feared, may be lost on professional staff people, who are likely to qualify for their jobs on the basis of technical competence rather than on their allegiance to the more expressive—and particularly the religiously informed—values that are the core of Habitat's ministry. They may also direct the organization toward complying with the logic of the market by over-emphasizing such instrumental values as maintaining professionals' status, implementing standardized rules and policies, and fixating on maximizing the efficiency of the operation. Whatever validity such fears may have, it is clear that professionalization—to the degree that it downplays expressive values and limits people's opportunities for acting in accordance with them—impinges upon Habitat's educative ideal at both the International and affiliate levels.

At the headquarters in Americus, the tensions wrought by professionalization are relatively new. As late as 1990, most positions within the organization were held by volunteers who received small stipends and whose work was managed by fewer than twenty salaried staff people. The compensation system, consistent with the "economics of Jesus," was based entirely upon individual need. This was generally deemed appropriate since the intangible rewards that came from working at Habitat were, in the main, sufficient for the organization's true believers. Salary adjustments were seldom instituted, formal performance evaluations were infrequent, and job assignments were broad enough to enhance the variety and enjoyment of people's work. The staff roster from that time was quaintly alphabetized by first names. With accelerating growth, however, came the need for change. According to Jeff Snider, Habitat's executive vice president at the time, the organization's single most important need was for "talented people" who could run the operation skillfully and thus should both be paid at competitive rates and held accountable for the quality of their job performance. As he put it, no longer could well-intentioned, but perhaps poorly trained, people self-righteously declare, "You can't tell me what to do—I'm doing something good."[6] His goal was to attract highly trained people and then expect them to perform to the professional standards essential for managing such a fast-expanding organization.

This was largely achieved during the ensuing years. Habitat International has a much more professionalized bureaucracy than it did before, and many in Americus consider this to be a welcome change. Delores Jarvie, who has a degree in nonprofit management as well as professional experience at the United Way headquarters in New York, is currently one of Habitat's executive staff members. She suspects that many of her support staff, who are primarily young women like herself, consider her to be "something of a tyrant" because she is very demanding of them. On most days, that does not bother her because she considers Habitat's mission to be too important to demand anything less than the highest level of efficiency from its employees. "This is a Christian ministry," she concedes, "but it's also an organization and it's got to be managed." When asked about the challenges that accompany managing a Christian ministry, she responds:

> Well, I think that sometimes we come in with the pre-conceived notion that, because Habitat is a Christian organization, it reserves the right for us to be really laid-back and unprofessional and not respect some of the things you have to respect in the business world. That's been a major challenge for me here. I think that the idea of us being a happy family is a nice fallacy, but we have a mission that needs to get accomplished. And I think

people have to be made accountable for that and you have to deal with them when they're not accountable. And we tend to say, "We're family, we can't hurt people. If they can't do the job, we'll just shift them to another job." So that's a challenge. A lot of people come to Habitat with that notion because it is a Christian ministry. That lackadaisical environment does exist here. And, unfortunately, it rests with some key people so it has permeated the entire environment.

For Jarvie, some of the work habits purportedly stemming from Habitat's identity as a Christian organization are in tension with the expectations of efficiency and accountability associated with professionalism. A similar point is made by Frank Riddell, an accountant with an M.B.A. from Dartmouth who worked for Merrill Lynch twelve years before realizing his job lacked what he calls the "GOOB factor." That job, he recollects, provided too little incentive to "get out of bed" in the morning, something he has recaptured upon moving to Americus. With him, he brought his professional expertise, which he claims benefits the organization by giving it greater credibility within the community. Like Jarvie, he considers this benefit of professionalism to be a corrective to a problem precipitated by Habitat's Christian identity. For him, this had to do with public mistrust:

> The community [in Americus] has been very slow to embrace us. It's sad, but I think that there's a mistrust of people who are so different and so contrary to just trying to get ahead, a mistrust of people who come in to help other people. I think it's getting better, though. As we bring in more professionals, I think the community will come around.

> *What is it about professionals that's so disarming for the community?*

> I think there's been a mistrust as to why someone would leave their home, travel hundreds of miles to southern Georgia and work for virtually no pay. But, I think the fact that many of us are professionals allows people to become more comfortable. We look more like them, we have similar background. It's not so foreign to their own experience.

Delores Jarvie's and Frank Riddell's assertions that professionalism brings more efficiency and credibility than if the organization were run according to religious values alone does not mean they are hostile to those values. In fact, Jarvie openly confesses, "I think that this is what God wants me to be doing with my life." Similarly, Riddell maintains, "I do feel that faith is better demonstrated through action; that's what works for me." They believe their professional skills actually accent their faith commitments, which, they further point out, do not have to be lived out in ways that are either inefficient or so unfamiliar as to breed mistrust among others.

Making an even stronger case for the compatibility between professionalism and religious faith is Melinda Deleon, a staff member in Habitat's Department of Human Resources. "I've always been more interested in contributing to something more important than doing work where all you worried about was whether or not the company makes a profit," she says. "If I help people as a human resource professional, that's the Lord's work." Not surprisingly, she had plenty to say when asked if professional priorities often conflict with people's religious commitments:

> If you have a child, do you take him or her to the Christian pediatrician with no experience and no degrees? Do you send your child to a Christian school where the teachers can't read? Most of us would say, "No, that's ridiculous." Then do you want your organization to be run by somebody, say a financial person, who can't count and wouldn't know a debit from a credit? Then do you want your people hired by a human resource person who doesn't know the law or how to check references and that kind of thing? It all amounts to this whole myth about professional people being secular. I tell people all the time—read the Bible, Jesus was the most professional, quality-orientated person we know. He didn't say to people, "OK, I'll give you one fish and everybody can take a little nibble." He said, "I'm going to feed everybody." Isn't that the level of professionalism we should be aspiring to?

Even if one is inspired by deep religious faith, she seems to say, doing something good for others is inadequate, and may even be harmful, unless one is sincerely committed to doing it right. A dedication to competence and efficiency seems entirely fitting since Deleon goes so far as to equate these marks of professionalism with divine attributes. Seeing no discrepancy between religious devotion and professionalism, she is more optimistic than Jarvie and Riddell, but she does not contradict them. They, after all, are just as convinced that inefficiency and a lack of credibility do not have to plague a faith-driven organization. Habitat, they and many others agree, can be managed professionally and still remain true to its founding religious vision.

That Habitat *should* be managed professionally is contested by none of the leadership in Americus. Their reasons nearly always focus on their high estimations of the organization's work or of their own role within it. Concerning first the organization, some unhesitatingly avow that Habitat is doing God's work while others, less comfortable with overtly religious claims, make more modest assessments. In either case, they are convinced that Habitat's work is making such a positive impact on the world that it should be done more thoughtfully, more noticeably, and in more locations. Such a worthwhile and important ministry, the consensus maintains, should have well-trained professional leaders who can manage it properly and ensure that the organization achieves the high level of success it deserves.

Regarding their own work, staff members in Americus consistently report that, since coming to Habitat, their occupations feel more like a "vocation," a "calling," "what I'm supposed to be doing," or "my contribution to humanity." Their work as white-collar professionals has gained a new stature in their own eyes. It is frequently seen not just as another way of making a living but as a way of making a life that can be lived according to a comprehensive set of values encompassing both home and office. They display a common desire to decompartmentalize their lives so their occupations can be as meaningful as they hope their private lives to be. No longer do they see themselves as simply managers or accountants or human resource personnel. These roles seem more meaningful because they contribute to a cause that dwarfs the comparatively petty goals driving the business world. With such a high estimation of their own work, it has become obvious to them that professionals should be an integral part of Habitat's ministry, despite the fact that its heavy reliance on volunteers has distinguished it from most other low-income housing organizations.

Since it is such a grassroots organization, it is understandable that, while Habitat has accepted a professionalized leadership, it has not done so uncritically. Many people at the international headquarters—even among the executive staff—remain wary of the potential consequences of professionalization, discussions of which inevitably center around the organization's religious identity. This is because Habitat's vitality is commonly believed to be contingent upon remaining faithful to its religious vision. The civic education of people associated with the organization would be impossible, many claim, if Habitat did not uphold its religious values. Indeed, it is these values that are said to initially stir the consciences of volunteers, enable them to see beyond their own selves, and, ultimately, undertake the edification process by which they grow in their understanding of social justice.

Fears abound about what could happen to Habitat's religious tenor and its continued ability to mobilize citizens if professionals become even more of a mainstay within the organization. I found that merely mentioning the topic of organizational growth and management was usually sufficient to get people talking about the difficulties of maintaining the religious character of the ministry. Habitat's current executive vice president, David Williams, talks about it quite a bit. Addressing the recent transition to a more professionalized work environment, he reflects:

> You know, in the early years of the organization, the Christian emphasis was exactly why people came here. But there was a shift because the success of the organization was really beginning to create some serious management problems. The whole issue was about the balance between faith and competence. In many cases we'd have people with great faith and yet not necessarily the tools to, you know, run an international human resource department or things like that. So, I would say that things have been done to increase the competency and technical skills. But maybe we did lose a little bit of the Christian element. People here don't sign a declaration of faith and I don't know if that's where we need to go. I would like to think that our faith is more than signing a piece of paper. But, if we are a Christian organization, somehow we have to define what that means. What does that mean in terms of our leadership? Part of the theology of Habitat is its inclusiveness. So the question becomes: How do we include everybody without losing who we are? And the more we're successful, the more that question will be there.

In her comments, Melinda Deleon attributed little credence to what she called the "myth about professional people being secular," but Williams does not appear to be so easily reassured. He gives the impression that he keeps a careful eye on the "balance between faith and competence" and does not always like what he sees. More clearly than Deleon, in fact, he sees that even professional people with religious faith, if they do not adhere to a common set of religious values, are apt to embrace more instrumental values commensurate with their common professional status and training. He seems to be grappling with this. He knows that hiring people based on their having the appropriate theology rather than appropriate skills is untenable given the complexities attendant to managing a worldwide organization. He also knows that imposing a dogmatic "party line" upon paid staff would be unimaginable for an organization that has, since its founding, prided itself on its inclusiveness and benefited from the broad support it has mustered as a result. All he can do is remain vigilant and endeavor to steer the organization so that it acts "in a Christian way," even though no firm consensus exists within the organization about exactly what that means.

Among those who share Williams's concerns about balancing faith and professionalism are people more certain than he that the professionalized ethos in Americus is ultimately detrimental to Habitat's ability to act in a Christian way. Their concerns fall into two broad categories: A professionalized leadership downplaying Christian values, they claim, is problematic both because of what it does and how it does it.

Clearly annoyed by some of the things the organization does is Carl Levering, another program director in Americus. As president of his own Michigan-based construction company, he tithed to Habitat for over ten years before learning of the opening for his present job. The position pays half of what he had been earning as a contractor, but he and his family prayed about their decision to come to Americus and ultimately "felt that it was what the Lord was leading us to do." Levering takes Habitat's religious values seriously. Consequently, he worries about the proclivity of some of the executive leadership to make decisions based on Christian values one moment and in the next to pursue utilitarian calculations intended to maximize the interests of the organization. This is tantamount to their "keeping one foot in the boat and one foot on the dock," which, in his view, is a particularly awkward posture for managers of a specifically Christian organization.

This awkwardness is exacerbated by the fact that Habitat does little to train its leadership in the founding principles that animate it and ought to guide its ongoing decision making. The result, says Levering, is that Habitat does certain things that are out of sync with its religious principles. For instance, he was disturbed by Habitat's application for an exemption, offered to certain nonprofits by the state of Georgia, from paying unemployment compensation to recently fired and laid-off employees. Elaborating on this matter, he says:

> I look at the way we treat our employees sometimes and I say, "Gosh, how can we call ourselves a Christian organization when we treat our people the way we treat them?" When I look at decisions like that, I see the problem of having people who aren't Christians in executive positions—because they're making decisions for a Christian organization without understanding what the principles are. They just say, "Hey, here's a way to save some money and, therefore, we meet the bottom line of building more houses." It's trying to use principles from a profit-making organization while being in a nonprofit and justifying decisions based on those principles. It doesn't work.

The faith component at Habitat will not be entirely lost as long as there are people like Carl Levering who ask questions that begin, "How can we call ourselves a Christian organization when . . ." These questions serve as reminders that the colonization of an organization by the logic of the market is best understood as an ongoing tension rather than an incontestable or irreversible process.

The people who voice a second category of concerns are another indication of this tension: They dislike how things get done. In many organizations, one hears complaints about bureaucratic rules, routinized tasks, elitism based on professional credentials, and impersonal work environments. These are predictable aspects of many fast-growing enterprises of both the for-profit and nonprofit variety. At Habitat, though, such issues are regarded as more than a personal annoyance or hardship; they are often seen as a digression from the religious ethos of the organization. While people accept that a faith-based organization can be professionally run, many insist it should actually be based on faith in God, not on excessive planning and bureaucratic procedures. In particular, some senior staff members—who can recall a time when the organization's most plentiful resource may well have been the religious commitments that goaded them on—believe that their work experience ought to be, as one put it, more "on the edge."

This is definitely the opinion of Gordon Knebel. Among his many stories about the times when Habitat "made it on faith alone," one of his favorites is the one about having on hand only a portion of the necessary vinyl siding halfway through the 1994 Jimmy Carter Work Project. With an excess of fifteen hundred volunteers on the site and an easily agitated ex-President expecting the siding the following day, he found it miraculous that the delivery truck—which had broken down, gotten lost, and been delayed by inclement weather—arrived at the Eagle Butte reservation just in the nick of time. He remembered feelings of exhilaration and purposefulness as he and a few other staff members unloaded the truck until three o'clock in the morning. "I don't think these kinds of events are just coincidences," he asserts. "I think the Lord likes what we're doing."

Knebel admits that such feelings have become less frequent. When asked why, he describes Habitat's organizational transition in terms of its effect on the once-prevalent sense that the success of the ministry is contingent upon faithfulness:

We're going through changes. And some are necessary—this is a big operation. And a certain amount of corporateness may be required. But it ain't
like it used to be. In the process of structuring itself, Habitat has come to
remind me of the early church. Jesus never intended to form a church.
After his death there was need to bring a certain structure, a vessel, to
carry the message—which made sense. But then, especially after Constan-
tine, you see how interlocking mazes of organization and hierarchies
started to form. And I feel that's where we're at in Habitat. It's not that
it may not be necessary, but we are sacrificing that organic, risk-taking
excitement as we become more risk averse, more bureaucratic, and more
structured. And those things bug me.

*This is a little surprising to me. Here you are, one of the main guys in the organi-
zation, saying you've got too much organization. What's going on here?*

Well, I fear for the organization as we install more and more of this structure. I find this stultifying after a while—this constant bureaucratic, political, form-filling stuff. It's necessary stuff, perhaps. But it ain't where the
action is. Let me say this: The notion of Habitat is essentially lunatic. If we
had decided to provide shoes for everybody on the planet, that could be a
doable thing. But we're providing houses, the biggest investment that most
people ever make in their lives. . . . This lunatic notion only works when it's
faith-driven. And I've seen it happen. I've worked with affiliates that aren't
faith-driven and they don't succeed. And I've worked with affiliates that are
and they do.

Knebel is frustrated with how the professionalized bureaucracy does
things. He seems to regret that, like the early church, the original
charism and countercultural verve of Habitat has undergone what Max
Weber has referred to as a process of "routinization."[7] This is the eventual transformation of fluid social movements into comparatively static
organizational forms. Knebel is right to concede that "It's necessary
stuff, perhaps" because, without some degree of institutionalization,
even the most commendable of movements cannot get their message
out and become sufficiently stable to have an appreciable impact on the
wider society.[8] At the same time, he is insightful enough to note that
this transformation, albeit necessary, comes with a tendency toward
stagnation, which has to be at least somewhat resisted if Habitat is to
continue inspiring people to support its ministry. This seems to be what
he is trying to do himself, in the hopes of allowing his own work to continue feeling like a calling instead of just another job.

There is another reason why Gordon Knebel seems frustrated. Positing the organization's "lunatic" mission as the reason for it to remain
faithful to its Christian roots, he echoes the familiar Habitat theme of

needing to be in partnership with God when setting out to do what is clearly an impossible task for mere mortals. So "lunatic" is this mission, he suggests, that it is pure hubris to think it can be accomplished by dint of the "bureaucratic, political, form-filling stuff" of professional management. For Knebel, the current organizational ethos at Habitat is upsetting because he interprets it as an indication that people are putting the ministry in the wrong (even if professional) hands, rather than remaining in a faith-driven endeavor in partnership with God.

Professionalization at a Local Affiliate

Knebel indicates that his concern about the international organization's fidelity to Habitat's religious vision extends to the local affiliates as well. Affiliates with professionalized staffs often have more opportunity to glean resources from local government and businesses instead of being tied to the surrounding churches from which most get their initial support. This does not mean such affiliates will become more secularized, however. The norm for most local affiliates, whether they have professional staffs or not, is to be supported by a mix of contributors, volunteers, and staff, some of whom are more overtly religious and others less so or, less frequently, not at all. The major reason, then, why professionalization poses tensions for Habitat's educative ideal at the affiliate level is not so much because it undermines the expression of religious values, which is how the problem is typically framed in Americus. Rather, it limits the opportunities for volunteers to act upon those values and learn to be better citizens in the process. When affiliates become larger and decide to hire paid staffs, professionals can hoard the responsibility and decision-making within the affiliate, in the process relegating volunteers to the ranks of those expected to just show up on occasion. The everyday operations of the affiliates can come to be directed more from above than from the grassroots. Given that there are more than fifteen hundred affiliates in the United States, about a third of which have paid staffs, it would be difficult to provide a comprehensive assessment of what increasing bureaucratization means in every instance. One way to get a sense of this is to observe the leadership transitions in a single affiliate whose location, for the purpose of protecting confidentiality, will remain undisclosed here.

Each of the first three leaders of this affiliate were introduced in the last chapter. The first, Francine Bromley, is a wife and mother of two grown children who had worked as a elementary school teacher for many years. Before being asked to start a Habitat affiliate by her church's mission committee, she had long been an active volunteer at the church, especially with its literacy program for Cambodian refugees. Expecting only a couple dozen people to attend the first informational meeting, she was surprised to see about 125 show up and even more so when they elected her chairperson of the affiliate steering committee, making her responsible for initiating the affiliation process with Habitat International. She accepted this role enthusiastically and, before long, had gained a reputation for being a tireless volunteer, the linchpin of the entire local organization. When Bromley describes volunteering between twenty and thirty hours every week during the affiliate's first three years, she does not convey the impression of a martyr who had flung herself upon the pyre of selfless altruism. "The good things people do are always good for them too," she says, and then goes on to describe how much she has received from her volunteer work:

> You must remember that Habitat is a gift to those who give and who receive. Those of us who volunteered were given a sense of what it is to be in relation with others and a sense of building community. I have such fond memories of working with people—of scraping plaster or hammering. We weren't always so efficient, but we did it. And we'd laugh about it and look back and say to each other, "Do you remember scraping all that plaster in that heat?" In a way, it was like a big craft project and it was like a party. I think Larry might have been upset with that attitude.

Francine Bromley and her fellow volunteers were construction amateurs in most respects, and their work may well have been comparable to a "big craft project." But they made a difference in the lives of their (admittedly few) homeowners. And, as she later put it, her voluntarism was "a way of feeling my strength."

In her comments, she mentions Larry Grierson, the affiliate's second leader and first paid executive director. It is not clear whether he was "upset" with the informal and less efficient character that marked the affiliate's early years. It is more than clear, however, that these were the very things he tried to change when he was hired two years after the affiliate began operations. Although she speaks highly of Grierson and recognizes that a full-time staff person had been needed, Francine Bromley still feels that the affiliate was never quite the same after he took charge. Describing the ensuing changes, she reflects:

At first there was the sense that it was just a bunch of folks doing things. Mind you, we were rather slow and erratic. But those houses got built and there was a feeling of people power. It was such a wonderful delight. But, to be honest, people did get a bit worn down and we were never very good at dealing with contractors or potential donors. It had to change—by growing larger. We started working on more houses, which meant more of everything else: paperwork, committees, everything!

Was this difficult for you?

It hurt a lot. To me, it [the affiliate] was like a small child that you keep so neat and combed and pretty until one day he becomes himself. And you know it's right. Larry has done so much for the affiliate. But his dream was for it to grow while my dream was for it to be run entirely by volunteers and just grow organically. We were at loggerheads, and I knew I had to go away—I just had to. Looking back on it, I suppose I wish I had the strength to keep the program more people-orientated and less, I guess, success-orientated.

When Bromley says "I just had to go away," there is a reason for this. Larry Grierson wanted the organization she loved like a child to mature in ways she would not have liked. As a one-time professional contractor, he had a facility for dealing with people in the construction trades and building supply business, and was able to secure their support. He was also concerned about better quality and more efficient work being done on Habitat houses. His degree in social work and experience in that field enabled him to better organize the affiliate and expand its productivity dramatically. There was a less ad hoc, "craft project" atmosphere at the affiliate, and it was apparent to everyone that the executive director, not the volunteers, was in control. Lastly, as an evangelical Christian, Grierson brought a certain missionary zeal to his work. Bromley describes herself as "somewhat of a skeptic," who sums up her sense of what it means to be a Christian with the nondogmatic phrase "lifting the burdens of others when we can." That was precisely what she tried to do when she led the affiliate. Grierson's approach, though, is different. "The success of the organization," he emphasizes, "comes from God, and I believe that it began with Millard's and Linda's call from God." As divinely ordained, Habitat's work is seen by him to be at once an expression of faith and a means of spreading that faith: "As far as our Christian faith goes, we can model the gospel even more by providing active service—this has frequently, and quite effectively, led people to Christ in the past."

With this kind of dedication to the religious foundations of the organization, it is small wonder that Grierson caught the eye of Habitat International and is currently serving as a regional director. During his tenure as executive director at his local affiliate, he incarnated the Habitat ideal: efficient, professional leadership deeply committed to Habitat's founding values and willing to witness to them when representing the affiliate in public. As he describes it, he never felt the need to waffle about his faith when seeking support from secular institutions. "You don't have to walk away from the avowedly Christian aspect of our ministry. It's been my experience that businesses and banks and so forth don't reject it either. When you tell them that you're a Christian organization, they're still listening," he declares confidently.

Given his earnestness, it is easy to see why people would be apt to listen. This is especially true of people in the churches with whom he established close bonds, again modeling the Habitat ideal. The churches, he explains, provide Habitat with a stable source of support while they gain an important outlet for their social mission. More than any other single factor, it was Grierson's commitment to nurturing this symbiotic relationship that allowed the affiliate to grow rapidly under his watch. His concerted effort to win the area churches over to Habitat eventually translated into increased financial support and organizational resources and more volunteer involvement. To Francine Bromley's way of thinking, this growth was an indication that the ministry was becoming more "success orientated" than desirable. But even she admitted, when reflecting on the recent house dedication for a new homeowner family to whom she is particularly attached, "I know they wouldn't be getting a home for a long time if the affiliate wasn't so large."

By the time of Grierson's "promotion" two years after first being hired, the affiliate had actually become so large that two people were hired to replace him, a construction manager and the new executive director, Gary Andrusz. Unlike Larry Grierson, who (like many people in Americus) has been described as everything from a "Habitat junky" to a plain "workaholic," these two men and the subsequently hired office manager have a much more compartmentalized understanding of their work with Habitat. It is not as all-consuming for them as it was for Grierson. "I would not sacrifice things to be involved with Habitat," says Andrusz, who frankly admits to being far more passionate about being a husband, father of three children, and a Republican state representative, for which the affiliate grants him an annual two-month leave while the legislature is in session. "I'm prohibited from close relationships at Habitat," he continues. "I'm a staff person and a professional and that, to me, dictates a certain distance. The interesting thing is that if the paycheck stops tomorrow, my involvement with Habitat stops tomorrow. End of point."

To quite a few volunteers, this distance is as apparent as it is disturbing. They tend to be impressed and, at times, even somewhat intimidated by Andrusz's knowledge and no-nonsense manner. Nevertheless, as one long-time volunteer observed, he "lacks an understanding of what the Habitat ministry really is." Those who work on the construction sites had grown accustomed to Larry Grierson working alongside them, often well into the night, and calling later to thank them or inquire how they were feeling after such a long day. This is not Gary Andrusz's style; he wears a suit and tie everyday, not a tool belt. Nor is he the back-patting motivator who likes to hobnob with members of the affiliate's operational committees after their monthly meetings. In short, many people feel slighted by Andrusz's businesslike manner and perceived reticence to interact with the volunteer regulars.

Others, while less concerned about such personality issues, claim that the current staff's desire to build houses even more efficiently compromises the affiliate's ability to "build community" with Habitat supporters in the city. For example, rather than borrow equipment from or wait for building materials and labor to be donated by the various construction-related businesses with whom the affiliate has painstakingly built relationships, Andrusz is more inclined to buy equipment and hire subcontractors to get things done efficiently and on schedule. Can Habitat remain a grassroots organization if it does this? Should individuals and churches continue to make donations to the affiliate when more of its resources are, as Francine Bromley notes, "going to overhead rather than houses"? These are the sorts of questions one now hears from some of the local Habitat faithful. In short, they are worried that the personal character of the ministry is being eroded.

Many are especially concerned that the ministerial character of the ministry is being eroded as well. They have noticed that the new construction manager does not begin each day of building with a prayer. Nor does Andrusz do so before meetings of the various operational committees, which gather together each month in the basement of a

Christian Reformed Church (where Larry Grierson is a member). Habitat is just not "this holy crusade type thing" for Andrusz. "I'd rather raise a hell of a lot more money and have volunteers build a lot more houses and forget about all this other peripheral stuff," he bristles. "And the way you're going to do that is by making the organization more professional." These are not the words of a man with an aversion toward religion. He has been a member of a nearby Baptist church for some time. It is simply that he, as a professional, feels that he needs to sell the organization any way he can. He cannot afford to target only those people with religious motivations as potential Habitat supporters, when he considers other motivations to be equally valid. Religious values, rather than being the driving force of the entire organization, are for Andrusz only what drives certain people; they should be appealed to, therefore, only when it is in the organization's interest to do so. Habitat comes off sounding decidedly less "lunatic" in his characterization:

> Habitat is, in essence, an effective program for accomplishing an important task. So people—for a variety of motivations—who believe that it is an important task will get involved with Habitat because it is an effective program. What they get out of it goes right back to why they believe it is an important task. Whether it's community building, or expressing their faith, or it's getting recognition, or it's feeling a part of a group—the motivations are many. People get a lot out of Habitat. None of those motivations are bad. But do they get something out of it? Yeah, they do.

People are utility maximizers, according to Andrusz. They determine what they desire—whether it be a sense of community, recognition, group solidarity, or the opportunity to live out their faith commitments—and then they do whatever is necessary to attain that. Individual actions are all melded together into a continuous cycle of exchanges. Do this, get that. It makes sense, then, that he would downplay the singular importance of religious values for the organization, just as it makes sense that, in doing so, he would alienate those volunteers who believe their religious commitments to be more important and less calculated than he imagines them to be.

In this respect, Andrusz is as opposite to Grierson as one could imagine. But, in another way, he is only an extreme example of a tendency that Grierson himself displayed when he was executive director. What they have in common is their tendency to limit the volunteers' ability to act upon their expressive values by playing a significant role in the operations of the affiliate. Much more than Grierson, however, Andrusz is intent on making all the decisions and managing the affiliate as he sees fit. The volunteers, meanwhile, are considered nonessential. The latent benefits of their participation do not seem to concern him. He sees little value in their becoming empowered citizens, feeling integrated into a community for which they accept responsibility, or being edified about social needs through their own hands-on participation. They merely want something from Habitat, and, when they no longer give something in return, they become expendable.

Missing from Andrusz's unsentimental, if not cynical, assessment of volunteering are signs that he appreciates, or even much understands, Habitat's long-standing goal of forming real partnerships among people as they work together to improve their communities:

> The fact of the matter is that you get a good value from your volunteers—and this is just being hard and cold. One is that they truly do lower the cost. Benefit number two is that a lot of people, including First Methodist Church [a covenant church], want to buy volunteer opportunity. That's exactly what they're doing. That's a worthy cause, a worthy program, a worthy thing they can't buy anywhere else. And so will we sell the service? Sure. We both get something. It's a great deal. I believe in volunteers, volunteerism is very important. But they should be valuable. You see, volunteerism for the sake of volunteerism is not a worthy goal. If it costs $30,000 to build a house with volunteers or without, I think you have to make the hard decision.

It is only since Habitat's dedication to "faith in action" has become entwined with the exigencies of managerial action that such a "hard decision" has even become thinkable. Gary Andrusz's willingness to run roughshod over the participatory character of Habitat reveals just how far the organization has come from the barn-raising spirit of its Koinonia Farm origins. Who, at that time, could have imagined Habitat as anything but a grassroots initiative born of the goodwill and sweat of volunteers?

The professionalization of Habitat at its international and local levels is a significant change from the organization's early years. This is not to say that professionalization is an inexorable curse destined to do away with opportunities for people to become involved in Habitat's ministry and realize the organization's vision of becoming more knowledgeable citizens as a result. If people sense that Andrusz, for instance, does not understand "what the Habitat ministry really is," they have opportunities to speak up. The thoughtful deliberations at affiliate board and committee meetings are testimony to that. Likewise, there are no grounds for demonizing all professionals within the organization. They are hired because, in light of the organization's growth and the resulting demand for full-time leadership, they are needed. They help to minimize the problems related to what voluntary-sector theorist Lester Salamon calls "philanthropic amateurism" and "philanthropic paternalism."[9]

The affiliate under Francine Bromley's leadership was a cadre of well-meaning amateurs compared to the sophisticated organization that Larry Grierson formed and Gary Andrusz has since fine-tuned. Furthermore, although many resent him for it, one of the benefits of Andrusz's professional distance from the volunteers is that he has a far more objective view of what the affiliate is doing. Recall from the last chapter, for instance, that he was one of the most vocal critics of the paternalism many volunteers display toward the homeowners (epitomized for him by the denunciation, "Television is bad!"). The affiliate has benefited from Andrusz's professional expertise and sense of equity, which complement Habitat's founding values. It is when professionalization brings with it a market logic that contradicts those values, as it is prone to do, that tension within the organization begins anew.

Freedom and the Issue of Commercialization

Organizational Freedom at Habitat

References to Alexis de Tocqueville's monumental *Democracy in America* are still the worn-smooth coinage of informed discussions regarding the importance of the voluntary sector for modern societies. "If men are to remain civilized or to become civilized," he memorably wrote, "the art of association must develop and improve among them at the same speed as equality of conditions spreads."[10] This is a bold claim. To comprehend it fully, note that he considered the burgeoning "condition of equality" to be an inevitable (even providential) development as nations progressed from the inequalities of status associated with the "old regime" toward greater democratization. From what he had witnessed during his travels, nowhere did this ideal seem to manifest itself more than in nineteenth-century America, where expanding political rights and educational opportunities, along with a general leveling of wealth, heralded what promised to be an increasingly egalitarian future.

As utopian as it may seem, this development was accompanied by a much darker side. In sundering feudal ties of status and obligation that had once bound people together, the modern age seemed to him profoundly atomized, permeated by individualism. With remarkable insight, Tocqueville discerned this "condition of equality" to be compatible—paradoxically—with both freedom and a subtle form of despotism. An unquestioned ethos of individual equality awakens people to the conviction that the goods of the world should be equally available to all, even though they are typically allotted on the basis of ability and good fortune. The ensuing discrepancy, he argued, breeds an intolerable level of frustration and envy among citizens, who, as atomized individuals, are impotent to effect any change.

But this is not true of the state, to which people willingly turn for the provision of material necessities, the direction of industry, and the protection of their individual rights. They do this, Tocqueville is loath to add, even though they may cede the freedom to control their own affairs in the process. The rather ominous outcome is a kind of "soft" despotism precipitated by an increasingly centralized administrative state: "It does not break men's will, but softens, bends, and guides it; it seldom enjoins, but often inhibits, action; it does not destroy anything, but prevents much being born; it is not at all tyrannical, but it hinders, restrains, enervates, stifles, and stultifies so much that in the end each nation is no more than a flock of timid and hardworking animals with the government as the shepherd."[11]

As disturbing as this vision may be on its own, Tocqueville further contends that people's inordinate "love for equality" not only corrals political liberty but constrains freedom of thought in a similarly herd-like fashion. Just as the ideology of individual equality cannot gracefully abide inequalities of wealth, it does not do much better with disparities in intellect or with minority opinion. Put differently, if everyone is deemed equal, then the views of some people cannot possibly be superior to others, in which case only those opinions held by the majority are accepted as valid. The unspoken popular mandate, therefore, gravitates toward conformity, and the effect is a pronounced tendency of democracies to drift toward mediocrity. Lamenting this pervasive "tyranny of the majority," Tocqueville declares, "I know no country in which, speaking generally, there is less independence of mind and true freedom of discussion than in America."[12]

By crowning equality, the citizens of democratic nations abdicate their own freedom to act and think for themselves, only to find that they have succumbed to a Janus-faced despotism marked by government centralization and mass conformity. Aware of this paradox, Tocqueville insisted on the value of certain "democratic expedients"—including local self-government, the jury system, the separation of powers, a free press, and the separation of church and state—that were operative in the United States and, if carefully preserved, could encourage public-spiritedness and protect individual freedom. Prominent among such expedients, of course, are voluntary associations. By engaging the energies of the populace, they prevent civic responsibilities from being swallowed up by the state and minority viewpoints from being put down by a mass mentality.

In Tocqueville's estimation, the ability to form associations based on freely chosen expressive values and then advance the goals of those associations without hindrance was the essence of democratic freedom. Voluntary associations were, for him, both a product of people's freedom and the institutional vehicles through which citizens could experience themselves as free moral agents. Although troubled by potential intrusions from the state sector and a penchant for groupthink on a massive scale, Tocqueville was less bothered by what, in the present discussion, has been identified as the logic of the market sector seeping into the organizational culture of voluntary sector groups. To overlook this problem when evaluating Habitat, however, would mean missing another of its organizational tensions. Habitat's freedom as an organization—its ability to uphold its distinctive values and act upon them as it sees fit—cannot be properly understood unless one is aware that that it is continuously challenged by a market-driven process of commercialization.

To understand this, consider the most important foundational choices constituting Habitat's freedom as an organization. The first is its reliance on volunteer labor, both to lower building costs and, most significantly, to build community in the places where affiliates operate. As mentioned earlier in this chapter, it is the process of professionalization that most constrains this organizational choice and thus threatens to compromise the educative benefits to be gained by people through their grassroots participation. Professionalization, in other words, represents a co-optation by the logic of the market because, in the hopes of maximizing efficiency and other instrumental aims, it minimizes the role of

volunteers within the organization as well as their capacity for being edified as citizens when filling those roles.

But what of the other organizational choices? The second is the fact
that Habitat has freely chosen to be a home-ownership organization
working with people from a specific income niche. These people must
not have sufficient resources to purchase a home at conventional market rates, but they still must meet Habitat's "ability to pay" criterion.
The organization, then, is not intended to serve people who can afford
suitable housing or those—the likeliest clientele for most nonprofit
housing groups—who have such low incomes that they must remain
renters or who have actually become homeless.

Third, as we have seen, Habitat has chosen to be a specifically Christian house-building organization committed to acting according to its
central religious values and then witnessing to them through its promotional literature, house dedication ceremonies, and other public
expressions. Here it is important to note that these latter two organizational choices are also not left unconstrained. They too are impinged
upon by the rationalized logic of the market. In these cases, however,
it occurs through a process of commercialization, the tendency for nonprofits to behave like for-profit enterprises by focusing on productivity
and charging increasingly more for their products.[13] As we will see,
commercial tendencies seriously constrain Habitat's freedom to abide
by organizational choices informed by two of its key expressive
values—its commitment to helping low-income families achieve homeownership and its commitment to articulating its religious vision while
doing so.

Commercialization and the Cost of Good Service

Habitat has made a free choice about the income niche it endeavors to
serve, but lately some within the organization have voiced concern that
this choice is becoming overly influenced by the market. Some people
fear that, like a for-profit construction firm, Habitat will need to cater
to higher-income homeowner "customers" in order to recover escalating building costs. Although the average cost of a Habitat house in the
United States—about $42,500—remains quite reasonable, these fears
are not imagined. As Habitat continues to spread beyond its rural southern origins (44 percent of U.S. affiliates are still located in the South)[14]
and builds more frequently in larger cities, especially in the Northeast
and West, it will feel the sting of rising housing costs ever more acutely.

This is already a huge problem for many of the affiliates in California. The Redwood City affiliate, for example, is in the process of completing a condominium complex in which each of its twenty-four units is being sold to homeowners for approximately $100,000. The Mount Diablo affiliate builds in three small cities where the average construction costs are $90,000 in Pittsburg, $110,000 in Concord, and $120,000 in Walnut Creek. So far, the sale price for homeowners is being kept at $70,000, but the difference will have to be made up through rigorous fundraising if ground is ever to be broken at new building sites. Calling these "construction" costs is not altogether accurate. The Mount Diablo affiliate typically pays from $35,000 to $55,000 just for the lots of land on which they build. City and county fees can add an additional $20,000 to $30,000 per house. These fees and their usual amounts include: building permits ($4,000); school district fees ($2,000); water connection ($8,600); sewer connection ($8,000); and traffic mitigation fees ($4,000). In short, the price of building "simple, decent homes" is rising, and this has left Habitat with the dilemma of how to continue partnering with, to use an organizational slogan, "God's people in need" rather than with higher-income customers from whom affiliates can more easily recoup costs.

That Habitat International is aware of this problem is evidenced by two basic responses to it, each directed toward a particular sector within the overall social ecology. The first is a subtle reassessment of its cautious attitude toward the state. One indication of change is the international board's 1994 decision to begin accepting government grants to cover administrative costs, an expansion of Habitat's longstanding policy of taking them only to pay for land and infrastructure. Another is the greater inclination and ability the organization is demonstrating, at both the international and affiliate levels, to take advantage of the rewards a closer partnership with government can bring. More than ever before, Habitat International is encouraging affiliates to work with local and state governments to get building permits and fees waived or reduced, and to gain access to unused, publicly owned properties. Many affiliates also work directly with federal agencies to acquire land made available by military base closings or to purchase foreclosed properties the state resells through Fannie Mae or the Federal Deposit Insurance Corporation (FDIC).[15]

Habitat's growing partnership with the Department of Housing and Urban Development is the single clearest sign of this shift in organizational culture. At the affiliate level, applying for HUD-sponsored

HOPE III grants, which are used to purchase and rehab publicly held buildings for resale to low-income buyers, is becoming as common an affiliate ritual as house dedication ceremonies. In 1993 alone, U.S. affiliates received more than $12.7 million from the HOPE III, about 15 percent of the total funds allocated by the program.[16] At the international level, Habitat's relationship with HUD is becoming even closer. In 1996 President Clinton signed the Housing Opportunity Program Extension Act mandating HUD to disburse $25 million (62.5 percent of the total funds distributed by the act) to Habitat in order to help defray land acquisition and infrastructure costs for 2,500 housing units.[17] Americus, in turn, is currently distributing the money to affiliates that submit applications, plan to undertake significant building projects, and agree to meet HUD's accountability guidelines.[18] Overall, this close partnership reflects the fact that Habitat has become something of an organizational darling within HUD as well as Habitat's own desire to continue serving families who are actually low-income.

In addition to reassessing its attitude toward the state, the second of Habitat's responses to this problem has been to reaffirm its longstanding critical perspective toward the market. Many who are concerned that the organization maintain its low-income service niche contend that others at Habitat are moving the organization away from that goal. Rather than espousing the countervailing approach to the market reminiscent of the "economics of Jesus," they argue that people involved in local affiliates tend to let the market's preference for bigger, costlier, and more luxurious homes unduly influence them. Many affiliates now build houses with such features as complicated floor plans, extra rooms, basements, brick facades, paved driveways, air conditioning, and other amenities, all of which raise the total price of the homes enough to make them less affordable for typical homeowners. This "creeping affluence," as some people call it, is considered by many to be an affront to the organization's founding charism and dedication to sheltering as many people as possible.[19]

This is the opinion of Millard Fuller, who also attributes it to a pervasive and wrong-headed tendency among many Habitat supporters to assuage, rather than authentically face, the guilt they feel about their own affluence. Barely disguising his disgust, he remarks:

> But what we're seeing in this ministry is that the guy with the 6,000 square foot house doesn't want to decrease the size of his house. So, to assuage his feelings of guilt, he increases the size of his neighbor's house. Every year

Habitat houses cost more and more and more. You build a certain number of these houses and the families that move in absolutely love them because they're such really nice houses. But, guess what? You run out of money. And then, at the end of the year, after you build six or eight houses, you don't have any money left and you have to shut down. So you have become Lottery for Humanity. A few lucky families get a few nice houses and everybody else has to stay where they are—in their shacks.

Fuller's pun, "Lottery for Humanity," seems to be a warning that, if Habitat begins to act like a commercial builder by meeting the demand of those consumers with enough money to pay, it too will dispense access to shelter as arbitrarily as the market itself. Habitat will become more commercialized because it will no longer endeavor to de-commodify housing.[20] Like any other commodity, in fact, housing will accrue primarily to the more affluent, "lucky families," a situation that is intolerable to Fuller because, as he later puts it, "God is the God of the whole crowd."

Habitat supporters who disagree with Fuller's religiously based egalitarianism usually do so with their own variant of egalitarianism. "Other people have nice houses, so why not our homeowner families?" they ask in justifying their position. This is not simply a matter of "keeping up with the Joneses," they often add. Building Habitat houses at least somewhat comparable to those surrounding them is a way of incorporating homeowners into their new communities without distinguishing them from their neighbors. To this, those in agreement with Fuller's way of thinking typically argue that distinguishing homeowners from their neighbors by putting them in "simple, decent houses" is precisely what should be done. In this way, Habitat can offer an unabashed critique of a housing market designed to convince people to live more extravagantly than they need to.

The debate does not lend itself to easy answers. That this debate is also a continuing one at Habitat was recently demonstrated when, just prior to blitz-building twenty-one homes for the 1995 Jimmy Carter Work Project in Los Angeles, a staff person discovered that zoning regulations required all units to come with fences and carports. This set off a concerted effort from Americus to overturn these requirements as well as an opposing effort by some supporters at the Los Angeles affiliate, who broke ranks by encouraging local authorities to enforce the zoning laws. After much dispute and plenty of ill feeling, the fences and carports were built and the houses, as some people grudgingly point out, were that much more expensive for twenty-one families.

To the outsider, intramural conflicts such as this no doubt seem much ado about nothing that a few extra dollars from contributors or home-owners cannot smooth out. For many within Habitat, though, they are important issues because they represent a betrayal of what the organization, at its founding, freely chose to be and whom it chose to serve. Seemingly trivial matters like fences and carports become important because they are perceived to cost more than just a few extra dollars. Many see them as compromising Habitat's most important values, which are intended to be diametrically, even prophetically, opposed to the logic of the market. This is why many supporters react to issues like the "creeping affluence" of Habitat houses and higher-income homeowners by reminding others of the religious values for which Habitat purportedly stands. Fuller's admonition that "God is the God of the whole crowd" is hardly an uncommon sentiment among people at Habitat. Such statements indicate that people are aware that commercialization can also be problematic for yet another of Habitat's initial organizational choices—its Christian identity.

The Process or the Product: A Commercialization of Partnership?

Habitat displays a commercial character when, along with its tendency to cater to higher-income homeowners, it becomes fixated solely on producing houses. The fact that this is widely understood as a distortion within a house-building ministry is testimony to the uniqueness of Habitat. Putting the matter in terms familiar to supporters within this unique organization, the *process* of building houses with others is every bit as important as the *product*. Carl Levering, the program director in Americus, states the basic idea clearly. He seems to fear the day when Habitat becomes so focused on its houses that it thinks of itself as merely a house-building enterprise. "The danger that comes with success is that people will get so focused on the product that they'll forget the process," he expounds, gesturing forcefully with callused hands. "I've been a contractor for years and I think I could build thousands of houses with the right organization and probably more efficiently and effectively. But part of the beauty of Habitat and what has made us what we are is *who* we are. The thing we have to remember is what Habitat's all about!"

Levering has built quality houses all of his professional life. He knows first-hand the value of that kind of work. But, with the nearly proselytizing surety of a nonprofit convert, he also values "what Habitat's all about" and "who we are" enough to remain faithful to the organization's founding principles. Levering, and many others like him, would prefer to see more people become part of the process of community building than watch the organization just produce more houses. Unlike the days when he tirelessly ran his own construction company, at Habitat he wants to hear the hammers stop pounding at least occasionally and then look up to see people talking to one another and laughing at the job site. He himself laughs when he describes one of his first experiences with Habitat, during which he witnessed an entire youth group play-fully covering one another with plaster instead of the walls of the house their church was financing. He realized then that there may be a fine line between wasting resources and creating fellowship, but it was not important enough to demand more efficiency from volunteers or be miserly about a few cans of plaster. To do so, in his opinion, would be to misunderstand Habitat's ministry.

The tension between emphasizing the product and upholding the process has a direct bearing upon the organization's Christian identity. Supporters enthusiastically exalt the building process, believing that this is when partnership, the cornerstone of Habitat's religious vision, is most likely to be realized. Whenever people discuss the issue of com-mercialization, it is always seen to be at odds with establishing true partnership, and thus it is perceived to be a distinctly religious issue. Keeping in mind that the entire organization is based upon the idea of a "dual partnership"—with others and with God—it makes sense that supporters regard elements of commercialization within Habitat as problematic for both of these partnerships. Attending to them in turn should serve to make the point.

As Carl Levering suggests, Habitat volunteers and staffs can get caught up in the desire to build more and more houses. And this is not unjustified; there is a real need for affordable housing in most local communities. But, say supporters, building houses should never inter-fere with the organization's capacity to partner with as many people as possible. The building process itself is less about building houses than it is about building partnerships within the wider community, argues Jason Boyer, an executive staff member in Americus. As he discusses the building process, skillfulness and efficiency are the least of his concerns:

> We've had some volunteers work with us who, in their religious zealous-ness, can screw the job up and we've had to go in later and fix it. But in their hearts, they are fulfilling one of God's basic tenets: "What you do to the least of my brothers, you do it to me."

Is it OK that they screw up?

Yeah. The reason why it's OK is because we're Habitat and we're not trying to make money off of these projects. We're not building the most efficient way that you can build. We're using volunteer labor that is often
unskilled. So we build in a much different way than other nonprofit devel-
opers. But, what is our purpose, again? It's to build houses with God's people in need and to live out the Gospel of Jesus Christ. It's not just to put
up a house. It's to do that, but also to build a community and a partnership
with that community across generations, across ethnic divisions, across
religious divisions.

If the goal of each Habitat project were "just to put up a house," then
there would be no problem with such practices as buying most of the
required materials, hiring skilled labor, and writing scores of grant proposals. Habitat is more than that, though. Affiliates sometimes engage
in such practices, but they are expected to rely more on the partnerships they forge with volunteers and contributors, so that their work
remains connected to the grassroots. This, and not the mere production of houses, is the telltale sign of an affiliate's success. Furthermore,
descriptions of this alternative understanding of success—of the real
bottom line—frequently employ the kind of religious language Jason
Boyer relies upon. Without such language, it would be difficult or
impossible for many at Habitat to make sense of their resistance to market norms. Because its organizational lexicon refers to such alternative
gospel values as serving others and creating fellowship, conversations
at Habitat are not inevitably dominated by those more fluent in the language of productivity maximization and cost-benefit analysis. Within
Habitat there is a market language focused on the product and another
language focused on the process, and both can be used to articulate the
meaning of the ministry. The alternative language is primarily a religiously informed one centering upon the critical theme of partnership
and rendering problematic anything that threatens it.

Habitat's commitment to partnership includes homeowners as well.
Commercialization impinges upon this relationship not because Habitat is a builder of houses but because it is a lessor of houses. The affiliates' partnership with homeowners extends beyond their move-in day
to the day when their mortgage is entirely paid off. Until then, affiliates are essentially landlords, and they show signs of commercialism
when they treat their homeowners as if they were simply tenants. This
tendency is not entirely unjustified. Volunteers and staff have little spare

time to work closely with homeowners having a hard time making their payments and who may not have maintained much more than a financial relationship with the affiliate since getting their home anyway. Because affiliates rely on timely mortgage payments to build new homes, they have an interest in dealing with homeowners in a resolute manner and are not inclined to think of themselves as heartless ogres for doing so. Even so, a tension is evident as once again Habitat's religious values come into conflict with the logic and language of the market.

Denise Kraybill, the staff member at the East Bay affiliate, seems well acquainted with this tension—so much so, in fact, that when describing her work with homeowners, she actually relies on both languages. She identifies herself as someone who is "trying to live by the Bible's influence instead of the surrounding culture's influence." When asked to elaborate, she responds:

> It's about following Jesus' example. He didn't live in a mansion. He was with the people, especially those who, in that culture, were considered undesirable like tax collectors and prostitutes.

> *What does following Jesus' example mean for your everyday life?*

> Giving my time and money is part of it and using my gifts to help others is too. I think I'm using my gifts at Habitat. But it's a fine line because, in my position, sometimes I have to be tough with people since I handle the money and so forth. I have to deal with things when people are delinquent with their monthly payments or when they're not doing their sweat equity hours.

> *How are you tough with people?*

> Mostly by setting boundaries. When I first started teaching Head Start, I had a class with ten boys and three girls. I got into the habit of asking what they wanted to do and maybe being overly nice. So they walked all over me. So I eventually started setting boundaries and it became a lot easier. That's what I have to do with the homeowners. Rather than letting them try to walk over us we say, "This is what we've set up, let's agree to abide by it." In that way, both sides have responsibilities they're expected to fulfill. I may lean more to the discipline than [the] grace end of things, but sometimes I find that I have to say that Habitat might not be the program that they want or need and then let them make the decision on their own.

Krabill personifies the tension wrought by commercialization. For her, Jesus exemplifies a willingness to lovingly partner with those who are considered "undesirable," and she wants to do the same through her work. Even with her unmistakable sincerity, she also finds that she has to set clear boundaries and be tough with people on occasion. She knows that there is a business side to Habitat's ministry that requires discipline, and it leads her, when comparing homeowners to the "little kids" in her Head Start class, to assume the patronizing attitude discussed in the last chapter. "This is what we've set up," she believes in telling the homeowners. "Let's agree to abide by it." In doing so, she seems to want to move from a covenantal relationship with them to more of a contractual one of the sort they would establish with, for example, a landlord or a realty company. Kraybill may deeply desire to live by the "Bible's influence," but the noticeable shift in her language indicates that, as Habitat is constrained to act like a commercial enterprise, the "surrounding culture's influence" is just as powerful within the affiliate as it is in the for-profit world.

Habitat wants to be productive. It does this by building houses and then making sure those houses are paid for by the homeowners. But if that is all it does, the organization's efforts will amount to little more than what voluntary-sector theorist Jon Van Til describes as "doing business tax-free."[21] That is why it must remain committed to the process of developing partnerships with the wider community and with the homeowners even while it builds the houses that are its product. The religious language institutionalized at Habitat serves as a reminder of how the organization is supposed to go about its business. That language functions as series of trail markers signaling the original direction Habitat chose to follow as an unapologetically Christian organization, and it makes sense that people like Jason Boyer and Denise Kraybill would rely upon it when discussing the quality of Habitat's partnerships.

What of the second component of Habitat's "dual partnership," its partnership with God? It too is a significant part of the organizational culture, and, as detailed in Chapter 2, it accounts for Habitat's determination to offer a prophetic witness against substandard housing and for its mustard seed faith in the efficacy of small acts. Supporters consider Habitat faithful to this partnership when it is forthcoming about the religious motivations of its founders and about its own continuing Christian identity. It is faithful when, in public, it uses the very same religious language that people associated with the organization privately rely upon to make sense of their obligation to others. Like partnering with others, therefore, faithfulness to its partnership with God is evidenced when Habitat privileges its process over its product. Enter commercialization. It becomes manifest when people in Americus or in the local affiliates are persuaded to downplay the organization's Christian identity in the hope of producing more houses.

Never is this more of an issue than when Habitat works with its corporate sponsors. The first of these was BellSouth Telecommunications, which, since 1990, has helped to build more than one hundred houses. Like many other corporate sponsors, the company contributes one quarter of the cost of each house, its local employees raise another quarter and then recruit volunteers to do the construction, and the local affiliate provides the remainder of the needed funds as well as most of the organizational resources. Similar partnerships have been established with such companies as Target Stores, Dow Chemical, Coldwell Banker, Maxwell House Coffee, America's Favorite Chicken, and the United Consumers Club, to name only a few. Other, more building-related companies partner with Habitat primarily by supplying in-kind support such as professional expertise, equipment, and various construction materials donated or made available at significantly reduced prices. In this category are, among others, Home Depot, HunterDouglas Window Fashions, Centex Homes, Sterling Plumbing Group, John Wieland Homes, Milwaukee Electric Tool Corporation, and Larson Manufacturing Company.

These corporate sponsorships are usually portrayed within the Habitat literature as the epitome of a "win/win proposition."[22] They provide the organization with much-needed support and important networking connections within the business world. For their part, corporations reap public relations benefits, since their partnering with a well-known and uncontroversial nonprofit allows them to market themselves as businesses that care about local communities. Corporate spokespersons also report that their partnerships with Habitat go a long way toward improving employee morale and, especially through their volunteering, serve as an effective "team-building" strategy.

Corporate partnerships that are driven by mixed, rather than purely altruistic, motives are generally not considered a problem within Habitat. As a rule, supporters do not regard corporations as a conservative social force influencing the political process and resisting progressive reforms in American society.[23] Instead, they talk about the decent, caring people working within corporations. They see corporations from the bottom up and have a much more personal view of them as a result. Few Habitat supporters, in fact, would question the sanguinity in

Fuller's assessment of the business world. "There's a secret about corporate America," he remarks. "It's made up of people who live in houses, have families, go to churches, and who know that being in business means not only producing goods and services but also helping neighbors—especially those in greatest need."[24] Corporations might not always be responsible citizens with the best intentions for the communities in which they operate, the message reads, but the individuals within them are sufficiently tutored by religious values and civic virtues to care about helping others.

This is the primary reason for Habitat's lack of suspicion regarding its corporate sponsors. Another is that, while Habitat believes in the people employed within corporations, it never claims to believe in the organizations themselves. Regardless of whatever unconscionable or unjust practices companies might engage in, Habitat's leadership maintains that it uses corporate resources to promote Habitat's own ends, not the ends of those companies. "The only tainted money is the money that'ain't ours," quips Fuller puckishly from time to time. The unimpeachable moral goodness of Habitat's work, he seems to say, supersedes any misgivings about how the money supporting it may initially have been earned. Among the many who agree with such sentiments is Gordon Knebel. That Dow Chemical manufactured napalm used during the Vietnam War seemed to him mildly ironic, not morally disquieting. "Using Dow's money to build a house? Cool," he declares, and then explains, "I think we can market that how we want; that doesn't mean we have to announce that Dow is redeemed!"

Victor Millman, in contrast, is less troubled about the religious status of Dow than he is about that of Habitat. He is one of the few members of the executive staff in Americus who does not share the prevailing optimism about corporate partnerships. Because corporations have an interest in projecting an all-inclusive—thus, nonsectarian—public image, Millman points out, they put subtle pressure on Habitat to downplay its religious identity when partnering with them. He cites the example of Target Stores, which recently entered into a two-year partnership with Habitat to build nearly one hundred houses throughout the United States. He has a hard time displaying the same level of enthusiasm some of his co-workers seem to feel about this joint venture. "I would prefer to see us live with one less house, one less dollar in our paychecks, one less piece of property," he admits, "if it meant that we had to either silence or deny our biblical roots and Christian witness." When asked about his reservations, he provides some interesting details:

> About a month ago there was a press release written from here in Americus about Habitat's relationship with Target. Now, I imagine that, being a nationwide organization, Target is an organization that has to be very concerned about equal opportunities for employment, equal opportunities for credit, nondiscriminatory hiring practices, nondiscriminatory customer service practices. They have to be very careful not to show favoritism to Christians, to Jews, to whites, to blacks, to Asians—that they are open to all races, creeds, and colors. And so the press release that talked about Target's corporate sponsorship did not mention that Habitat is a Christian organization. That stuff [acknowledgment of Habitat's Christian identity] gets set on the shelf and we become just two organizations engaged in a humanitarian effort.
>
> *Is that frustrating to some folks?*
>
> I think so.
>
> *I can imagine that Millard Fuller would be frustrated by that.*
>
> Probably. But he's not here to micromanage. Some folks might say he micromanages more than enough [laughter]. But, at some level, he trusts a group of either senior management or program directors to make sure that that stuff happens.

Victor Millman seems to have a slippery slope in mind. If, in the interests of accommodating Target, Habitat allows itself to be portrayed in public as just another organization "engaged in a humanitarian effort," will it do the same for every corporate sponsor? Will it, over the course of time, actually become a nonsectarian organization? In the end, he, like Fuller, seems willing to trust the organizational leadership to make the proper decisions in ensuring that Habitat remains close to its Christian roots and identity.

Millman's implied vote of confidence in his fellow staff members assumes that the rest of Habitat's leadership are as concerned about the issue as he is. In reality, they are not equally dedicated to ensuring that "that stuff happens" at all. Consider, for example, another staff member in Americus, Teresa Breines. She assists in coordinating Habitat's fundraising and public relations efforts and helps to arrange its corporate partnerships. On occasion, she hears "little snipes" from other employees regarding their qualms about a Christian organization working so closely with major corporations. Singled out by Breines for particular disapproval was one staff member who, during a recent discussion of some of the financial challenges facing Habitat, assured the others present that "God will provide." "Well, when it came time for her paycheck, if we stood there and said, 'Sorry, God will provide,' I wonder if it would still have had the same impact," she mused censoriously.

As this incident suggests, Breines is not altogether comfortable with Habitat's religious language. Indeed, she is much more comfortable dealing with corporate sponsors than she is with some of her faith-driven co-workers. Discussing Habitat's Christian identity, she gives the impression that she would welcome a more businesslike work environment:

> I am going to treat this department—in our dealings—as though we were a corporation. To do the job in this department, I think we've got to be selling the sizzle, as they like to say. As I say to people here, "If you don't raise the money, then they can't carry out the programs; if they don't carry out the programs, then people aren't getting the houses; and if the people aren't getting the houses, then we're not fulfilling the mission of the organization."

> *I assume you package the organization as a Christian organization.*

> I package the organization as a house-building organization. It's an organization that builds affordable homes for people in need, and we were founded as a Christian ministry and this is what we adhere to. Our materials will indicate our basic goals, our mission. What I use is on our letterhead—"Building houses in partnership with God's people in need"—I have no problem with that line.

> *I'm sensing that you do have some problem with Habitat's religious character.*

> Well, I'm not one of those more vocal people. I remember what my mother always taught me: It's what you do, not what you say. I don't constantly refer to our *Christian* ministry. It is in our literature. I do not hide that. I make sure that it's there. But I'm not going to sign my letters, "Yours in Christian partnership." To me, I feel like I'd be discriminating against people. The fact that we are a Christian housing ministry, that's how we were started, that's the purpose—a lot of people here are very vocal about that. I'm very much in keeping and respectful of what they say. But when people talk about things being a blessing, well those aren't words in my corporate vocabulary.

Without doubt, Teresa Breines is committed to building houses for people in need. That does not mean she is as protective of Habitat's Christian emphasis as Victor Millman is counting upon the leadership in Americus to be. Her mother's pragmatic maxim, "It's what you do, not what you say," only partly resonates with Habitat's fidelity to faith in action. As people like Millman firmly assert, the organization's partnership with God demands that it remain steadfast in what it *says*—that is, in witnessing to its Christian faith in the public sphere. To such people, Breines's "corporate vocabulary" is not a neutral language. They are uneasy about the prospect that, should it become the lingua franca of the organization, it could have a profoundly negative effect on Habitat's ability to articulate its belief in the important process of establishing partnerships between people. The religious language with which many at Habitat make sense of their solicitude for their fellow citizens might then become something of an arcane dialect, less heard and rarely understood.

Such misgivings do seem justified. Overtly religious language could be a liability as Habitat becomes increasingly intent upon "selling the sizzle" to secular or non-Christian constituencies. Organizational efforts at getting the "best deal for Habitat" actually reflect, rather than resist, the competitive logic of the market. The difference between them and efforts designed to get the best deal for Dow Chemical or for Target Stores, for example, is indeed minimal since they all share a common commercial spirit concentrating on such matters as stimulating greater productivity and organizational growth.

To say Teresa Breines's intention to help run her department "as though we were a corporation" exemplifies the potential for Habitat's religious identity to be undermined does not mean that individuals like her are the source of the problem. That would be both inaccurate and unfair. This potential is more a function of Habitat's being an organization with a minimalist, inclusive theology. Because it is not dogmatically defined, its religious vision is not always something people would proselytize or even necessarily defend if it actually were being undermined. Soft-peddling the religious aspect of Habitat's ministry can be easily rationalized by self-assurances that the practical, house-building aspect is being better served as a consequence. The tendency to be cavalier about religious language, then, is due more to Habitat's organizational culture than to specific individuals like Breines. The following advice about corporate sponsorships actually appears in the operations manual published by Habitat International and distributed by it to every local affiliate:

> Most Habitat affiliates occasionally face the dilemma of how to approach a potential donor who is not excited about or may even be offended by the Christian identity of Habitat. If an affiliate has acknowledged itself as

Christian in its general literature (brochure and newsletter), then it should not be disturbed by pangs of conscience in presenting to a particular donor a proposal that does not call attention to the fact that the organization is Christian.[25]

Affiliates, in short, are not to deny their faith for the sake of appeasing donors; nor are they expected to witness to it at the cost of condemning themselves to a lion's den of inadequate funding.

Following this advice with regard to its own corporate partnerships is not the only thing Habitat does to perturb staff members like Victor Millman. Some consider the 1995 decision to revise the Campus Chapters covenant, giving it less explicitly Christian language, to be a mistake. The director of the program claims the new wording makes "Habitat's Christian identity more accessible to students from different walks of life and faith journeys,"[26] whereas others see the omission of the previously used phrase "to witness to the Gospel of Jesus Christ" as an intolerable compromise of that Christian identity. Still others are critical of what they see as an excessive preoccupation with marketing the organization. The leadership in Americus, they maintain, simply bothers too much with such peripheral concerns as "gross impressions" (estimated number of times an organization is mentioned in the media), "Q-ratings" (a measure of an organization's public image used by television advertisers), and what rank Habitat holds among the nation's most productive home construction organizations. Some fear that Habitat's religious character will not be deemed a marketable asset by such calculations and will thus seem unimportant as a result.

These concerns cannot be written off as simple alarmism. In 1995 Habitat commissioned a study of its donors and prospective donors and discovered that they responded positively to four "core messages" communicated to them by the organization.[27] First, they appreciate that Habitat "produces tangible, measurable results," emphasized in the countless before-and-after stories of homeowner families in its promotional literature. Second, Habitat is "efficient and effective" (read: businesslike) in its use of donors' resources. Third, it addresses a pressing need—America's housing woes—which, the study suggested, Habitat should make better known to its donors. Finally, they see Habitat as representing "strong values and integrity in its principles and operations," which most elaborated to mean the specific values of hard work and self-sufficiency.

Hardly mentioned are Habitat's religious values. This is a problem for some supporters because they fear that the organization will itself downplay them in order to conform Habitat's message to what donors most want to hear. Writing about the results of the donor research, the director of marketing and public relations in Americus only justifies such fears. "Now that we know why people give to Habitat, we can focus our communication to donors on those points that are most important to them," he writes.[28] It is easy to anticipate that the Christian emphasis, which has long reflected Habitat's partnership with God, will get less emphasis if the consumer demand of potential donors comes to govern the way the organization presents itself.

"The market now reaches into every institution and every relation," reads the excerpt from C. Wright Mills at the outset of this chapter. Habitat, it seems, is no exception. The market reaches into this institution when the organizational decisions that were freely made at its founding are constrained toward greater commercialization, and when professionalization curtails the grassroots participation that develops increasingly edified citizens. Likewise, as the previous chapter explored, the market reaches into every relation when class inequalities distort Habitat's vision of equal empowerment and social integration for both volunteers and homeowners. By threatening to co-opt the long-recognized latent benefits of civic participation, the rationalized capitalist market shows itself capable of reaching into the very heart of democratic civil society—voluntarism.

It is common to think of voluntarism as average citizens giving of their time and talents to accomplish some social good. Voluntarism is about rising above individual interests and contributing to the commonweal. It is asking what one can do for one's country, city, neighborhood, or even one's next-door neighbor. Civic participation, in other words, is typically envisioned as a pulsing and beneficent component of pluralist societies. In many respects, this reputation is deserved. The single caveat offered here is that paradenominational groups like Habitat, as well as other voluntary associations and non-profits, do not airily transcend the constraints of the market. Like the Cheshire Cat's, the broad smile of voluntarism's beneficence is easily discernible. Unbeknownst to many observers, however, it can be attached to the weighty but less visible body of the market. The temptation is to glance upon that smile and to feel good, and not to wait to see what else appears along with it.

6

Habitat's Construction of "Real Religion"

It is ten o'clock on a scorching July morning in Charlotte, NC. Millard Fuller is pounding nails into roof sheathing on one of 14 houses rising simultaneously. Around him, 350 volunteer builders, many of them veteran Habitat workers bused in from out of town, are hammering, drilling, toting boards, fitting windows—building a neighborhood ... Fuller gazes out at the bedlam.

"Who's paying for all this?" a passer-by asks.

"Nobody," Millard replies.

The man looks dubious. "Folks don't do this sort of thing for nothing."

"It's worse than that," Millard says cheerfully. "They paid to come." He explains that the volunteers—from churches around the country—simply want to help.

"Man," says the onlooker, "that's real religion!"

Reader's Digest, June 1988

Ritualizing Voluntarism: A Habitat High Mass in Minneapolis

The morning had already proven to be a full one for the approximately 120 staff and supporters of Twin Cities Habitat for Humanity® who gathered that Saturday in the huge Central Lutheran Church in downtown Minneapolis. Beginning with coffee and doughnuts at 8:00 A.M., faithful volunteers and newcomers alike had been in the church's main hall and adjacent rooms participating in the affiliate's annual planning

179

meeting. They had been busy. Along with their meeting or catching up with one another, most of them attended two one-hour workshops selected from a variety of offerings. These included sessions on new house construction, rehabilitating old houses, and doing interior work during non-building months (October to April). There was a session to explain volunteer opportunities on affiliate committees and boards, and another to discuss how partnerships with homeowner families could be improved. Resource procurement was also a prominent topic in workshops addressing everything from fundraising to soliciting in-kind donations.

By late morning, the general session had begun. An affiliate staff member, Scott Quinley, kept the group's attention by recounting their accomplishments for the year: By Christmas, twenty-eight homes would be completed and all the families moved in; the affiliate would be relocating to their newly purchased office and warehouse facility during the first week in December; an innovative foreclosure-prevention program was showing early signs of success among struggling homeowners; new house plans were designed to add variety to Habitat houses and cut building costs; and many new partnerships with churches and corporations had been forged in recent months. Following him were representatives from each of the five affiliate chapters, who informed the group of what they had achieved in the past year and what they anticipated doing in the next. Finally, testimonials were given by various people—homeowners, volunteers, a minister of a covenant church, and a mid-level executive from the sponsoring Pillsbury Company—all of whom spoke glowingly of Habitat and appreciatively of their own opportunity to participate in its work.

People listened intently. Short speeches like these are an important facet of Habitat's organizational culture. They provide listeners with a stock of models and reasons for volunteering, which are often in short supply amid the hectic hum of modern life. With middle-class Americans on average working longer hours than ever before and compensating for their hard work by doing things—or, more accurately, by buying things—for themselves, such testimonials are critical for making sense of volunteers' decisions to extend themselves still further by doing things for others.[1] Without occasional words of assurance, it would be harder for many to set aside a Saturday morning like this one for Habitat. And it would be well nigh unimaginable that they could do so with the light-heartedness they displayed when the group finally broke for lunch in the church cafeteria.

Shortly afterward, as tables were being cleared of cups and dishes, the sound of piano music trickled in from the main hall, reminding people of the most important part of the day's agenda. Returning to their seats, they reconvened to celebrate the completion of the affiliate's hundredth house. "Celebrating this remarkable achievement is also part of our work," Quinley began as the sound of the piano receded. "It's important that we bear witness to the wonderful things that can result from people coming together out of compassion for those in need." He then led the group in singing "Called as Partners in God's Service," after which he introduced Felix Mishel, one of Habitat's regional directors. "Christ is the center of this ministry," Mishel explained while describing the affiliate's work as one part of a world-wide movement building thousands of homes with the help of God. An accomplished flutist, Mishel then offered a rendition of "Amazing Grace" that was well received by the assembly, many of them with heads bowed. This was followed by remarks from Sylvia Harriman, the affiliate's first homeowner, who had been living in her house since 1985. She described how well her two children were doing in school and some of the satisfactions she and her husband experienced running their own catering business. None of this, she tearfully assured those present, would have been possible without Habitat's assistance. Closing the prayer service was Stuart Blanchard, a Methodist minister who had been a supporter of the affiliate since its early years. "God is working in the world today through your actions," he told the group. "You are a blessing to the people you volunteer with and the families you care about because you are demonstrating the love that God has for all people."

At that point, the piano began to play a processional hymn—"We are One in the Spirit"—well known in many Protestant churches but, interestingly, with the word *builders* used to replace the *Christians* in the original lyric. People sang along:

> We are one in the Spirit, we are one in the Lord [repeat].
> And we pray that all unity may one day be restored.
> And they'll know we are builders by our love, by our love,
> Yes, they'll know we are builders by our love.

Still singing, each person walked to one of the surrounding walls, against which leaned no less than a hundred eight-by-ten-inch glossy photographs, one of each individual Habitat house, handsomely matted and connected to a wooden slat for easy carrying. Smiles beamed everywhere as the singing intensified:

> We will walk with each other, we will walk hand in hand [repeat].
> And together we'll spread the news that God is in our land.
> And they'll know we are builders by our love, by our love,
> Yes, they'll know we are builders by our love.

Two of the younger staff members, with a large purple and white Habitat banner held between them, marched toward the double-door exit and motioned for the rest to follow. They did. Grabbing coats with one hand and holding their photographs aloft with the other, they embarked upon the 1.8-mile walk through the city to the recently completed hundredth Habitat house for its dedication ceremony, singing all the while:

> We will work with each other, we will work side by side [repeat].
> And we'll guard each one's dignity and save each one's pride.
> And they'll know we are builders by our love, by our love,
> Yes, they'll know we are builders by our love.

In time, the singing stopped. People talked to each other excitedly as they paraded through the most congested part of the city, occasionally interrupted by the horn of an approving driver or a question from a curious pedestrian. Winding its way into the residential Southside, the procession passed the affiliate's first house, where the Harriman children, clad in Habitat T-shirts, were outside waving enthusiastically. Then they went by its twenty-fifth house, at which some of the marchers, who had worked on it years ago, hooted and cheered with a proud bravado.

But most of the marchers, it seemed, were unfamiliar with this modest neighborhood and were not entirely sure where they were being led. As they turned the corner onto Fifteenth Avenue, however, they saw a sight familiar to most Habitat supporters: the setting of a house dedication ceremony. The house was wide open, and tarps had been placed over the carpets so volunteers and staff could come in and inspect their work and congratulate the smartly dressed homeowner family. A makeshift stage and public address system had been set up in front of the main entry, facing rows of folding chairs arranged neatly on the still unsodded "lawn" and sidewalk. Helium balloons floated from strings here and there or darted through the crowd in the hands of running children. Some people sipped soft drinks and many munched on apples donated by a nearby orchard. A local television crew hurried into position as an a cappella women's quartet launched into a selection of show tunes and gospel arrangements. That was a signal that the dedication ceremony was about to begin.

After a few songs and a polite ovation from the crowd, a board member from the Southside Minneapolis chapter, Pam Lorentzen, welcomed the assembled crowd to the celebration. As is typical of a Habitat house-dedication ceremony, she spent several minutes thanking the volunteers and donors who had made the event possible and then singled out for special recognition those groups that made the most significant contributions. For this particular house, the most notable of these was the Lord of Life Lutheran Church, which covenanted with Habitat to pay for half of all the building costs and sent teams of volunteers to the building site throughout the previous summer as a congregational service project. Covering one-quarter of the costs and also providing volunteers was the Minneapolis-based Residential Funding Corporation, a mortgage financing company that has supported Habitat projects in various parts of the country. Other groups providing money and volunteers were the Eagan Jaycees, Mounds View Lions Club, Calvary Presbyterian Church, Mayflower Community Congregational Church, and Holy Trinity Lutheran Church.

Finally, Lorentzen thanked the following businesses for their free or minimally priced contributions to the house: Ames Construction (excavation and foundation); Colonial Craft (moldings and kitchen cabinets); Home Valu Company (carpets); HunterDouglas (windows and mini-blinds); Larkin, Hoffman, Daly and Lindgren (legal services); Robillard Plumbing (bathroom fixtures and plumbing hook-ups); University of Minnesota (roofing materials and nails); Valspar Company (paint and varnish); and Wong Electric (wiring, switches, and outlets). Her concluding message: "I want to thank everyone who has given so much to this project and also encourage all of us here to give even more in the future. When we come together like this, we're reminded that ours is truly a caring community and that the possibilities are limitless when we cooperate with one another." It would be difficult to imagine a Habitat house dedication ceremony that did not have this message as one of its dominant themes. Recognizing it, the crowd applauded and waited for the next speaker to emphasize it further.

Pam Lorentzen introduced and gave a friendly embrace to Rita Hernandez, the affiliate's twenty-fifth homeowner, who lived with her husband and five children in a Habitat house just three blocks away. Clearly overwhelmed by the loud reception she received from the crowd, she spoke shyly of her pleasure at seeing many familiar faces. She had taken time to choose a Scripture passage appropriate for this occasion, she said, and wanted to share it. "It's a summary of everything Habitat is about, in my opinion," she added, and then read from Paul's letter to the Philippians:

> So if there is any encouragement in Christ, any incentive of love, any participation in the Spirit, any affection and sympathy, complete my joy by being of the same mind, having the same love, being in full accord and of one mind. Do nothing from selfishness or conceit, but in humility count others better than yourselves. Let each of you look not only to his own interests, but also to the interests of others. (Phil. 2:1–4)

"The Spirit of Christ was present in the building of my house, and the Spirit is still working in my family today," she declared, clapping and pointing at certain people in the crowd as they, in turn, applauded her. Her entire family then came onstage and she gave brief descriptions of how their lives had improved since 1991, when they moved into their rehabbed brick home. Her husband had a room in the basement for pursuing his various hobbies and enjoying rare periods of privacy after work; the children had a quiet place to do homework and a big backyard to play in; she had her own garden and shared some of her vegetables with her neighbors. She clearly could have gone on.

Soon, however, she relinquished the stage to Debbie Mazur, a single mother with four children who all lived in the affiliate's fiftieth house. She told the crowd that their lives had also improved in the two short years since they moved into their house across town. But what she most wanted to do was to thank people associated with the affiliate for "the opportunity for me to get on my feet and take care of my family the right way." Whenever she thought of Habitat, she said, she thought of the many volunteers "who gave of themselves so generously" and most of whose names she could not recall. "But I see your faces everyday," she insisted. "I don't think of my house as just one house. I think of it as lots of small pieces that were put in place by different people. When I see a door or just a screw in a door, I can still see the face of the person that screwed it in there. When I look at one of my windows, I see a bunch of people holding it up and setting it into its frame so carefully. I just want you all to know that you're still present in my house and I love having you there." A wide smile flashed across her face and, just as quickly as she had scampered onstage, she refolded the paper from which she read and exited with a parting wave to her audience.

The next speaker walked onstage slowly and seemed more comfortable talking to a large group about Habitat. As most people already knew, Morton Ringgren was one of three people who, after reading Millard Fuller's books ten years ago, drove to a Habitat meeting in New Jersey, where they met Fuller and former President Carter. He seemed to revel in telling the crowd how moved he was when Carter asked him, "Don't you think Christians like you should be doing more for the world than just teaching Sunday School and singing in the choir?" "I was stunned," intoned Morton, actually looking quite stunned for the crowd's benefit. "The scales fell from my eyes, and I knew the only possible answer to that question was 'Yes.' I knew I had to do something more so my actions matched my beliefs more closely." That something, he explained, was to spread the word about Habitat—first at his own Lutheran church and then, after gaining affiliation, to other churches in the area. He and his wife have been avid volunteers ever since, and both have been "blessed with a feeling of purpose and fulfillment" as a consequence.

To illustrate, he gave a number of examples: the close friends he had met volunteering; the hope he felt for the future when he saw young people contributing to their communities; the daughter of a homeowner who had graduated from college the previous spring . . . Ringgren was rambling a bit. Catching himself, he told the group that he wanted to end with two of Fuller's most frequently quoted Scripture passages that, in their "straightforward simplicity," were worth keeping in mind as the affiliate began work on its next hundred homes:

> And if your brother becomes poor, and cannot maintain himself with you, you shall maintain him; as a stranger and a sojourner he shall live with you. Take no interest from him or increase, but fear your God; that your brother may live beside you. You shall not lend him your money at interest, nor give him your food for profit. I am the Lord your God, who brought you forth out of the land of Egypt to give you the land of Canaan, and to be your God. (Lev. 25:35–38)

"God cares for people who are in need and we should do likewise," Ringgren continued, and then explained that the same message appears in the New Testament as well. Directing them to listen to the simple exchange between Jesus and his followers in Luke's gospel, he quoted:

"And the multitudes asked him, 'What then shall we do?' And he answered them, 'He who has two coats, let him share with him who has none; and he who has food, let him do likewise'" (Luke 3:10–11). "I think what Jesus said about coats and food also applies to houses," Ringgren concluded. "Most of us have houses more than big enough for what we need. So I think when we help those who lack housing, we're doing more than we sometimes even know—we're living according to God's view of things."

Ringgren stepped off the stage, and the women's quartet returned to sing a couple of slow, inspirational numbers. By the time they finished, the mood of the event had become quieter, more reflective. Almost gratuitously at this point, the program called for a reading from Scripture. Former affiliate board president, Wendy Farganis, with a sheet of paper in her hand, took the microphone and announced softly, "This is a reading from the Gospel of Matthew." She then read the account of Jesus' Sermon on the Mount during which he blessed, among others, the meek, the merciful, and those who mourn and hunger for righteousness, and concluded with his exhortation:

> You are the light of the world. A city set upon a hill cannot be hid. Nor do men light a lamp and put it under a bushel, but on a stand, and it gives light to all in the house. Let your light so shine before men, that they may see your good works and give glory to your Father who is in heaven. (Matt. 5:1–10; 14–16)

After a moment of silence, Scott Quinley again stood before the crowd, this time to offer a brief reflection on the gospel verses just read. He confided that he had thought about the famous passage numerous times since becoming an affiliate staff member five years ago. Knowing that the people whom Jesus considered most "blessed" are precisely the kind one meets through Habitat has constantly reminded him that his own decision to become involved with the ministry was a wise one. "The message we usually get from our society is that it's better to be happy all the time rather than being sensitive enough to mourn about some of the problems that surround us. It's better to be a go-getter climbing the corporate ladder rather than behaving meekly and kindly. It's better to hunger for a life of luxury for oneself rather than for righteousness for all," he said, raising his voice slightly with each sentence. "This passage has always reminded me that that message is only one way of looking at it. There are other ways of being in the world."

He could have ended his comments there. He appeared ready to do so, in fact, before admitting to the crowd that he had forgotten that the verses about people bringing light to the world through their good works were also part of the Sermon on the Mount. But he had not given these much thought, unlike the preceding verses. "You know, it occurs to me that they really relate to what you're doing in this work too," he said, and then told the crowd about a nearly completed Habitat house in St. Paul that had been vandalized just two weeks previously. After a brief newspaper article reported the incident and a couple of TV stations picked up the story after that, a virtual flood of calls came into his office with offers of assistance and of money toward the twenty thousand dollars needed to repair the damage. "The point is," he explained, "most of these people have never had anything to do with Habitat before." He went to make this point clearer:

> They just wanted to help us because they know we care about other people. And so, when they helped us, I think it showed that the idea of caring for other people has taken root throughout the whole community. I think that the fact that there are people who do things like volunteering to build houses for others gives people a sense of hope. It tells them that hope is real. It's a rational way of thinking. And that's an incredibly valuable idea to have in a community. It means that Habitat's achievement exceeds even the building of one hundred houses. And you are the face of it, the sweat of it. God bless you in this work and may you continue to be a light for the people around you.

"Now for the main event," Quinley declared abruptly, with a wide grin. Immediately, everyone knew what was about to occur. Some of the people in the back who, up to that point, did not mind having their view obstructed by those in front of them suddenly sought out better places to stand. Coaxing their four children ahead of them, Dae and Eunhee Chuan climbed up on stage and shook hands with Quinley. Whispering something to them, he was able to elicit a few nervous giggles from the couple before Pam Lorentzen took the microphone once again. They glanced bashfully downward as she told the crowd what a joy it had been to work with this family of recent Korean immigrants who attended a Presbyterian church a mile away. Dae Chuan's full-time job at a package delivery service during the week was physically demanding, but he was a dependable and pleasant worker at the building site on many evenings and, without fail, all day on Saturdays. Eunhee Chuan worked part-time at a restaurant and, often with her children, helped out with mailings and other projects at the Habitat office, where she was much appreciated among the staff. "This family is part of the light that shines from Habitat," Lorentzen told the crowd. Then, turning to Dae and Eunhee, she presented them with the keys to their house and a Bible, something done at every Habitat housing dedication ceremony. "Our hope is that this house will keep your family safe and warm and this Bible will nourish your spirits throughout your lives. On behalf of Habitat's Southside chapter, let me be the first to welcome you to the neighborhood."

Everyone, Lorentzen and Quinley included, applauded the family. With his arm around his wife, Dae Chuan, whose broken English was still considerably better than hers, addressed the gathering. "Just two years ago we came to this country. We never thought we could buy a house for a long time, but now we're so thankful. We're thankful for this chance to live in a happy home." With his wife nodding in assent, he concluded to still more applause, "We'll never forget Habitat for our whole lives." That, as everyone seemed aware, was the climax of the event. Some people even rose from their chairs to leave or, if they had not already done so, to take a tour of the house. They quickly sat down again when Gail Dorsey-Johansen, a minister at the Lord of Life Lutheran Church, which had contributed so much to this particular house, began to give the closing prayer:

> God, we thank you for this wonderful spirit of community, knowing full well that it is a reflection of your divine purpose for our lives together. We thank you for the many people who have cared enough to build this beautiful house and for the Chuan family, whose lives will bless it and turn it into a home. Finally, we thank you for allowing us to have celebrated the occasion of welcoming a new family into our community one hundred times now. We pray that you will guide this ministry and permit us to experience that blessing again and again. Amen.

"Amen," came the celebratory response of the crowd, followed almost immediately by the banter of conversation, the refolding of chairs and, eventually, the sound of cars starting and heading homeward. The ritual appeared to have been effective. It conferred public recognition on a worthy homeowner family and, perhaps more importantly, did something similar for the volunteers who were present. Indeed, it placed their voluntarism within a larger conceptual framework that rendered it meaningful, even if only for the moment. Whatever private motivations individual volunteers might have had for contributing to the affiliate's work, during the house dedication they were connected to a distinctly public sensibility and purpose. The ceremony, in other words, permitted their efforts to be woven into what anthropologist Clifford Geertz evocatively calls "webs of significance."[2] It allowed people to envision their voluntarism as being intricately enmeshed with thriving (and grateful) homeowner families, with a wider community filled with caring churches, corporations, fellow volunteers, and with a divinely sanctioned order in which the light of people's good works glorifies God. As efficacious for people in need, as part of an ongoing community concern, and as a moral response to the divine will, therefore, their own work was interpreted and presented to them as enormously significant. It is on such occasions that voluntarism is constructed as a meaningful activity. People at Habitat perform the disparate acts of hammering, fundraising, and attending meetings, to give just three examples. Yet when the fuller significance of those acts is displayed during rituals like the one on Fifteenth Avenue, they take on a cohesive meaning that transforms them into voluntarism as collectively, not just privately, understood. Such rituals also demonstrate that, as the previous chapter discussed, the deeper meaning of voluntarism is usually constructed and publicly expressed at Habitat through religious language.

The Churches: Habitat's "Primary Partner"

What Habitat Gets from the Churches

The Chuan family's house dedication ceremony suggests how important the churches are to Habitat and why Fuller has long considered them to be the organization's "primary partner."[3] That the dedication took place at all was largely due to the financial contributions of several local churches, especially Lord of Life Lutheran Church. Together they account for about one-quarter of the Twin Cities affiliate's entire annual revenues. This figure is modest in comparison with some, particularly Southern, affiliates, which receive twice that percentage from churches, but it exceeds others like the Mount Diablo affiliate, which gets only 2 percent of its funding from area churches.

And what of other kinds of resources? A church was hardly an unusual place to hold the planning meeting that preceded the dedication ceremony. Church basements and halls are where most affiliates have their planning, orientation, training, and committee meetings and also where their offices—if they have them—are most often located. Active church leaders like Stuart Blanchard and Gail Dorsey-Johansen are critical for legitimating Habitat's work, spreading the word about it, and involving congregants as volunteers. Finally, as discussed in Chapter 1, Habitat is so successful in mobilizing the people in the pews because churches are institutions that generate substantial "social capital." For example, Pam Lorentzen, a homemaker and mother of three, might never have become a board member at the Southside chapter were it not for the leadership skills she gained from serving on the social concerns committee at her Presbyterian church. Without the dense social networks maintained within his Lutheran church, Morton Ringgren might never have read his first Habitat book (given to him by his pastor) and probably would not have been able to recruit a sufficient number of like-minded others to join him in founding a new affiliate. Many of the people attending the house dedication ceremony were informed about it at their churches, the very same places they likely heard about volunteer opportunities with Habitat in the first place. But skills, networks, and access to community information would mean little without a set of shared values capable of uniting people in cooperative ventures such as Habitat. Those values are also nurtured by the churches. The songs and Scripture readings that are so important for bringing people together in worship also give expression to ideas such as love, service, faith, and righteousness that are used to make sense of their voluntarism.

Since most Habitat affiliates get their start and often their initial funding from local churches, they tend to be well aware of the resources and social capital possessed by religious institutions. They usually make every effort to partner with whatever congregations are within their proximity. Even newer affiliates targeting other sources of support and having fewer religious ties, like Mount Diablo, eventually must also turn to churches if they are to grow. The fact that more and more affiliates are forming their own church-relations committees indicates a widespread understanding that, absent the churches, Habitat is less likely to succeed as a grassroots organization.

This view, of course, is shared by Habitat International. Its goal for the coming years is to enter into partnerships with at least 50 percent of all churches in every local area where an affiliate is located. While so far only the affiliate in Sarasota, Florida, has reached this benchmark, the organization clings to the high hopes expressed by former President Carter: "Well, the fact is, that there is no large church in this nation that couldn't build five or six homes for poor people every year and have a very exciting and adventurous and gratifying experience," he urges. "And even a small church can build one or two houses a year or renovate an old one. If all the churches did that, and if all the Christians and members of synagogues would do that in a year, it would just totally transform the problem of housing and homelessness in the United States."[4]

Hopeful statements like this one seriously underestimate how tight church budgets generally are and also overestimate the willingness of most congregations to throw themselves into the issue of housing when they are busy with so many other concerns including, some congregants would be sure to emphasize, the spiritual well-being of their members.[5] A critical reading of such statements would see them as a defense of the federal government's shedding its responsibility for housing its poorer citizens onto the voluntary sector. By a more sympathetic reading, they are an enormously ambitious goal and a call for Habitat to make its case to the churches in new and creative ways.

This is the preferred reading at Habitat. The organization is forever coming up with innovative ways for churches to get involved with its work. For instance, in 1997 it instituted its Global Church Challenge, whereby congregations in the United States partner with those in developing countries where building projects are under way. American churches supply volunteers and 90 percent of the funds, and the host congregations provide most of the labor and hospitality for their American visitors. Another innovative partnership is the one Habitat formed in 1996 with the National Council of Churches to rebuild the predominantly black churches that had recently been damaged or destroyed by racially motivated arson. These smaller initiatives come and go depending on the level of interest they generate at the local level. Three larger initiatives are being pursued by the international organization in earnest, and are thus worth closer attention.

The first is a concerted effort by Habitat's Church Relations Department to involve more black and conservative churches in the ministry. Most of the 17,281 American churches (4.9 percent of the U.S. total) that contributed a full $16.4 million to Habitat in 1995 (the last year for which reliable data are available) were affiliated with primarily white, "mainline" denominations. The only denominations, in fact, to exceed $1 million in their contributions were: Presbyterian, USA ($3.9 million); United Methodist ($3.4 million); Roman Catholic ($1.6 million); Lutheran ($1.4 million); and Episcopalian ($1.3 million). Of the most conservative Christian churches, only the Southern Baptists ($723,000) approached this level of giving to Habitat, and none of the historically black churches did.[6] To be sure, the organization wants the support of these churches and certainly needs it if its lofty goals are to be taken seriously. There is more at stake, however. According to many among the organizational leadership, its heavy reliance on the liberal white churches of the mainline makes Habitat no different from many other charity organizations that have been bankrolled by them in the past. Habitat, however, envisions itself as a thoroughly ecumenical partnership incorporating the entire Christian community—rich and poor, white and black, liberal and conservative—into its ministry. Mobilizing predominantly black and more conservative churches is necessary if that vision is to be fully realized.

Second, Habitat has lately become more attentive to forming partnerships at the denominational level. So far, these efforts have been modestly successful and have resulted in various forms of denominational assistance. Some denominations have allocated funds to Habitat through their own social service programs. For example, in 1994 the American Baptists, through their "One Great Hour of Sharing" program, paid for ten houses ($350,000) built in Homestead, Florida, after the devastation of Hurricane Andrew; then they gave the Jefferson City affiliate enough money for two more houses ($60,000) to assist with flood-recovery efforts in Missouri. Between 1993 and 1995, combined contributions from the Lutheran Brotherhood and the Aid Association for Lutherans brought in more than $3 million for Habitat affiliates. Also, the United Methodist Committee on Relief (UMCOR) has for more than a decade donated approximately $50,000 each year to Habitat projects abroad. Other denominations have opted for another means of demonstrating their support. They strenuously endorse Habitat as a mission outlet for their member churches. The Lutheran Church, for example, passed a resolution declaring itself in partnership with Habitat and pledging to encourage its member churches to involve themselves with the organization's work and pray for its continued success. The United Methodist Church exceeds even this by permitting member churches to give money to Habitat in lieu of financial gifts to their own denominational conference. Finally, since the late 1990s, annual denominational meetings have become still another way for churches to support Habitat. The Disciples of Christ blitz-built three houses during one General Assembly; another five were built during the national meeting of the Cooperative Baptist Fellowship. A full twenty houses were constructed by participants of the Mennonite Church's yearly general conference. These are significant developments. Habitat has always been close to individual congregations at the grassroots level. Its focus on denominational structures indicates it is now becoming more intentional in attracting religious backing at the regional and national levels, a logical next step for an expanding ministry.

Third, as a way of attracting more religious support, Habitat has heavily promoted its relatively new Building on Faith event, a week-long blitz build specifically targeted to its religious constituencies throughout the country. Preceding the Habitat-sponsored International Day of Prayer and Action (the third Sunday in September), the event is intended to build houses, spark interest in the organization, gain media attention, and incite affiliates to create new partnerships among the churches closest to them. In 1999, 200 North American affiliates participated and built a total of 300 houses, using money and volunteers derived almost exclusively from local churches.[7] From Habitat International's perspective, these houses may very well be merely the frosting on the cake. The enormous resources it expends promoting both the blitz week and the concluding day of prayer suggests that these events are mainly public-relations tools for reminding affiliates of Habitat's religious character and for signaling to the churches that they are indeed the "primary partners" to whom it looks for assistance.

What Habitat Gives to the Churches

Like any partnership, the one between Habitat and supportive religious institutions works both ways. The latter provide Habitat with various resources and with concerned individuals, who, partly due to the social capital generated within the churches themselves, are likely to be mobilized as volunteers for its house-building ministry. In return, Habitat proves itself to be a "real gift" to the churches, says Robert Krailsheimer, an evangelical minister at Zion Lutheran Church in downtown Sioux Falls. One of the first things he did upon taking his current position in 1993 was to raise $32,000 from within the congregation; as a covenant church, the congregation then donated the money to the local Habitat affiliate. Since then, Zion Lutheran has sponsored three houses, and each year more than two hundred of its congregants contribute to the organization and about 125 of them volunteer with it.

Krailsheimer is impressed with the impact Habitat has had in the community; he is especially vocal about its positive effects within his own church:

> Habitat gives us an opportunity to carry out the ministry the churches are supposed to be undertaking. The church is the only institution I know of whose greatest responsibility is to nonmembers. So a church that just concentrates on self-perpetuation is not really accomplishing its mission. In addition to bringing people to Christ, the church has to do service in the world. And that does two things. It helps with evangelization because people tend to see hands-on ministry and can't help but be drawn into communion with those who open their hearts to them. And, secondly, it gets people out of the various board and committee meetings and revitalizes the church by offering an important avenue for service. We need fewer meetings and more ministry. Habitat, in particular, is important here because they're so well organized and have proven their effectiveness. So we can get involved and make a substantial impact without having to reinvent the wheel.

Speaking with reference to his own church, Krailsheimer nicely summarizes three of the major themes to which church leaders typically allude when describing the benefits of partnering with Habitat: evangelization, revitalization, and mission.

Many religiously conservative church leaders who are deeply concerned with evangelization agree with Krailsheimer that a commitment to social service is an effective way of "bringing people to Christ." Less expectedly, religiously liberal respondents are apt to make a similar observation. Their usual claim is not that Habitat helps the churches save souls but that it carves out a social space in which religious values are taken seriously. The result, says Victor Millman, is that Habitat may actually demonstrate the power of religious faith better than the churches can. "When somebody comes to a project and says, 'I really like Jimmy Carter and that's the only reason I'm here,' we're going to expose them to morning devotions; we're going to have them working side by side with people who have a biblical basis in their lives. So," he continues, "they become exposed to devotions, to a Christian focus and to principles in an organization that are absolutely biblical." Just as actions are said to speak louder than words, Habitat supporters like Millman say that being exposed to "faith in action" is the surest way for people to become convinced of the importance of religious faith for their own lives.

Habitat is also frequently praised for revitalizing church communities. A greater sense of solidarity and excitement, enhanced feelings of fellowship, firmer connections to the surrounding community, new volunteer roles for lay people to live out their faith commitments, burgeoning awareness of religion's relevance to the real world—these are the sorts of benefits church leaders gladly attribute to their partnership with Habitat. "We set out to be a blessing to others and we had no idea what a blessing this effort would be to our own church," summarizes Jeffrey Hoy, a Methodist pastor in Florida, who, along with some of the benefits listed above, also cites the 60 percent increase in annual giving as a sign of Habitat's role in revitalizing his congregation.[8]

Habitat boosts the churches' evangelism and promotes their revitalization because it also provides them with a third important asset: a mission outlet through which they may undertake outreach to their wider communities. The benefit of churches being able to join preexisting and well-organized ministries like Habitat's without having to, as Robert Krailsheimer puts it, "reinvent the wheel" should not be underestimated. Local churches are usually occupied with too many other activities to allow them to maintain such ministries on their own. This opinion is shared by Rebecca McNab, a former employee of the California Council of Churches hired by the Redwood City affiliate for the specific purpose of making contacts and forming partnerships with area churches. She is very aware of how important the churches are to the Redwood City affiliate. It might never have begun without the $250,000 contribution it received from Menlo Park Presbyterian during its first couple of years and would not be as vibrant as it currently is without the church-based volunteers who account for roughly 93 percent of all those who show up at the construction site every Saturday. The church leaders with whom McNab works are enormously forthcoming about how important Habitat is to their congregations' social ministry. "They [religious institutions] can't be experts in a lot of the things that are needed in our society. It's very difficult for an individual church or an individual denomination to do something about providing shelter for families that need it. But, with Habitat, they can make a significant contribution toward tackling the problem," she explains. "Habitat allows for the praxis. It leaves it to the churches to do the theological reflection that gets people motivated and gets people to see a deeper meaning in what they're doing for their neighbor."

This is not just true for individual churches. Mission outlets like Habitat enable the entire religious community to contribute more to the common good because a focus on service can unite the tremendous variety of churches on the higher ground of social ministry. McNab makes an argument reminiscent of the organization's own unifying "theology of the hammer"—that Habitat further serves the churches by giving them an opportunity to come together, overcome their relatively petty doctrinal differences, and emerge as a more effective institutional presence in American society. "I think faith communities have been shooting themselves in the foot by being so divided and suspicious of one another," she complains. "But Habitat is dealing with something for which liberal churches and fundamentalist churches can come together. We don't talk about abortion on the work site for goodness sake!"

Implied in McNab's frustration with the divisiveness among the churches is a fourth benefit Habitat renders to churches, one mentioned almost exclusively by the more liberal religious leaders associated with the organization. They perceive Habitat as a flexible, nondogmatic counterpart to more traditional religious institutions, which often appear outdated and calcified by comparison. That is, they understand Habitat as posing a critique of the churches. This actually constitutes a service because it allows people, especially progressive religious leaders, to express whatever discontent they may feel toward their religious institutions by working with Habitat, rather than by disrupting those institutions with internal dissent. Habitat is a mission outlet and also serves as something of a pressure valve, releasing dissent before it reaches a critical stage and providing church leaders less at home in traditional religious structures with alternative forms of ministry.

Caroline Roth is one such leader. She was an associate pastor at an affluent Lutheran church in Minneapolis for a couple of years, but in time she found that work dull and overly consumed with simply keeping the church running. That had been a spiritually stultifying experience, so she became a chaplain for two funeral homes and the St. Paul Fire Department and began volunteering extensively with Habitat. She finds these new commitments more fulfilling and exciting, and Habitat particularly so because it brings laypeople together and mobilizes them on the basis of their shared convictions—something, she claims, the doctrines and values preached by the churches are no longer capable of doing. "All the churches are trying to do is survive as institutions," she says, but groups like Habitat are actually "showing people what to do." Continuing this vein, Roth explains:

> I sometimes think of the church as this big semi-truck that's barreling down a narrow road. We know we're going the wrong way, but the thing's too big to be able to turn around and it's tough to stop anyway. But I imagine people jumping off the truck, hopping on bicycles and peddling the other way—the right way. Well, I think of Habitat as one of those bicycles. And, I'll tell you, I've jumped off and I'm going the right way. I'm happy about it. Although, I must admit, it's lonely at times because I can see myself and the church going in opposite directions.

The image is compelling. And even if it is not entirely true that Habitat is peddling in a direction away from that of the churches, it does typically ride along the edges rather than in the center of the narrow road of parish ministry. It seems that Caroline Roth, albeit not without a sense of loss, is grateful for the opportunity Habitat has given her to go along for the ride.

The same could be said for Martin Concina, a Southern Baptist minister who has long been a community activist and is currently a staff member at the San Francisco affiliate. Like Roth, he is wary of staid and narrow ministerial routes. "I've always felt more at home outside the institutional church than inside of it," he divulges. When discussing "the institutional church," he more often refers to denominational structures than to the congregational-level issues Caroline Roth addressed. This is because Concina is an unmistakably liberal minister who, because of his stands on issues ranging from U.S. foreign policy to homosexuality to inner-city homelessness, has had to grapple with his place within a predominantly conservative (particularly among its clergy) Protestant denomination. He has high regard for the traditional Baptist principles of "soul competency" and the "priesthood of all believers," but also acknowledges he is a "highly eclectic" practitioner of Zen meditation with an avid interest in Quaker spirituality.

In a way that is characteristic of Habitat supporters in general, Concina is wary of denominational labels. "Denominational structures are based on somewhat arbitrary definitions. I don't think people necessarily cling to their beliefs and values in ways that exactly correlate with the way denominations have broken them up. Those boxes, if you will, no longer contain all of what people believe." About being Southern Baptist, Concina laughingly exclaims, "Basically, I was just born into it—I probably never would have chosen it." And indeed most of the denomination's institutions would almost certainly never choose him for a ministerial or other leadership position. He considers himself to be an outsider and consequently feels at home working with Habitat:

> Right now there's no place in the institutional church for me in terms of being able to exercise my calling. There's no Baptist structure that would hire me at this point because of the positions that I've taken on a number of issues. My support and affirmation of gays and lesbians? That would eliminate me from about 95 percent of the Baptist community as well as many other communities. So a good chunk of Christendom has written me off right there. Plus, I've done a few other things that would probably cut me off from many other folks. So this is my place to do what I see as good work. A denomination can't live with the diversity of values in our society, but a group like Habitat can.

Concina, echoing Caroline Roth before him, cites the inability of traditional religious institutions to accommodate people's increasingly diverse religious directions and values as the principal reason why organizations like Habitat are gaining in popularity. The vast diversity of paradenominational groups, with their wide array of causes, are thought to better accommodate those diverse, religiously informed commitments. The irony is that the partnership between Habitat and the churches is actually strengthened when such people, both lay and ordained, are drawn to find a place within Habitat's ranks. Progressive clergy like Caroline Roth and Martin Concina may be critical of the churches, but they still have ties to them, and, as Habitat leaders, they are likely to sustain the ties their affiliates have to them as well.

Rationalization: Keeping "Real Religion" Religious

The Predicament of Rationalization

The partnership Habitat maintains with a wide assortment of religious institutions means that people from disparate religious traditions (or none at all) contribute to its ministry. Those who understand their involvement in explicitly religious terms tend to see their volunteering in the same light as the onlooker mentioned at the outset of this chapter. Upon observing a blitz build, he proclaimed, "Man, that's real religion!" Working with the organization makes religion more real to them, supporters typically say, because at Habitat faith yields demonstrable results; it, in short, gets things done. This is the brand of faith most at odds with an otherworldly piety that is less concerned with transforming a present-day society marked by injustice. Usually unnoticed is the fact that this brand of faith also displays a kinship with the instrumental reason that governs the rationalized spheres of public life that are similarly devoted to getting things done. When the perceived reality of people's religious convictions is contingent upon their capacity to produce results, that is an indication that their faith has likewise become rationalized to a certain extent.

One way the trend toward rationalization impinges upon Habitat is by affecting its methods of operation. As the last chapter described, its organizational culture is prone to being colonized by the rationalized logic of the market, as manifested in the processes of professionalization and commercialization. These processes inject a distinctly pragmatic attitude into the organization, creating tensions with the more expressive attitudes promoted by Habitat's founding religious vision. Rationalization has similarly shaped the locus within which Habitat does its work. In the "disenchanted" world that is our rationalized society, religious groups—especially paradenominational organizations—seeking public relevance very frequently undertake ministries in ways that have not traditionally been considered particularly religious. In other words, the sacred is now largely represented by them through ostensibly secular activity in the workaday world.

Building houses is one such secular activity. One of the more interesting aspects of Habitat's organizational culture is the way in which that activity becomes reconfigured as a manifestation of the sacred. House dedication ceremonies like the one described at the beginning of this chapter are the best example of how this is done through ritual. Even the language commonly heard at Habitat contributes to this subtle reframing. The organization does not simply raise structures of cement and wood. According to Millard Fuller, "Habitat houses are sermons—sermons of pure truth"[9] because they reflect God's will that people love and cooperate with one another. Lower-income families moving into newly completed homes are not just fortuitous exemplars of upward mobility; they are the consequence of, as one homeowner explained it, "God's love in action, hammering away for His people." Similarly, a group of suburbanites spending part of their weekend clearing a newly acquired plot of land of brambles and debris are actually, in the words of one of them, "part of the movement of the Spirit seeking to make the world a better place for everybody."

These statements, which portray the secular work of house building as a sacred activity, raise few brows at Habitat. They indicate more than the fact that people possess an understanding of the sacred and its ethical mandates and then attempt to fulfill them by building houses. This happens, of course, but something more subtle is also implied. Such statements depict the act of volunteering as not only a consequence of one's sense of the sacred but as a manifestation of the sacred itself. It is as if people associated with Habitat are so struck by the power of individuals working together or by the extraordinariness of their willingness to act on primarily altruistic impulses that attributions of divinity seem appropriate. Housing construction, an apparently secular locus of activity, becomes in effect re-enchanted, since it is reframed as the locus of God's moral command and, beyond that, as the locus for God's action in the world.

Articulating Habitat's work in terms of the sacred, as exemplifying "real religion" in the secular world, has been part of the organization's official ideology from the very beginning. But this creates a significant problem. Since "real religion" is so pragmatic and generative of good works, it is attractive to those who desire to be part of a pragmatic organization dedicated to doing good, although not out of any explicitly religious motivation. Because so many perfectly legitimate reasons exist for wanting to get involved with Habitat, the religious tenor of the organization may become watered down as its emphasis shifts to the common denominator uniting everyone's participation: the secular, rationalized activity of house building. This is ironic. The rationalization of modern society makes the secular activity of house building a locus of the sacred, of ministry. That coalescence of the secular and sacred, however, means that Habitat's ministry can become inundated by supporters with mixed or principally secular motivations. There is a very fine line, in short, between sacralizing the secular and secularizing the sacred.

These are not terms Fuller would use; he is nonetheless keenly aware of the tension. "Our purpose, so stated in our articles of incorporation, is to witness to the gospel of Jesus Christ," he insists, and then describes how Habitat's growing popularity and success threaten to undermine that original purpose:

> When you become very successful, other people get interested in what you're doing. Often they don't want to witness to the gospel of Jesus Christ—they want to build houses. So those people get involved with

Habitat's Christian values but, since these values are "absolutely not needed" to describe the organization, who end up portraying the ministry in more instrumental terms.

This is particularly true of organizational leaders, who inevitably discover that many supporters are more interested in practical, not religious, matters. They learn to package the organization accordingly. Regional director Victoria Gillespie recalls facilitating her first few volunteer orientation meetings and being surprised by people's indifference to the religious character of the organization with which they were preparing to volunteer. "People come to an orientation and, you know, you give a ten-minute history thing. It started at Koinonia Farm, it was a Christian thing, blah, blah, blah. But questions come up: 'When are we building?' 'What are we going to do?' 'Do we have a project?' *Those* are the questions people care about!" This still seems to surprise Gillespie, who shakes her head in wonderment as she speaks. Other organizational leaders, perhaps just as surprised, have learned a valuable lesson from similar encounters with Habitat supporters: They have learned to cater to the demands of their audience. For example, Charlene Konolige, a board member of the Jackson, Mississippi, affiliate, has no qualms about jettisoning Habitat's religious language when soliciting support for the ministry. "The Christian element doesn't run the show because, if you get on your theological high horse, no houses get built," she declares. This is why, when she represents her affiliate's interests before people working in local government, she presents them with a smorgasbord of good reasons to assist Habitat projects:

> I say it all. I say it's a reflection of pure, decent Christianity, we need to get rid of the poverty that's in the very center of the city, it'll get people on the tax rolls. Any way you look at it, it's a sexy program because it's not a giveaway. It's an easy sell. There are a lot of reasons to help Habitat and they're all good ones. If you and I are running a marathon together, and you are running because you want to win and I'm just out to lose a few unwanted pounds—what difference does it make? The race is getting run.

What difference *does* it make? As long as the organization is getting houses built—as long as the "race is getting run"—what difference does it make why people are helping to build them? What is wrong with organizational leaders tailoring Habitat's vision so that it suits each particular occasion and makes for a more comfortable fit for supporters with disparate agendas? These are good questions. Among those who think it does make a difference, most say that preserving Habitat's religious character is essential for remaining true to its founding values and mission. But there is a second, more implicit, reason why downplaying the religious tenor of the organization is so disturbing to people at Habitat. It is significant that so many people perceive the organizational tensions precipitated by inequitable class power (see Chapter 4) and by the colonizing processes of professionalization and commercialization (see Chapter 5) in distinctly religious terms. This suggests that religious language is the principal means available within Habitat's organizational culture by which people can identify these tensions as problematic. Religious language renders Habitat's central notion of partnership meaningful, and it is uniquely capable of expressing resistance when purely instrumental considerations threaten to undermine the spirit of partnership within the organization. Unquestionably, these concerns—even if they are not always stated as such—are at the heart of the persistent efforts of people throughout the organization, and particularly at the international headquarters, to ensure that Habitat remains an avowedly Christian ministry.

Two Tentative Positions Regarding Christian Identity

Among those who perceive it as a dilemma, there are two main answers to the question of how to sustain Habitat's Christian identity while remaining attractive to a broad constituency. The first, the confessional position, contends that the organizational leadership ought to be composed of professed Christians. Executive staff member Gordon Knebel states it forcefully.

> If we're going to succeed, it's going to be our faith that takes us there. And losing that is the greatest threat we face. We have affiliates now that call themselves interfaith affiliates or don't mention religion at all. How we fail them here is in our hesitance to get right in the middle of that real quick. This is what you need to say: "Yeah, we're a Christian organization. But we'll take your help, we'll take anybody's help. You don't have to be a Christian to help out." But when we're talking about executive directors and presidents of affiliates, when we're talking about the senior leadership in Americus, when we're talking about regional directors—I don't think we can survive as a Christian organization if we don't have Christians in those positions. Now, I'm very broad in my definition of Christian. But I think there needs to be some acknowledgment of: "Yeah, I believe in Jesus Christ, I believe in the gospel of Jesus Christ and I believe that this work is a manifestation of that gospel or it's an effort to manifest the gospel." If we don't do that, we're going to find ourselves secularized.

1

Religious Pluralism and Spiritual Selves within Habitat

Leader: **Friends, do you promise to prayerfully and humbly serve God, witnessing to the love and teachings of Jesus Christ in your assignments as International Partners?**

International Partners: **Yes, with God's help.**

Leader: **Do you affirm that you and your partners in Christ will construct simple, durable, and affordable houses at no profit and with no interest according to Habitat for Humanity® principles, building relationships, communities, and hopes to the glory of God?**

International Partners: **Yes, with God's help.**

Leader: **Do you commit yourself to work in partnership with representative local leadership in areas of your assignment and participate in the selection of future homeowner families, selecting families in greatest need first and without favoritism or discrimination?**

International Partners: **Yes, with God's help.**

Walking Humbly with God: A Commissioning Service in Americus

The questions quoted above were posed slowly, with deliberation. The response, "Yes, with God's help," echoed back each time with the resonance of nineteen voices speaking in unison. The voices came from the front of an unadorned chapel within a one-story building that also houses offices for some of the Habitat staff in Americus. Watching raptly—

although squinting as the last shafts of November daylight pierced surrounding windows—were about one hundred volunteers, staff people,
and family members. They smiled and then began clapping when the
leader officially pronounced her group of respondents Habitat's newest
international partners.

The group consisted of five single people and five married couples.
Two of the couples were each bringing two children along with them
for their three years of service abroad. Along with language school for
some, they had spent two months training together in Americus and
were now eager to begin their work. Their destinations—nine separate
countries within four continents—were a reminder of just how international this house-building ministry truly is. And the commissioning
service itself was a reminder of what a *ministry* this house-building ministry is for those participating in it.

The partners had promised to witness to "the love and teachings of
Jesus Christ" and to work toward the "glory of God"—both, as stated,
with God's help. They then sat silently before the crowd with heads
bowed, the parents among them calming fidgety children. Soon Mark
Sievers, in about his late thirties and easily the eldest of the partners,
stood before a simple wooden pulpit and read from the prophet Micah
(6:6–8):

> With what shall I come before the Lord, and bow myself before God on
> high?
> Shall I come before him with burnt offerings, with calves a year old?
> Will the Lord be pleased with thousands of rams, with ten thousands of
> rivers of oil?
> He has shown you, O man, what is good;
> And what does the Lord require of you but to do justice, and to love kind-
> ness and to walk humbly with your God?

This passage, depicting a God spurning the petty offerings of ritual and
requiring the most sublime of deeds, was selected by the group, and it
displayed their grasp of the organization's pragmatic theology. Again
heads were bowed and people were asked to reflect on those words as
another partner, Kevin Hargous, performed a skilled rendition of
"Amazing Grace" on his violin. Stillness now, a few of the partners
holding hands, people looking on reverently, some with their heads in
their hands. The room was quiet, breathing.

Rising slowly, the leader, an International staff member, asked each
of the partners to come forward for individual recognition and to receive

compassionate actions because these are reflections of "God's love." The organization is simply the "space" where such actions can occur. The Spirit, the sacred, is conceived as a verb and not as a noun. The particular religious traditions that shape individuals and perhaps inspire their social convictions are usually considered less important to Habitat supporters like Victoria Gillespie than whether those convictions are translated into action.

Gillespie feels free to call upon her Native American heritage, and, in keeping with Cheyenne tradition, she considers the effects her present actions with Habitat will have seven generations hence. Habitat's inclusive religious vision is such that everyone associated with the organization is similarly encouraged to interpret their voluntarism with reference to their own spiritual traditions. Most of these people, of course, are at least nominally Christian. More and more, though, non-Christians are coming to feel just as comfortable doing this at Habitat. For example, Anna Sonneschein has been actively involved with the organization for more than four years. Working as the Hillel director at a Pennsylvania university, she is a Reformed rabbi who, in addition to being a regular at Jimmy Carter Work Projects, organizes groups of students volunteering at a local affiliate two Sundays (to avoid the Jewish Sabbath) each month.[1] She is frustrated with what she sees as a tendency among many students to equate their Judaism simply with resisting anti-Semitism or with support for the state of Israel. Volunteering with Habitat, she tells them, permits them to express their religious identities in a less defensive and more positive way, a way that puts into action a Jewish tradition richly laden with the values of righteousness, charity, and social justice. Apparently, it does the same for her:

> I think Habitat's overall direction fits very well with my Judaism. You see, Judaism is based on a this-worldly, works-based spirituality that puts a lot of emphasis on a type of praxis that seeks to repair the world. I never needed to work with an organization that had this or that theology or that was even God-centered. What I wanted was a place where I could dedicate myself to concrete works. The spirituality was secondary because I had my own spirituality that I could bring to good works.

Another volunteer who considers Habitat a worthwhile "place" to dedicate himself to concrete works is Jesse Loucks. After five years working in London as the executive director of a nonprofit devoted to building houses for homeless people, he found himself "completely burnt out on a basically endless project." He quit his job and went to Tibet for two years, where he began to take his spiritual life more seriously; he has been a devoted Buddhist ever since. Setting aside time for daily meditation is extremely important for Loucks, but his volunteer work with Habitat is a way for him to balance inwardness with an active engagement with the world. "I have a sort of congenital need to do something. My meditation teachers would be giggling right now if they heard that!" he says, giggling quite a bit himself. "But I really like to make things happen. So I guess Habitat basically complements that interior aspect of my spiritual life."

Finally, one of Loucks's fellow volunteers at the Marin County affiliate, Audrey Polanco, provides the extreme example of someone whose deepest beliefs are enacted, not learned, at Habitat. A resolute atheist since her late teens, she nevertheless seems to epitomize the basic pattern that has emerged. Reflecting on her involvement with Habitat's ministry, she remarks, "I have a suspicion of people who emphasize the revealed aspect of religion. What is it—faith, hope, and charity? The faith bit is the one, obviously, I don't have anything to do with. But hope and charity—they're the legs Habitat seems to be walking with." Since Audrey is someone who believes in putting legs to her own belief in helping others, she finds herself volunteering fifteen to twenty hours each week with the affiliate, and doing much of her work with churches in the area. Laughing about her dedication to this Christian organization, she throws up her hands and concludes, "Hey, atheists don't pool together and help build houses for poor people—we've got to go somewhere!"

Pluralism and the Demise of Religious Boundaries

Because Habitat qualifies as a legitimate "somewhere" for so many different people seeking to enact their deepest convictions through service, its religious character is startlingly pluralistic. Indeed, its eclecticism raises doubt about the commonly heard argument that maintaining the organization's religious tone will suffice to keep it true to its foundational Christian values and steer it away from the class divisions and instrumental logic associated with the market. The religious voice within Habitat is too multivocal for that. Most of the organizational leaders in Americus recognize and actually appreciate this religious inclusiveness. Nevertheless, they usually claim that, since Habitat's religious supporters are still overwhelmingly Christian, the organization will continue to be run at the grassroots level according to widely agreed

questioning early beliefs,"[6] and a full four-fifths agree that "an individual should arrive at his or her own religious beliefs independent of any churches or synagogues."[7]

This propensity to minimize doctrine is exactly what one would expect in a culturally plural context in which the well-defined edges of people's religiosity are increasingly blunted by being rubbed up against competing worldviews. Small wonder, then, that the ethical ramifications of faith frequently loom larger in the minds of many than belief itself. For example, in his study of religious conviction among baby boomers, Roof found that only 14 percent of conservative Protestants and a mere 8 percent of mainline Protestants in that generation felt that one could be a good Christian without being concerned for the poor. For mainline boomers, this emphasis on social justice measured higher than did even the degree to which they felt one must believe in the divinity of Christ to be a good Christian.[8] Overall, it seems that theology, to borrow another phrase from Caroline Roth, is increasingly likely to be "out the window."

As with denominational labels, the dismissal of doctrinal correctness as unimportant is legitimated and significantly encouraged by Habitat's ideology of service. The comments of Pauline Tanner, a staff member at the San Francisco affiliate, are typical:

> Habitat is about people who are open and determined to honor other people's understandings of what is spiritual and holy to them. To me, that's not about saying, "I'm right and you're wrong"—which I think a lot of the churches try to do. But I can't say that. I can say what I believe. And I think those are good things *for me*, but I don't know if it would be good for you or not. I don't have all the answers and probably never will. I definitely believe I'm a Christian seeker because I think Christ's example of love and acceptance of others is what I hold to be good. Some might say that, "Well, you're not a Christian unless you believe in X, Y and Z about Jesus Christ." But I'm not going to say that.

As a self-proclaimed "Christian seeker," Tanner is at ease with her realization, "I don't have the answers and probably never will." Whatever possibilities exist for her to find what she is seeking, they, in her opinion, have little connection to theological doctrines and plenty to do with what she describes as "people getting to know each other and helping others, not caring who believes this or that."

Interestingly, this outlook is shared by many of the religious conservatives within Habitat. Daryl Collingsworth, an evangelical staff member at the Redwood City affiliate, is a good example. Also a volunteer youth leader at his Presbyterian church, he tries to read the Bible daily and to live his life according to a passage from Paul's letter to the Philippians, which he quotes from memory: "Do nothing from selfishness or conceit, but in humility count others better than yourselves. Let each of you look not only to his own interests, but also to the interests of others" (Phil. 2:3–4). While his understanding of faith commitment is more centered upon Jesus, Collingsworth is actually quite similar to Pauline Tanner in his deemphasis of dogmatic distinctions. "I don't think regulations and doctrines are the point. Jesus is the point," he asserts. Displaying a seriousness conferred by his theological education, he continues, "I think that when you worry about transubstantiation or constubstantiation or whether or not you should drink alcohol or just a little or whatever— it gets kind of annoying. Caring for and serving others, it seems to me, was what Jesus was all about."

Just as Habitat's integrative citizenship ideal envisions the barriers between different types of people coming down, there also exists within the organization a strong suspicion of the doctrinal differences that distinguish religious communities from one another and maintain the boundaries between them. These are likely to be seen as human constructs that, by being divisive and superfluous to the main point of helping others, are basically "annoying." The organizational culture, therefore, is strikingly unkind to religious boundaries. It looks far more favorably upon a religious consciousness marked by universalism and simplicity of service, two notions that will be examined in turn.

Service to Others: The Universal Simplicity of the Lay Liberal Faith

In their recent study of Presbyterian baby boomers, sociologists Dean Hoge, Benton Johnson, and Donald Luidens conclude that approximately one-third of their sample qualify as "lay liberals."[9] These are people who evince a distinctly universalist view of faith because they reject the notion that Christianity, or any other religion, qualifies as the one true religion. They usually acknowledge that their own faith is an accident of birth or upbringing, or that it is true "for them" because it meets their spiritual needs. Beyond that, they make few particularist claims. Roof's study of baby boomers also highlights the widespread sense of religious universalism among American adults. Nearly half of his sample agreed with the statement, "All the great religions of the world are equally true and good." An even larger percentage displayed an openness to investigating other religions. When posed the question,

makes perfect sense that acting according to the more universalist, ethical ramifications of those beliefs would be an acceptable way of expressing them. One of the most fascinating things about Habitat supporters is that acting according to the relatively simple ethical ramifications of those beliefs is considered to be the single most meaningful way of expressing their religious commitments. It is as if they would be willing to distill two thousand years of Christian theological reflection into the single, prosaic slogan used in advertisements for Nike sportswear: "Just do it."

The problem, as Farganis, Berryman, and Roth all suggest, is knowing just how much one ought to do. Wendy Farganis is worried about maintaining her "safe lifestyle," and Josh Berryman wonders about the consequences of being too selfless if others do not reciprocate in their turn. Such concerns keep them from totally dedicating themselves to the service of others. Both also cite responsibility to their children as limiting the time they can reasonably volunteer. These fears are understandable. Indeed, Caroline Roth goes so far as to argue that such fears are precisely what cause many people to sidestep the stark simplicity of Jesus' example of service by making the Christian faith more complicated than it actually is. This is scarcely an insurmountable problem for these three volunteers. Their fears do not keep them from acting, partly because Habitat provides them with identifiable volunteer roles that facilitate their service to others while limiting it to manageable levels appropriate for their busy lives and multiple responsibilities.[12] Habitat has a distinctly segmental, on-again/off-again understanding of volunteering, whereby people are considered empowered by making modest, not necessarily martyrly, contributions to the common good. Its organizational culture, therefore, extols a faithfulness that is both simplified by being defined by service and rendered achievable through clearly demarcated volunteer roles that come with no expectations of boundless, self-sacrificial heroism.

One of the ways people legitimate this variant of "real religion," the nonparticularist commitment to service, is by expressing it *negatively*. In other words, it is exactly what conservative evangelical Christianity is not. This is surprising given Habitat's own evangelical roots. Yet even self-identified evangelicals within the organization are apt to describe Habitat's work as being the very antithesis of the dogmatism, exclusivity, intolerance, and other-worldliness that are taken to characterize the more conservative segment of the evangelical community with which they are no longer (if ever they were) in accord.[13] Often relying on caricatures of evangelicalism, contrasts between it and Habitat's ministry abound. Victor Millman's thoughts on the issue are typical. "There are images you can conjure up when you say the word evangelical: Charismatics with their hands lifted in prayer or people demonstrating outside of abortion clinics or the whole 700 Club kind of mentality," he declares. "Habitat is not that. But I think that Habitat is very definitely the kind of organization that, with our hands and our hammers, we do what evangelicals do with uplifted hands and bibles."

Another executive staff member, Frank Riddell, expressed similar sentiments. Like most of the executive staff who came to Americus from another part of the country, he confessed to some initial apprehensions, which were ultimately assuaged, about moving to the heart of the Bible Belt. In time, he too came to see Habitat's ideology of service as being at odds with a more conservative sort of Christianity. He told a story about a friend who was a board member of an organization sponsoring people to sail from city to city witnessing to their faith and passing out bibles. When asked by his friend to join him on the board of directors, Frank knew he had to "set him straight." "I told him, without trying to totally bust his balloon, that that's not my motivation—to land and pass out bibles and say, 'Come to Jesus.' At Habitat, we're leaving tangible results by acting on our faith."

Although Habitat supporters are not inclined to proselytize or publicly urge people to "come to Jesus," their commitment to acting on faith is often expressed as following the example of Jesus. Predictably, they give priority to the humanity of the historical Jesus over assertions of divinity attributed to the Christ of faith. Jesus is depicted mostly as a man, a universal Everyman, who exemplified a life of service and taught his followers that it was God's will that they do likewise. Even Millard Fuller, who is thought by many within the organization to be too religiously conservative, gets frustrated when people piously focus on Christ's divinity at the expense of living by his example. "People will worship the hind legs off of Jesus, but they won't obey him," he exclaims, shaking his head in exasperation. "He taught by word and example that we are to practice relevant religion in the here-and-now, in the real world!"

When he centers on the humanity of Jesus, Fuller strikes a chord to which nearly everyone within the organization, even the most religiously liberal, is inclined to listen. "I think if Jesus were here today,"

so-called religious tone, it will almost certainly be in a different, perhaps less perceptible pitch than much of the leadership in Americus would like to hear. This is particularly disturbing to many since it also calls into question whether the class divisions and instrumental logic wrought by the market will be rendered problematic and resisted at the affiliate level by people with a shared religious language they are willing to voice and set of religiously informed values they are willing to act upon.

Subjectivization: Constructing the Spiritual Self

The Subjectivization of Religion at Habitat

To say that modern religion is subjectivized means that its ideas and symbols are considered to pertain primarily to the individual self. Thus they are secure from being contested by the instrumental reason prevalent within other public domains (rationalization) or by myriad competing worldviews with their own distinct truth claims (pluralization). What is religiously valid is what works for the private, spiritually autonomous self free to choose among an assortment of "religious preferences" rather than declaring allegiance to the particular ideas and symbols of a given religious community. Sociologists have long maintained that religion ultimately attends to two principal foci of concern: the quest for personal meaning and social belonging.[15] The subjectivization of religion basically amounts to the first of these becoming more dominant. The spiritual needs of the self have begun to weigh more heavily upon the modern religious consciousness than commitment to the gathered community.

Some might ask what this trend has to do with the Habitat's housebuilding ministry. Habitat, they might say, is not principally about self-improvement, as the religious offerings within the human potential movement are. It does not offer greater self-realization and self-mastery, as some religious disciplines imported from the East do. It is occupied with serving others, not with preaching what sociologist Philip Rieff once called the "gospel of self-fulfillment."[16] Even Habitat's promotional literature touts the benefits of partnership and shows scant evidence of Americans' religious individualism, which goes back at least as far as Thomas Paine ("My mind is my church") and Thomas Jefferson ("I am a sect myself"), to mention two of its more celebrated exemplars.[17]

These are important reservations. Yet to end the matter there would be to miss the more subtle ways in which the individual self rises to prominence when Habitat supporters discuss their religious lives. Witness, for example, the following exchange with Nancy Douthwaite, a member of the executive staff in Americus. After college, she spent three years as a Habitat International Partner in Botswana and then, upon completing a master's degree in public administration, worked for Catholic Relief Services in Zimbabwe for another two years. She attributes her desire to work with the poor to the religious instruction she received while growing up. Our conversation continues:

Do you think of your work at Habitat as a calling from God?

I think I do. It might change.

Do you consider yourself to be a religious person?

Yes, in the sense that my decisions are based on faith. I wouldn't consider myself religious in terms of going to church regularly or in terms of commitment to a church body. But if the definition is faith and trying to reflect my faith in my life decisions and in where I go and what I do, then I'd consider myself religious.

But you're Presbyterian officially?

Yes. Well, I sing their songs.

I noticed that you attended devotions this morning.

Sure. That's an ecumenical service. It's not really connected to any church body. But it's not church. Habitat doesn't want to be a church because that's what the church's job is [laughter]. This is an action organization. It's putting your faith to action.

It would be easy to miss some of the meaning of this exchange. It is so typical of sentiments heard at Habitat that it would seem to warrant no further consideration. But, probing these remarks further, we find a reflexively religious self that is autonomous, changeable, and discriminating. Douthwaite's current work in Americus, like her earlier jobs in Botswana and Zimbabwe, seems to be what God wants her to do, but, she admits, "that might change." She left her foreign posts because she was tired of feeling like a cultural outsider and wanted to build closer relationships with her co-workers. Her personal needs changed, and she expects that they may do so again. So she remains reflective and self-monitoring, open to the changes and growth occurring within her own psyche and willing to make future adjustments in her work life accordingly.

distances them from a rigid, pharisaical intolerance not expressive of who they are as individuals.

The same dynamic is at work regarding a third failing said to be prevalent within congregations: hypocrisy. The dissonance between what is preached on Sunday morning and what typical churches and congregants do during the remainder of the week is a source of frustration for many Habitat supporters and one of the more frequent reasons they give for becoming involved with the organization. Pauline Tanner, a staff member at the San Francisco affiliate, recalls the first time she understood the depth of religious hypocrisy as a teenager in South Carolina. "My family was very loyal to the Southern Baptists," she acknowledges. "But I could not and still cannot understand how, if you truly believe in Christ's example, you can judge a person on the basis of their skin—and not let them in the church, for heaven's sake!" As soon as she was old enough, Tanner left the church and did not return until her early thirties. Today, about twenty years later, she is still critical of religious hypocrisy. Wiser and less angry now, she chalks much of it up to the fact that "because we're human beings, we get misguided and misdirected." She realizes that she can do more than simply drop out of her church:

> I feel organized churches are valuable institutions in many ways for seekers to get together and go on their search in the company of others. But as places for people who know all the answers, I don't want anything to do with that kind of church. No one has all the answers. That's why I'm working here [the San Francisco affiliate]. It lets me live out what I think is true. And that lets me stay with my church because now I feel like I'm doing it with integrity.

Notice that belonging to a church takes a back seat to establishing an authentic sense of self. Rachel Whetton expresses a variant of this leitmotif. She is just as derisive about religious hypocrisy as Pauline Tanner: "The church says it's about *this*, but they're doing *that*. But they still tell me to do *this*! So I just do what feels right for me." Unlike Tanner, Whetton finds that belonging to a church is no longer "what feels right," so, while still considering herself Catholic, she no longer attends Mass. So concerned with maintaining her own integrity is she that, when visiting local congregations to talk about Habitat, she usually brings one of her affiliate's homeowners, someone who, as a "devout Christian," is comfortable using overtly religious language. "He talks about Habitat as God's grace in the world," she explains. "I tell you, he has the women in tears every time—and I'm almost convinced every time myself." She admits to finding some humor that, as an affiliate executive director, she has to bring in a "ringer" to pitch Habitat's ministry to local churches. Still, she insists, it is also indicative of a serious attempt to avoid hypocrisy: "My faith is so personal and searching, it's difficult for me to profess to others what I'm still trying to understand myself."

This emphasis on personal integrity is another example of how the religiously concerned self takes priority over belonging to religious groups that are so often pinned with disparaging labels like formalistic, judgmental, and hypocritical. Not everyone is as scornful as Gordon Knebel, who gruffly asserts that the churches "don't show me much except, possibly, why the Romans were so hard on the Christians." Most Habitat supporters would stop short of implying, even sarcastically, that the shortcomings of local congregations justify persecution. Nonetheless, with impressive frequency, they point to these institutional shortcomings to explain why, faced with a choice between religious belonging and the authentic self concerned with informality, tolerance, and its own integrity, they tend toward the latter.

"I'm Not Really Religious, I'm More Spiritual"

Another discursive habit common among people at Habitat is their tendency to distinguish the religious from the spiritual. "I'm not really religious, I'm more spiritual," they avow in near-mantralike fashion. The effect of this disclaimer is to accent their subjective, individually based understanding of faith. It serves as a kind of code privileging the self's direct experience of the sacred, which is typically understood as coming from within, over secondhand exposure to a religious tradition that one acquires from the outside, by belonging to a religious community. Spirituality implies that the religiously autonomous individual discovers the sacred through his or her own efforts, which may include engaging in various religious practices, exploring new and perhaps esoteric teachings, reading devotional literature, participating in a self-help group, or becoming involved in a paradenominational ministry. Religion, in this oppositional usage, is meant to refer to doctrines, ethical mandates, and professional clergy, all of which, because they represent heteronomous sources of truth, tend to be written off as less authentic and less real.

Evidence of the ascendancy of spirituality language among the broader population is readily available. Eighty-six percent of the baby

because they experience themselves as having been moved to action by something—whatever they may call it—greater than themselves. Their voluntarism, to use Peter Berger's terminology, often functions as a "signal of transcendence"; by providing glimpses of the sacred, it reminds them that there is more to life than the predictable and practical unidimensionality of everyday routines.[27] When they act upon these other, more ultimate concerns, they construct an understanding of themselves as spiritual persons, as people with something to do with the sacred.

In addition to being a tenuous endeavor, the construction of this kind of self-identity is also an ongoing one. It requires constant affirmation that the edifice of the spiritual self continues to stand and that it still affords a view to the sacred. People need demonstrable evidence of their relation to the sacred, which is exactly what working with Habitat seems to provide. Over and over again, Habitat supporters describe themselves as spiritual persons, and, to prove it, they typically point to three closely related ways in which their involvement with the organization helps them *feel* like spiritual selves.

One way Habitat does this is by giving them access to experiences of the sacred. Scholars have long noted the importance of what theologian Harvey Cox calls "experientialism" for sustaining a sense of wonderment and piety, which makes the sacred more real within people's daily lives.[28] When one talks with Habitat supporters, accounts of the experiential dimension of the organization are typically the first thing people convey, and inevitably the thing that inspires the most enthusiasm. Some people agree with long-time Sioux Falls–affiliate volunteer Adrienne Clark that house-dedication ceremonies are enormously moving experiences. "I really feel that God is working through Habitat's ministry," she says. "If you could just be present at one of the home dedications and experience the thrill of seeing the family get their house keys for the first time, then you'd just know that there's something beautiful and sacred happening in this ministry."

Others like regional office staff member Michael Quattrone point to Habitat's cooperative, hands-on work as partaking in the sacred. The experience of working with other caring people has provided him with a "spiritual awakening," which he describes as follows:

> In the last three years there's been some sort of change occurring within me. I feel much more spiritually in tune in my work life. The feeling of solidarity at building events, working in the office here, meeting new and

really wonderful people at training sessions—it all makes me feel like I'm part of something that's bigger than I am. It makes me feel like I'm an agent in the world doing God's will to the best of my ability together with other people. That's what I think spirituality is.

As Quattrone's comments suggest, powerful feelings of solidarity with other people in pursuit of a shared and noble goal is the quintessential way in which experiences of the sacred are framed at Habitat. Experiences of working side by side with others not only break down the barriers between people but often result in stirring feelings of sanctity and wholeness. They serve as affect-laden proof for self-monitoring individuals searching for assurances that their own lives are not divorced from the life of the spirit.

A second kind of proof emphasized by many respondents is the capacity for personal growth their involvement with Habitat affords. Practically by definition, being spiritual means the self is discontented with any fixed religious location and, instead, moves constantly toward new vistas of awareness and meaning. This appears to be what sociologist Tex Sample has in mind when he argues that baby boomers tend to see life in terms of an ongoing "journey" toward greater spiritual development and, oftentimes, away from formal creeds and fixed religious boundaries.[29] The metaphor of a spiritual journey resonates deeply among Habitat supporters. They frequently allude to the need for continuous spiritual development, and, just as often, they credit Habitat with instigating some of that growth in their own lives.

For instance, when asked if she is a religious person, volunteer Deirdre Schorske responds that she is instead a "principled person." To her, the distinction is clear: "Faith isn't something that's demonstrated solely through church involvement. I think it's something that requires constant growth in order to be real and that growth only occurs when it's put into practice." Her involvement with Habitat, she later clarifies, is the primary means by which she puts her faith into practice. The same is true of executive staff member Melinda Deleon, who, after describing herself as a "spiritual person," explains, "I think being spiritual means that it's not necessarily that you have to have a big C on your head that says, 'I'm a Christian.'" "I think it's an ongoing struggle," she says in concluding her interview, "that's what the word *spiritual* conveys, to know that there's always more and better things that you can do." Like Schorske, who insists that faith requires "constant growth," Deleon knows that being a person of faith is an "ongoing struggle" during

supporters, they elide into one another in different ways. Yet together they represent the need many people have for discerning signs of their own spirituality and of the part that Habitat plays in allowing them to do so.

The Irony of Habitat's "Religious Tone"

A subjectivized religiosity is promoted within Habitat's organizational culture by a first set of discursive symbols that highlight the shortcomings of conventional religious belonging. The organization offers a contrasting model that sensitizes its supporters to the formalism, judgmental attitudes, and hypocrisy frequently perceived within their congregations. It allows them to put their faith into action in ways that are consistent with these contrary values. By being critical of the churches, Habitat supporters uphold the religiously enfranchised, autonomous self over the strictures of the gathered community. This subjectivized religiosity is also promoted by a second set of discursive symbols that focus on the ongoing achievement of a spiritual self. As Habitat supporters undertake the project of constructing a self-identity with a relation to the sacred, they find the organization attractive because it enables them to feel that their efforts are successful, that they are "on the right track."

Significantly, as with the processes of rationalization and pluralization, this sort of subjectivized religion poses problems for Habitat. Societal rationalization has affected both the methods by which groups like Habitat operate and the secular, pragmatic loci in which they operate. This, as we have seen, means its ministry inevitably comes to be shared by people without much concern for its founding religious vision. Pluralization, on the other hand, accounts for people's loosened grip upon denominationally tied and doctrinally defined understandings of religious truth. This contributes to a religious sensibility at Habitat that is so inclusive that it can inhibit the expression of any particularist faith perspective at all. Finally, subjectivization has a different effect, but one no less problematic for the leadership's expectation that maintaining Habitat's Christian emphasis will enable the organization to achieve its citizenship ideals. Forgotten in this expectation is the fact that Habitat caters to and even encourages a subjectivized religiosity that asserts the preeminence of the individual self over institutional commitments. As a result, the self's quest for meaning can become paramount, reducing Habitat to simply one option, among many others, for seeking personal fulfillment. It is an open question, therefore, whether these spiritual selves can be counted on to create the religious tone that many among the organizational leadership deem necessary for solving some of the problems Habitat now faces.

The spiritual self, for example, can become more concerned with its own relation to the sacred than with establishing a strong sense of accountability to a larger community of people. This trend has been recognized at least since the early twentieth century, when Ernst Troeltsch wrote of the spread of individual-based "mystical religion," which he contrasted to more community-based "church" and "sect" forms of religion.[31] What this means for Habitat is that it is unrealistic to think that the discrepancies in class power between homeowners and volunteers described in Chapter 4 will be ameliorated simply by faithful adherence to the organization's founding religious vision. Many Habitat supporters tend to associate themselves with the organization in order to actualize their own spiritual selves. They tend to be less concerned with ensuring that their volunteering occurs within an organizational community undistorted by inequitable levels of empowerment or a skewed understanding of social integration.

Nor do they always appear to be overly concerned with resisting the increasing professionalization and commercialization addressed in Chapter 5. When volunteers detect the logic of the market creeping into their local affiliates, they do not invariably rush to make reforms. Rather, when the operations at Habitat come to resemble the passionless offices and impersonal bureaucracies with which many are familiar, they may simply go elsewhere for volunteer opportunities that are better fitted to actualizing their spiritual selves. Enough other service options exist that offer the self comparable possibilities for transformative experiences, spiritual growth, and personal satisfaction for individuals not to shop around when discontented. The self picks and chooses as it will. There is a certain pathos to this quest, however. The same spiritual selves that embark upon their search for the sacred—for that which is more than human—can end up leaving Habitat less humane and less personal when, in their quest for greater fulfillment, they abandon this ministry as soon as it is confronted by the organizational tensions precipitated by the market.

This is all extremely ironic. Habitat owes much of its enormous success to the fact that, as a paradenominational organization, it serves as an institutional space for a pragmatic, nondoctrinal, and individualistic religiosity well adapted to the secular climate of modernity. Ironically, however, it is precisely this form of religiosity that appears least likely to engender the religious language and values that can create a religious tone capable of resisting the market's instrumental logic and class-based effects. It is too early to tell whether this means that, in producing a religious tone so suited to contemporary society, Habitat has, as Marx and Engels once put it, also produced "its own grave-diggers."[32] Yet the most helpful perspective on Habitat's organizational culture, and the tensions it contains, may come from keeping in mind that Habitat represents a distinctly modern social form of religion and that it abuts a larger social ecology in which the rationalized market holds considerable sway.

8

Building Upon a Sturdy Foundation

If you look closely you will see that almost anything that really matters to us, anything that embodies our deepest commitment to the way human life should be lived and cared for, depends on some form—often many forms—of volunteerism.
Margaret Mead[1]

Habitat and the Voluntary Sector

How can one sum up an organization that currently establishes an affiliate every two days and builds about ten houses per day, that each year mobilizes more than a quarter of a million volunteers, including approximately twenty thousand affiliate board members, in the United States alone? The difficulty of capturing Habitat's vitality serves as a reminder that it exists within a voluntary sector that is itself enormously eclectic and vital. This is important to keep in mind. Giving short shrift to the nonprofit organizations and various other associational forms that compose the voluntary sector would mean underestimating their role in delivering the social services mandated by the welfare state as well as their significance for sustaining a pluralistic, participatory democracy. Without an appreciation of the voluntary sector, then, one's perspective on the social world is incomplete.

Reflecting upon the considerable time and energy that so many dedicated volunteers and staff put into their work with

Habitat further reminds us that, despite the contrary evidence one finds in the daily newspaper and elsewhere, our society is still a caring one. Average people still contribute everything from their discretionary incomes to old clothes to pints of blood for the benefit of strangers they will likely never meet, and they spend time with fellow volunteers they probably would otherwise never have met. When asked how important "helping people in need" is to them, nearly three-quarters (73 percent) of the American public say it is absolutely essential or very important, while just a quarter consider it to be only fairly important (23 percent) or not very important (2 percent).[2] Thus, without an appreciation of the caring and cooperation embedded within the voluntary sector, one's perspective on the social world is not only incomplete, it is also likely to be overly cynical.

If we overlook the ways in which our higher selves find expression within the voluntary sector, we risk being blind to the remarkable depth of solicitude that exists in our society. As if corroborating the dour view of humankind captured in the Roman dramatist Plautus's famous phrase, "man is a wolf to man,"[3] today the self-regarding inclinations of the human person still appear to be grabbing most of the attention. Psychologists, for example, overwhelmingly attribute individual motives and actions—even ostensibly altruistic ones—to the egoistic satisfaction of deep inner drives for social status, personal integration, immortality, and so forth. Neoclassical economics, now the dominant approach to the discipline in the United States, assumes that producers and consumers are primarily concerned with maximizing their own self-interests within the market. A similar assumption is made by many sociologists; influenced by "exchange theory," they attempt to explain individual human behaviors as calculated means of accruing various types of social reward. American politics is also largely grounded upon the presumed selfishness, if not wolfishness, of the average citizen. Political debate often consists of a cacophony of people claiming their individual rights, and no principle is upheld more vigorously than that of noninterference—the notion that people are free to do as they choose as long as they can refrain from harming others. The fact that our presidential candidates ask us to consider little more than whether we are better off financially than we were four years ago indicates just how central self-regard has become to our political life.

The problem with these prevailing discourses is twofold. First, they tell only half of a larger story that must also include the selflessness and sacrifice that are also a part of most people's everyday reality. Second, as these discourses become ingrained within American culture, they can become a sort of self-fulfilling prophecy. As psychologist Alfie Kohn has put it, "we tend to 'live down to' the assumption that we are basically selfish, or up to the assumption that we are given to act prosocially."[4] This is one reason why the voluntary sector is so important. The grass-roots initiatives that emerge from within it assume that the wider public, from whom they must derive their support, is indeed disposed to act in the interests of anonymous others. By its very existence, this sector accosts people with the presumption of their own goodness and challenges them to live up to it. The voluntary sector reminds us that we are better than current intellectual discourses typically describe us as being, that we generally endeavor to live according to commendable values, and we are willing to care for others when we can. It presents us, in sum, with a more positive perspective on people and on society itself.

Writing in the early years of the twentieth century, social theorist Charles Horton Cooley stated the matter this way: "Those who dwell preponderantly upon the selfish aspect of human nature and flout as sentimentalism the 'altruistic' conception of it, make their chief error in failing to see that our self itself is altruistic. . . . The improvement of society does not call for any essential change in human nature, but, chiefly, for a larger and higher application of its familiar impulses."[5] Carving out a social space for the "larger and higher application" of people's noblest impulses is the voluntary sector's primary contribution to American society. The groups and organizations that succeed in institutionalizing our highest values allow us to live according to them in much the same way that commercial organizations, for instance, permit us to live out our more acquisitive values.

The tremendous success Habitat has experienced in its brief history is testimony to its ability to institutionalize expressive values such as putting one's religious faith into practical action, ecumenical inclusiveness, economic justice, and personal responsibility. To say that these values have been institutionalized means that they inform certain practices and mores that, in turn, pattern people's behavior.[6] For example, these values generate and give meaning to manageable volunteer roles—part-time builder, committee member, financial supporter, and so forth—that people can plug into in order to live out their concern for others. These values are enacted and acknowledged in such public

rituals as blitz builds and house-dedication ceremonies. They are reinforced by an impressive selection of stories embedded in Habitat's
organizational culture. Millard Fuller's "riches to rags" story, Jimmy
Carter's transition from working in the White House to working on
his next Habitat house, accounts of the organization's incredible
growth, countless tales about average people joining in partnership
with one another—these are the scripts Habitat's voluntary actors learn
by heart. These values, finally, are carried forth by the language one
hears from Habitat supporters, which is often overtly religious and
also likely to emphasize the citizenship themes discussed in previous
chapters. The importance of such language for shaping people's actions
should not be underestimated. "Over time," warns the astute political
columnist E. J. Dionne, "when people stop *saying* things publicly, they
stop *believing* them privately. And when they stop believing them, they
will, over time, stop *acting* on them."[7]

To the extent that Habitat successfully institutionalizes its own
expressive values, it ensures that its volunteers and staff will continue
to act upon them. And as they build houses and display care for their
fellow citizens, they demonstrate that our society—despite also being
rife with individual hard-heartedness and structural injustices—is still
a caring one. This conclusion does not mean we can ignore our most
pressing social problems, nor does it mean that they are even remotely
solvable through volunteer efforts alone. America's unmet housing needs
are a telling example of the inadequacy of even the most impressive voluntary initiatives to address the nation's social problems without a sig
nificant policy commitment from the federal government. Rather, the
point of emphasizing the importance of institutional vehicles for, as
Cooley put it, the application of our "familiar impulses" is to insist that,
while the state's role in social service provision is critical, it ought to
complement and support work already being done by nonprofits within
local communities. In order to live in a caring society, citizens must have
access to well-organized opportunities to care for one another. If nothing else, Habitat's success has been a indication of people's willingness
to take advantage of such opportunities.

Habitat and the Secular Climate of Modernity

Paradenominational groups like Habitat are especially interesting
because they appear so well adapted to the climate of modernity. If public

institutions were not so thoroughly rationalized, it would be difficult to imagine caring citizens being so concerned to represent the sacred through a rationalized activity such as house building. Without religious pluralism, there would be little room for innovative new forms of religious entrepreneurship—exemplified by paradenominational groups—within the bustling marketplace of American religion. There would also be little inducement for people to transcend denominational boundaries and join together in such ecumenical ministries. And if religious subjectivization did not leave it to individuals to construct their own spiritual selves, then Habitat and other paradenominational organizations would probably not be as popular as they have become. Because of its adaptability to the processes of secularization, therefore, the paradenominational social form of religion has thrived in the United States. It has become an increasingly important manifestation of what religious historian Martin Marty refers to as the "public church," the ongoing mobilization of religious constituencies in addressing matters pertaining to the common good.[8]

Many at Habitat, and especially its leaders, would almost certainly agree with this assessment. They seem less aware that the process of secularization also accounts for some of the key tensions within their organization. We have seen that the rationalized nature of Habitat's work threatens to undermine the Christian character of its ministry. This problem presents the organization with two major challenges pertaining to its religiosity. First, it must grapple with the effects of religious pluralization within its organizational culture, which has the effect of encouraging inclusiveness at the expense of particularist expressions of faith. Habitat must, to use sociologist Philip Selznick's categories, attend to the balance between "piety" and "civility."[9] Without witnessing to the religious convictions that have fed the ministry for years (piety), Habitat can neither remain true to its original charism nor serve as a social space in which people may express their own religious commitments. But without an emphasis on the values of tolerance and diversity (civility), Habitat is unlikely to garner enough support from individuals, corporations, and the state to even approximate its construction goals for the future. How well Habitat is able to balance these sets of values will partly determine its ability to remain a distinctly Christian organization.

The second religious challenge the organization faces is that Habitat supporters must care about its Christian character. Because their religious convictions tend to be so subjectivized, many people are apt to show more concern for their spiritual selves than for maintaining the religious tone of the organization. If the organization fails to meet their inner needs, they frequently feel free to move on. Even though Habitat certainly has its share of "regulars" with a deep sense of loyalty to its ministry, many volunteers base their involvement with the organization on what it does for them. Indicative of the "expressive individualism" in American culture, their commitments typically function, in the words of Robert Bellah and his colleagues, "as enhancements of the sense of individual well-being rather than as moral imperatives."[10] Thus, the challenge for Habitat is to generate a sense of moral imperative among its supporters, to encourage them to see their voluntary involvement as an obligation and not a mere choice. "Commitment mechanisms" could take a variety of forms.[11] Conferring membership status on certain volunteers, enhancing volunteer education about the origins and values of the organization (which currently tends to be minimal), providing opportunities for volunteers to interact apart from the construction site or affiliate office, making higher demands of volunteers— the possibilities are numerous. Perhaps they are also too onerous or time-consuming for the organization to pursue. Yet, if Habitat is serious about preserving its religious tone, it will have to extend its efforts in new directions.

Habitat and the Larger Social Ecology

Habitat would also be wise to acknowledge that it exists within a larger social ecology that includes, most prominently, the megastructures of both the state and market. To date, it has been far more intentional regarding its relation to the state. Its early anti-statist rhetoric moderated as the organization has grown, and now there is willingness to partner with all levels of government, albeit with some restrictions. A comparable display of attentiveness has not been shown to the market, however. The "economics of Jesus" has proven to be an accessible way to express a mandate to care for lower-income families feeling the harsh effects of capitalism. Yet it is inadequate as an analytic tool for assessing the impact the market has had on its own organizational culture. Habitat often extols its capacity for molding supporters into empowered, socially integrated, edified and free citizens, but it has not been sufficiently alert to the ways this objective is undermined by the class effects and instrumental logic of the market.

Considering the latter, the colonizing processes of professionalization and commercialization described in Chapter 5 often compromise
the edification of volunteers (and some staff) and organizational freedom at Habitat and thus prevent supporters from directing the operations of their grassroots affiliates as they see fit. Specifically, the rationalized, instrumental logic of the market tends to supersede the
nonrationalized, expressive values that have been the bedrock of the
organization since its beginning at Koinonia Farm. The reason for this
tendency is not mysterious. Professionalization and commercialization
are the hallmarks of an efficient, accountable, and ultimately successful
organization. More houses get built, and few people, especially inadequately housed prospective homeowners, would complain about that.
Nevertheless, it does leave the organization with a dilemma if it is also
interested in building homes and, as the Habitat slogan continues,
"building communities" replete with an active citizenry. The very things
that can make an organization most successful can be least effective in
attracting people who want to experience their volunteering as personally meaningful.

Identifying this dilemma as pervasive throughout the voluntary sector, Robert Wuthnow contends, "To combat totalitarianism from above,
voluntary associations must achieve some success in solving societal
problems, even if this means large bureaucracies and instrumental programs. But to combat the withdrawal of individuals from public life
itself, voluntary associations need to remain small, informal, personal,
and diverse."[12] Habitat must attend to this fundamental tension if it
aspires to be more than a house-building organization and remain true
to its stated objective of being a grassroots and unmistakably religious
movement. Even if, as Calvin Coolidge once quipped, "the business of
America is business," if it becomes the primary business of Habitat, one
can expect fewer citizens to buy into its ministry.

How the major effects of the market—the discrepancies in class
power between Habitat's primarily middle-class supporters and its
homeowners—compromise the goals of equal empowerment and social
integration among these two groups is another issue the organization
must address more deliberately. Chapter 4 enumerated specific imped-
iments such as middle-class paternalism, the emphasis on the needs of
volunteers, and expectations of homeowner compliance. But these problems are only symptoms of a larger tension about how Americans view
their responsibilities to their fellow citizens in need. Should access to

basic social goods like adequate housing depend on the voluntary "kindness of strangers," or should it be considered, as T. H. Marshall first put it, as a "social right" to which every member of society is entitled?[13] While individual activists would offer a wide range of answers to such questions, Habitat, as an organization, has not faced up to the fact that it appears to be presenting the public with the first option in no uncertain terms.

The reason for this actually stems from Habitat's widespread popularity and visibility. It was listed in a 1996 *U.S. News and World Report* survey of America's fifty favorite charities.[14] Fuller himself continually receives accolades including, in 1996 alone, induction into the National Housing Hall of Fame and the Presidential Medal of Freedom, the country's highest civilian honor. Habitat's impressive accomplishments remind us that we live in a caring society, but its broad-based appeal may lull us into forgetting that we also live in a unequal society for which voluntarism and charitable giving, although commendable, are not realistic remedies.

As long ago as the turn of the twentieth century, this same issue concerned Jane Addams, the renowned social work pioneer and founder of the settlement house movement. She observed, "Probably there is no relation in life which our democracy is changing more rapidly than the charitable relation—that relation which obtains between benefactor and beneficiary; at the same time there is no point of contact in our modern experience which reveals so clearly the lack of that equality which democracy implies."[15] Habitat's emphasis on partnership is a worthy goal to which the organization should continue to aspire. Yet it must recognize that the "charitable relation" between the volunteers and homeowners is a "relation which obtains between benefactor and beneficiary," one that is at odds with its ideal of equal partnership.

As Habitat's operations and popularity grow and the organization becomes increasingly well known, maintenance of this "charitable relation" will become more problematic. For instance, that the organization received $25 million in 1996 from the federal government to assist in implementing the nation's affordable-housing goals indicates that Habitat affiliates have become part of the structure of the American welfare state. By virtue of using public funds, they represent the state to ordinary citizens at the grassroots level. But while state programs are intended to be universally available to qualified applicants, Habitat has always been more particularist, choosing families that seem most likely to become successful partners on its terms. It is no accident, for example, that while 76 percent of families using public housing nationwide are female headed, only about a third of Habitat families are. But as the organization receives more government funds, its preference for "traditional" families will undoubtedly arouse the ire of watchdog groups with little taste for affiliates distributing public funds only to people who meet their own values-based selection criteria.

Although what sociologist Lester Salamon calls "philanthropic particularism" is a serious concern, the greatest problem with the "charitable relation" embedded within Habitat is its "philanthropic insufficiency."[16] Simply put, Habitat is incapable, even in combination with other housing groups, of solving America's housing problems, and the voluntary sector as a whole is insufficient to meet the remainder of the nation's social welfare needs. Habitat's organizational leadership certainly recognizes this fact, but they should be more conscientious about conveying it to the general public. Instead, they present a "can do" attitude that, while inspiring, can serve to legitimate, not challenge, the inequitable class divisions that are the effect of the capitalist market. It may also inadvertently provide ideological support for political conservatives intent upon dismantling the welfare programs and social services targeted to low-income citizens.

Habitat projects are considered great investments by the federal government, and they make great photo opportunities for politicians running for office; they suggest an appealing message about communities coming together, personal responsibility, and getting things done. The problem is that, because of its vast popularity and symbolic appeal, Habitat has come to represent in the public mind the phenomenal achievements of voluntarism; there is far less mention of its insufficiency. Promoting this image creates excitement and attracts potential supporters. Unfortunately, it also gives the erroneous impression that groups like Habitat are adequate to the task of solving the nation's housing woes, a problem for which the organizational leadership must assume greater responsibility.

Similar observations can be made regarding the symbolic, perhaps ideological, uses of voluntarism in general within American society. For instance, the 1997 presidential summit on voluntarism received enormous media coverage and seemed to give an inspired nation a collective lump in its throat. Yet rare were the news stories that compared the $27 million President Clinton allotted for a new initiative to encourage volunteering with the billions of dollars he slashed from domestic programs on the eve of the 1996 election. This example raises the question of whether Habitat also serves as a feel-good symbol diverting public attention and resources away from deeper, more structural sources of social injustice. Thus, the "charitable relation" fostered within the organization may strain its ideal of partnership. But the larger issue concerns Habitat's complicity in perpetuating the notion that basic social goods like housing should be contingent upon the occasional generosity of benefactors rather than constitute the "social rights" of beneficiaries. No one gets involved with Habitat unless they want to see lower-income families living in simple, decent houses. However, unless the organizational leadership becomes more vocal about the structural inequities of the market, the overriding message heard by the public may actually be that volunteers, not the federal government, ought to bear most of the responsibility for building them.

Religious Tradition, Modern Structures, and Paradoxically Virtuous Citizens

Some Habitat supporters are young mothers or fathers who help out in the local affiliate office while their children are in preschool. Some are businesspeople or construction workers who are gratified, and sometimes even surprised, to discover that the occupational skills they acquired supporting themselves can be useful for helping someone else. Among their ranks are retirees who shudder at the thought of spending their newfound free time on golf courses or at yard sales. At a typical blitz build, one might encounter college students on summer vacation, newlyweds on their honeymoon, convicted felons on furlough programs, and spiritual seekers hoping to find more meaning in their lives. One may encounter a mix of first-time (and perhaps last-time) volunteers, extremely dedicated board or committee members, and staff people working well more than forty hours each week to keep their affiliates running. People come to Habitat from diverse backgrounds, for different reasons, and with various levels of commitment. Perhaps the only attribute they share is a willingness, even if only for a while, to contribute to the larger common good.

This attribute is often referred to as civic virtue or, more prosaically, good citizenship. It is through institutions like Habitat that individuals learn, however imperfectly, to become responsible moral agents. Writes philosopher William Sullivan, "The general character of people in any society will bear the marks of the moral pedagogy fostered by that society's institutional order, the round of life it makes available and, to varying degrees, obligatory."[17] For some of its most dedicated supporters, Habitat seems to make the practice of civic virtue obligatory. For others, Habitat makes it at least culturally possible. Although the capacity to learn civic virtue *at* Habitat varies from person to person, what can be learned about it *from* Habitat can be stated more generally. Insofar as this lesson is as paradoxical as the organization itself, it ought to serve as a fitting conclusion to this discussion.

Habitat demonstrates that civic virtue is at once traditionalist as well as thoroughly modern. First, a specific religious tradition was essential to Habitat's founding and remains central to its identity. Without the traditional truth claims and moral norms embedded within the Christian tradition, Habitat would neither exist nor play an appreciable role in forming virtuous citizens. This observation is consistent with the findings of Robert Bellah and his colleagues. They note that, "Religion is one of the most important of the many ways in which Americans 'get involved' in the life of their community and society."[18] This is because religious institutions of all kinds build the social capital that enables people to become engaged in the public sphere, and they pass on the symbols and stories that tell people they ought to do so. "Human unity is not something we are called on to create, only to recognize and then make manifest," wrote William Sloane Coffin.[19] Bringing people to recognize and act upon their interdependence, their underlying unity, is precisely what religious traditions contribute to sustaining civic virtue in our society. This fact may explain the leadership's perduring concern for Habitat's Christian identity. Not simply an expression of cultural conservatism or an interest in wooing church-based support, this concern about Habitat's religious tone may reflect an awareness that, without the moral language articulated by traditional faith communities, its capacity to nurture civic virtue would be seriously undermined.

Civic virtue is also deeply embedded within the fabric of modern society. The differentiated social structures (especially democratic polities and capitalist economies) that marked the transition from traditional to modern societies actually require civic virtue for their own viability. The American political system, for example, is grounded in a philosophical liberalism that, agnostic about moral ends, is concerned with maintaining the proper means by which individual and group interests may compete with one another in the public sphere. However, such an arrangement would scarcely last a single day if the populace were not deeply concerned about moral questions and widely disposed to acting and often sacrificing for the public good. The necessity for a virtuous citizenry to humanize the modern political system has been acknowledged since the earliest days of the republic. "To suppose that any form of government will secure liberty or happiness without any virtue in the people is a chimerical idea," declared James Madison.[20] And, in his celebrated "Farewell Address," George Washington noted that "of all the dispositions and habits which lead to political prosperity, religion and morality are indispensable supports."[21]

The same can be said of the capitalist economic system, which is typically envisioned, as Adam Smith described it, as an "invisible hand" pushing social progress to the extent that individuals are able to maximize their individual well-being. This, too, is a fallacy. Sociologist Alan Wolfe explains that "there has never existed, properly speaking, such a thing as a capitalist society ... one reason capitalism was able to flourish was that it could count on those *not* committed to its vision to provide the morality that made it work."[22] Such people acting upon moral, frequently religiously informed, worldviews instilled with the values of self-restraint, charity, voluntarism, and compassion—the stuff of civic virtue—have long corrected some of the most glaring abuses of the capitalist economy and, consequently, contributed to its continued viability.

Just as people in Habitat continue to draw heavily on religious tradition, they are also caught up in modern social structures. At its best, the organization promotes a laudable citizenship ideal; at its worst, it merely perpetuates unrealistic expectations of what volunteers can accomplish that can be used to justify a backlash against the welfare state. Either way, Habitat is inescapably political. And who could deny that it has been drawn into the capitalist system? Certainly not the roughly twenty-nine thousand families in the United States who, since 1976, have come to realize a part of the American Dream that might have been denied them without Habitat.

What seems to be required is for Habitat to recognize this. Its next challenge is to acknowledge that its work fosters a sense of civic virtue that abets the operation of political and economic systems, and that these impinge upon it as well. Just as Habitat ought to tend thoughtfully to its religious roots, it must critically reflect upon the inevitable growth in its ministry, which, given the complexities of modern society, will ideally include cogent social analysis. What should be the organization's approach to a federal government that is supportive of its house-building efforts but stops short of the commitment necessary to resolve America's housing crisis? To what degree does Habitat's ministry of extending homeownership to lower-income families legitimate, rather than contest, a capitalist market that allots basic social goods so inequitably? Is Habitat becoming more like a business and less of a ministry? These are the sorts of questions the organization now faces and from which it would be ill advised to turn away.

It is also possible that posing analytic questions more attuned to the pervasiveness and power of modern social structures is the surest way for Habitat to tap into its own religious roots. These questions, after all, will undoubtedly elicit answers that uphold such notions as the common good, human interdependence, and love of neighbor, which will require religious language to adequately convey and understand. If such conversations are conducted with integrity, Habitat supporters will discover themselves to be paradoxically virtuous citizens to the extent that they are willing to bring the wisdom of premodern religious tradition to bear when grappling with the problems attendant to modern social structures. In the end, however, pursuing that paradoxical goal appears to be precisely the main purpose of Habitat as well as for paradenominational groups more generally.

Appendix A

Affiliate Covenant:
A Basic Covenant between
Habitat for Humanity® International
and an Approved Habitat Affiliate Project

Preface

Habitat for Humanity® International and the Habitat for Humanity® affiliate work as partners in this ecumenical Christian housing ministry. The affiliate works with donors, volunteers and homeowners to create decent, affordable housing for those in need, and to make shelter a matter of conscience with people everywhere. Although Habitat for Humanity® International will assist with information resources, training, publications, prayer support and in other ways, the affiliate is primarily and directly responsible for the legal, organizational, fund-raising, family selection and nurture, financial and construction aspects of the work.

Mission Statement

Habitat for Humanity® works in partnership with God and people everywhere, from all walks of life, to develop communities with God's people in need by building and renovating houses, so that there are decent houses in decent communities in which God's people can live and grow into all that God intended.

Method of Operation

Habitat for Humanity® sponsors projects in habitat development by constructing modest but adequate housing. Habitat also seeks to associate with other organizations functioning with purposes consistent with those of Habitat for Humanity® International and the affiliate, as stated in the Articles of Incorporation of both Habitat organizations.

Foundational Principles

1. Habitat for Humanity® seeks to demonstrate the love and teachings of Jesus Christ to all people. While Habitat is a Christian organization, it invites and welcomes affiliate board members, volunteers and donors from other faiths actively committed to Habitat's Mission, Method of Operation, and Principles. The board will reflect the ethnic diversity of the area to be served.
2. Habitat for Humanity® is a people-to-people partnership drawing families and communities in need together with volunteers and resources to build decent, affordable housing for needy people. Habitat is committed to the development and uplifting of families and communities, not only to the construction of houses.
3. Habitat for Humanity® builds, renovates, and repairs simple, decent and affordable housing with people who are living in inadequate housing and who are unable to secure adequate housing by conventional means.
4. Habitat for Humanity® selects homeowner families according to criteria that do not discriminate on the basis of race, creed, or ethnic background. All homeowners contribute "sweat equity"; they work as partners with the affiliate and other volunteers to accomplish Habitat's mission, both locally and worldwide.
5. Habitat for Humanity® sells houses to selected families with no profit or interest added. House payments will be used for the construction or renovation of additional affordable housing.
6. Habitat for Humanity® is a global partnership. In recognition of and commitment to that global partnership, each affiliate is expected to contribute at least 10 percent of its cash contributions to Habitat's international work. Funds specifically designated by a donor for local work only may be excluded from the tithe.

7. Habitat for Humanity® does not seek and will not accept government funds for the construction of houses. Habitat for Humanity® welcomes partnership with governments that includes accepting funds to help set the stage for the construction of houses, provided it does not limit our ability to proclaim our Christian witness, and further provided that affiliates do not become dependent on or controlled by government funds thus obtained. Setting the stage is interpreted to include land, houses for rehabilitation, infrastructure for streets, utilities, and administrative expenses. Funding from third parties who accept government funds with sole discretion over their use shall not be considered as government funds for Habitat purposes.

Agreement to Covenant

In affirmation of the Mission, Method of Operation and Principles stated in this Covenant, we, _____ , a Habitat for Humanity® affiliate, covenant with other affiliates and Habitat for Humanity® International to accomplish our mission. Each partner commits to enhancing that ability to carry out this mission by: supporting effective communication among affiliates, Habitat for Humanity® International and regional offices; sharing annual reports; participating in regional and national training events; and participating in a biennial review and planning session between each affiliate and the regional office.

This Covenant is valid upon approval by each member of the affiliate board of directors and a designated representative of Habitat for Humanity® International.

Appendix B

Steps to Affiliation

Note: Some of these steps to affiliation are performed concurrently with other steps. Some of these steps can be accomplished in a short time period while others may require many months.

Laying the Foundation

1. Discuss your community's interest in Habitat with your regional director. (See the regional center map to identify the regional director for your state. Call the Habitat Help Line at ext. 551 or 552 to obtain the current map.) Your regional center sends you *Welcome to Habitat, Part I*. Read this handbook.
2. Read one or more of Millard and Linda Fuller's books. Read issues of *Habitat World* and *The Affiliate Update*.
3. Make arrangements through your regional center to attend a Habitat regional event.
4. Make arrangements through your regional center to visit an established affiliate.
5. Look at issues of diversity, minority involvement and low-income involvement in your community.
6. Determine the need for Habitat in your community. Conduct a housing needs assessment. Look at the issues of obtainable land and availability of volunteers to do the organizational and operational work.
7. Learn about other agencies and ministries that are addressing housing needs in your community.

253

8. Learn about other Habitat affiliates near your community. (Later on you might form partnerships with some of these affiliates, when feasible.)
9. Speak to as many people as possible about Habitat—on an informal basis and through presentations to churches, civic groups and other organizations throughout the community. Get names and addresses of interested community members.
10. Learn more about your local government. Get to know your community leaders.
11. Identify one or more locations that may eventually become the focus area(s) for your Habitat work.
12. Get to know the "community of need"—their real needs, feelings and goals. Involve them in organizing your affiliate.

Becoming a Prospective Affiliate

Note: Many of these steps are performed concurrently with "Legal Considerations" steps.

13. Form a steering committee of at least twelve people. Your steering committee must be made up of men and women of diverse ethnic, economic, religious, occupational and age groups. Select a steering committee chairperson.
14. Inform your regional center that your steering committee is formed and meeting regularly. Send to your regional center the names and addresses of committee members so that they can begin receiving *Habitat World* and *The Affiliate Update*.
15. Define the geographic area to be served by your affiliate, and choose a descriptive name for your affiliate.
16. Submit your completed housing needs assessment to your regional center.
17. Request permission from HFHI to use your affiliate's name as well as the Habitat for Humanity® International name.
18. HFHI sends you its written permission to use the Habitat name. When your group has sent your steering committee's names/address to your regional center (Step 14) and received official permission to use the HFHI name (Step 18), your group has achieved prospective affiliate status.
19. With your notification of prospective status, you also receive *Welcome to Habitat, Part II: Application for Affiliation Workbook* from

your regional center. Read this workbook carefully, even though you may not be ready to answer the questions at this point.

20. Purchase the 5-volume *Affiliate Operations Manual* (AOM) from Habitat headquarters. Order additional volumes for committee members, as needed. The AOM includes information that is essential to the formation and operation of an affiliate, including board and committee formation. Do not fail to utilize this valuable resource!

Enlarging the Base of Support

21. Obtain a telephone number and a listing for your affiliate in your local phone book.
22. Acquire and use HFHI resources: brochures and other promotional materials, articles, videos.
23. Begin to do public relations work.
24. Develop an "interests/skills survey." Distribute the surveys at every Habitat presentation and other community events.
25. Develop a mailing list and a database.
26. Begin raising funds.
27. Determine a way to receive donations until your tax-exempt status is decided.
28. Continue making speeches and giving presentations about Habitat.
29. Establish and nurture partnerships with churches.
30. Schedule one or more public meetings to broaden your partnership base and establish your presence in the community. Arrange for a speaker from your regional center or from a nearby affiliate.
31. Establish partnerships with the business community, local media, local government and the neighbors in your focus area(s).
32. Consider the role of volunteers in your affiliate. Develop a plan for the coordination of volunteers.
33. Begin to design brochures and newsletters.

Legal Considerations

34. Secure the services of a business attorney.
35. Form a nonprofit corporation (i.e., incorporation of your prospective affiliate).

36. Obtain a federal taxpayer (employer) identification number by filing Form SS-4 with the Internal Revenue Service.
37. Decide on the fiscal year your affiliate will use. (For inclusion under HFHI's group tax-exemption, your fiscal year must be the calendar year.)
38. Decide whether to secure tax-exempt status under HFHI's group tax-exemption or to seek tax-exempt status independently. (If you choose to be included under group tax-exemption, you will include a letter of authorization with your application for affiliation.)
39. Draft the articles of incorporation, making certain to include the specific purposes and provisions discussed in Volume 2 of the AOM. Have the articles reviewed by your attorney.
40. Submit the articles of incorporation to your regional center for approval.
41. File the articles of incorporation with the necessary state agencies.

Note: At this point a permanent board of directors is elected.

42. Draft the affiliate bylaws and have them reviewed by your attorney.
43. Get approval of the bylaws from the board of directors.
44. Examine issues of tax-exempt status within your state, as well as other legal issues.
45. Begin to develop your fiscal safeguards policies/procedures.
46. Become familiar with the *Affiliate Accounting Policy Manual*, which is available from HFHI. (1-800-HABITAT, ext. 312 or 140.) Some affiliates eventually secure the services of an accountant.
47. Become familiar with other corporate formalities and necessities relating to affiliate operation.

Board of Directors

Note: The formation of committees must come prior to the formation of the board of directors.

48. Appoint a nominating committee to select the board of directors.
49. Elect a board of directors from those nominated. The board should be composed of at least 12 people (and no more than 20). Your board must be made up of men and women of diverse ethnic, economic, religious, occupational and age groups.

50. Make certain board members receive a board member packet, including the *Welcome to the Board of Directors* booklet.
51. Instruct the board to elect officers: president (or chairperson), vice president (or vice-chairperson), secretary and treasurer.
52. Instruct the board to discuss these issues: partnership with HFHI and partnership with the community.
53. Instruct the board to discuss the expectation of affiliate tithing to Habitat's international affiliates.
54. Instruct the board to review and sign the affiliate covenant.

Committee Formation

Note: The formation of committees must come prior to the formation of the board of directors.

Family Selection Committee

55. Form a family selection committee of 5–12 members.
56. The committee begins to develop a sweat-equity plan.
57. The committee begins to develop family selection criteria.
58. The committee begins to design the homeowner application.

Family Nurture Committee

59. Form a family nurture committee of at least 6 members.
60. The committee begins to develop a plan for family nurture/partnership.

Development Committee

61. Form a development committee of at least 5 members.
62. Board members must pledge financial support of the affiliate to the extent that they are able. Some affiliate boards ask their members to sign a "covenant among board members." See a sample board covenant in Volume I of the AOM.
63. The affiliate demonstrates fund-raising capability by raising at least $3,000 from at least 15 different sources.
64. The committee begins to design an affiliate development plan. The plan looks at all aspects of the affiliate's public relations and fund-raising efforts (both short-term and long-range plans).

Site Selection Committee

65. Form a site selection committee of 3–5 members.
66. The committee begins to develop a site selection plan, including a description of the focus area(s) selected.

Building Committee

67. Form a building committee large enough to support the affiliate's house building work.
68. The committee begins to develop a construction plan.
69. The committee becomes familiar with the Habitat house design criteria; the criteria are listed in the "Building Committee" section in *Welcome to Habitat, Part I.*
70. The committee estimates the cost of building a Habitat house; consult your regional director.
71. The committee calculates the selling price of a Habitat house, using the "HFHI Guidelines on Determining the Selling Price of Habitat Houses." See *Welcome to Habitat, Part II* for these guidelines.

Application for Affiliation

72. Complete the *Application for Affiliation Workbook* (Part III of *Welcome to Habitat*). The board contributes some of the information and supporting materials, and the specific committees provide the remainder. Use the "Affiliate Application Review" at the end of the workbook for instructions on assembling the application's cover sheets and attachments.
73. Contact your regional director for information about submission of your application. Arrange for a meeting with your director to review your application.
74. Submit the completed application to your regional center. Upon approval by the regional director, the application goes to the area director for review. The HFHI board of directors grants final approval of affiliation.

Affiliation Approval

75. Following affiliation approval, your affiliate receives *Welcome to Habitat, Part III: A Housewarming Package.* Congratulations! You are now a Habitat for Humanity® affiliate!

76. Also, following affiliation approval, your affiliate receives the U.S. Affiliate Insurance Program handbook from HFHI's insurance broker. (Prospective affiliates can order the insurance information packet before their affiliation is approved by HFHI. Call Acordia Insurance Company at 1-800-824-9245.)

77. Save all parts of the *Welcome to Habitat* handbook and related appendices as a reference handbook as your affiliate enters into operation.

Note: The affiliate organizational process takes at least six months, and more commonly nine to twelve months from start to finish. There are no shortcuts!

Appendix C

Habitat's Local Affiliate Structure

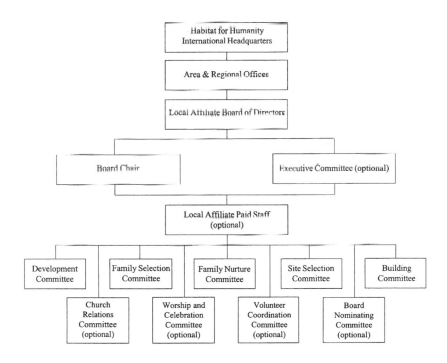

Notes

Chapter One

1. Alexis de Tocqueville, *Democracy in America*, trans. George Lawrence (New York: Doubleday, 1969), 517.

2. Lester M. Salamon, *America's Nonprofit Sector: A Primer* (New York: Foundation Center, 1992); Michael O'Neill, *The Third America: The Emergence of the Nonprofit Sector in the United States* (San Francisco: Jossey-Bass, 1989).

3. Waldemar A. Nielsen, *The Endangered Sector* (New York: Columbia University Press, 1979), 5.

4. For his normative analysis of the three social sectors, see Robert Wuthnow, "The Voluntary Sector: Legacy of the Past, Hope for the Future?" in *Between States and Markets: The Voluntary Sector in Comparative Perspective*, ed. Robert Wuthnow (Princeton: Princeton University Press, 1991), 3–29.

5. Alan Wolfe, *Whose Keeper? Social Science and Moral Obligation* (Berkeley: University of California Press, 1989), 20.

6. Robert N. Bellah, Richard Madsen, William M. Sullivan, Ann Swidler, and Steven M. Tipton, *The Good Society* (New York: Vantage Books, 1991), 12.

7. Peter L. Berger and Richard John Neuhaus, *To Empower People: The Role of Mediating Structures in Public Policy* (Washington, D.C.: AEI Press, 1977), 6.

8. Gabriel Rudney, "A Quantitative Profile of the Independent Sector," Working Paper 40 (New Haven: Institution for Social and Policy Studies, Yale University, 1981), 3.

9. O'Neill, *The Third America*, 6–8; Burton A. Weisbrod, *The Nonprofit Economy* (Cambridge, Mass.: Harvard University Press, 1988), 170.

10. Virginia Ann Hodgkinson, Murray S. Weitzman, Christopher M. Toppe, and Stephen M. Noga, *Dimensions of the Independent Sector: A Statistical Profile* (Washington, D.C.: Independent Sector, 1994), 29.

11. For these figures and others, see Virginia Ann Hodgkinson and Murray S. Weitzman, *Giving and Volunteering in the United States: Findings from a National Survey* (Washington, D.C.: Independent Sector, 1996), 1–4.

12. Ibid.

13. Hodgkinson et al., *Dimensions of the Independent Sector*, 7.

14. Ibid., 9.

15. See "Economic Competition Involving Charities" in Alan Ware, *Between Profit and State: Intermediate Organizations in Britain and the United States* (Princeton: Princeton University Press, 1989), 73–104. Also informative is J. G. Gallagher's *Unfair Competition? The Challenge to Charitable Tax Exemption* (Washington, D.C.: National Assembly, 1988).

16. "Church Attendance Unchanged As We Enter the 1990s," *Emerging Trends*, June 1994, 4. For a challenge to this widely quoted 40 percent figure by researchers who claim that weekly church attendance is actually about half that for Catholics and Protestants, see C. Kirk Hadaway, Penny Long Marler, and Mark Chaves, "What the Polls Don't Show: A Closer Look at U.S. Church Attendance," *American Sociological Review* 58 (December 1993): 741–52.

17. Stephen V. Monsma, *When Sacred and Secular Mix: Religious Nonprofit Organizations and Public Money* (Boston: Rowman and Littlefield, 1996), 2–10.

18. See Daphne N. Layton, *Philanthropy and Voluntarism: An Annotated Bibliography* (New York: Foundation Center, 1987). Peter Dobkin Hall pointed out the dearth of religious research in Layton's listing in his article, "The History of Religious Philanthropy in America" in *Faith and Philanthropy in America*, ed. Robert Wuthnow and Virginia A. Hodgkinson (San Francisco: Jossey-Bass, 1990), 38.

19. In addition to this covenant theme, Kenneth D. Wald also points to the themes of original sin and chosen people as important religious influences on American democracy; see his *Religion and Politics in the United States*, 2d ed. (Washington, D.C.: Congressional Quarterly Press, 1992), 41–68.

20. This is the contention of one of the more insightful and prolific commentators on the importance of voluntary associations, James Luther Adams, and of many of his colleagues. See James Luther Adams, *Voluntary Associations: Socio-cultural Analyses and Theological Interpretation*, ed. J. Ronald Engel (Chicago: Exploration Press, 1986), and *The Prophethood of All Believers*, ed. George K. Beach (Boston: Beacon Press, 1996); Michael Novak, ed., *Democracy and Mediating Structures: A Theological Inquiry* (Washington, D.C.: American Enterprise Institute, 1980); D. B. Robertson, ed., *Voluntary Associations: A Study of Groups in Free Societies* (Richmond, Va: John Knox Press, 1966); Max L. Stackhouse, "Religion and the Social Space for Voluntary Institutions," in Wuthnow and Hodgkinson, *Faith and Philanthropy in America*, 22–37.

21. Weber even goes so far as to suggest that the critical voice of autonomous prophecy was a direct precursor to the institutionalization of a free press. See Max Weber, *Ancient Judaism* (New York: Free Press, 1952).

22. Alfred North Whitehead, *Adventures of Ideas* (New York: Macmillan, 1933), 69.

23. James Luther Adams, "The Political Responsibility of the Man of Culture," in J. Ronald Engel, *Voluntary Associations*, 146–47.

24. According to George H. Williams, this sort of group discernment and respect for minority opinion was the root of the notion of "loyal opposition" within parliamentary democracies. See his "The Religious Background of the Idea of a Loyal Opposition" in D. B. Robertson, *Voluntary Associations*, 55–90.

25. This is a point that Adams derives from his close reading of Ernst Troeltsch, whose work Adams considers an important supplement to Weber's thesis regarding the unintended consequences ascetic Calvinism had in stimulating the rationalization

of the capitalist economy. Troeltsch expanded this view with his assessment of Calvinism's impact in democratizing the political sphere, which it did partly by providing the ideological support for a proliferation of voluntary associations. As Troeltsch put it in his masterpiece, *The Social Teaching of the Christian Churches* (Louisville, Ky.: Westminster/John Knox Press, 1931), "The sectarian ideals which had been absorbed from the New Testament and from the Anabaptist criticism of the Reformation were thus fused with the idea of the Church as an organ of grace, and merged in the idea of predestination, which by its active character intensified the sectarian ideal, and yet kept the balance by its emphasis on the ideal of the Church. . . . This leads Calvinism everywhere to an organized and aggressive effort to form associations, to a systematic endeavor to mold the life of Society as a whole, to a kind of 'Christian Socialism'" (p. 602).

26. Tocqueville, *Democracy in America*, 513.

27. Ibid., 47.

28. Ibid., 444–45.

29. Robert D. Putnam, "Bowling Alone: America's Declining Social Capital," *Journal of Democracy* 6 (January 1995): 65–78. For a fuller exploration of social capital and its significance for enhancing civic life, see also Putnam's book on regional governments in Italy, *Making Democracy Work: Civic Traditions in Modern Italy* (Princeton: Princeton University Press, 1993).

30. Peter Dobkin Hall, "The History of Religious Philanthropy in America," in Wuthnow and Hodgkinson, *Faith and Philanthropy in America*, 38–39.

31. Virginia A. Hodgkinson, Murray S. Weitzman, and Arthur D. Kirsch, "From Commitment to Action: How Religious Involvement Affects Giving and Volunteering," in Wuthnow and Hodgkinson, *Faith and Philanthropy in America*, 97.

32. Virginia A. Hodgkinson, Murray S. Weitzman, Arthur D. Kirsch, Stephen M. Noga, and Heather S. Gorski, *From Belief to Commitment: The Community Service Activities and Finances of Religious Congregations in the United States* (Washington, D.C.: Independent Sector, 1993), 31–33.

33. John A. Coleman, S.J., "Under the Cross and Flag: Reflections on Discipleship and Citizenship in America," *America* 174 (May 1996): 6–14. The original survey was taken by *The Nation*.

34. *The Connecticut Mutual Life Report on American Values: The Impact of Belief* (New York: Research and Forecasts, 1981), cited in Robert Wuthnow, *Christianity in the Twenty-first Century: Reflections on the Challenges Ahead* (New York: Oxford University Press, 1993), 34–35.

35. Sidney Verba, Kay Lehman Schlozman, and Henry E. Brady, *Voice and Equality: Civic Voluntarism in American Politics* (Cambridge, Mass.: Harvard University Press, 1995), 312.

36. Robert N. Bellah, Richard Madsen, William M. Sullivan, Ann Swidler, and Stephen M. Tipton, *Habits of the Heart: Individualism and Commitment in American Life* (New York: Harper and Row, 1985), 20.

37. A. James Reichley, *Religion in American Public Life* (Washington, D.C.: Brookings Institution, 1985), 359.

38. Michael R. Welch, David C. Leege, Kenneth D. Wald, and Lyman A. Kellstedt, "Are the Sheep Hearing the Shepherds? Cue Perceptions, Congregational Responses, and Political Communication Processes," in *Rediscovering the Religious*

Factor in American Politics, ed. David C. Leege and Lyman A. Kellstedt (Armonk, N.Y.: M. S. Sharpe, 1993), 235–54.

39. James R. Wood and Elton Jackson, "Religion and Public-Spirited Behavior in Indiana: A Research Report." The findings in this unpublished report are discussed in James R. Wood and James G. Hougland, Jr., "The Role of Religion in Philanthropy," in *Critical Issues in American Philanthropy: Strengthening Theory and Practice*, ed. Jon Van Til (San Francisco: Jossey-Bass, 1990), 99–132.

40. Verba, Schlozman, and Brady, *Voice and Equality*, 373.

41. Hodgkinson and Weitzman, *Giving and Volunteering in the United States*, 10. Hodgkinson and her colleagues discovered that less than one-quarter (21 percent) of the 54 percent of the American population who were not asked to volunteer their time in 1993 actually volunteered anyway; meanwhile, among the 44 percent who were asked, a full 82 percent agreed and did volunteer.

42. Putnam, "Bowling Alone," 69.

43. See his sixth chapter, "The Growth of Special Purpose Groups," in Robert Wuthnow, *The Restructuring of American Religion: Society and Faith Since World War II* (Princeton: Princeton University Press, 1988), 100–131.

44. These ten categories are: religious coalitions against nuclear warfare; prison ministries; world hunger ministries; holistic health activities; positive thinking seminars; group therapy sessions; Bible study or fellowship groups; the charismatic movement; social protest and activism; and healing ministries. See Wuthnow, *The Restructuring of American Religion*, 118–21.

45. Ibid., 120.

46. Ibid., 112–18.

47. This insight comes from Robert Wuthnow, who, in his *Producing the Sacred: An Essay on Public Religion* (Urbana: University of Illinois Press, 1994), argues that, in addition to "special interest groups," the sacred is also represented in society by congregations, denominational hierarchies, religiously sponsored academic institutions, and public ritual.

48. Emile Durkheim, *The Elementary Forms of the Religious Life*, trans. Karen E. Fields (New York: Free Press, 1995). See also Mircea Eliade, *The Sacred and the Profane: The Nature of Religion* (New York: Harcourt, Brace and World, 1959).

49. See Niklas Luhmann, *The Differentiation of Society* (New York: Columbia University Press, 1982). Also, for a penetrating essay discussing the effects of societal differentiation on religion, see Robert Bellah, "Religious Evolution," in *Beyond Belief: Essays on Religion in a Post-Traditionalist World* (Berkeley: University of California Press, 1970), 20–50.

50. The classic statement of the meaning of differentiation for the secularization of society is Max Weber's "The Religious Rejections of the World and Their Directions" in *From Max Weber: Essays in Sociology*, ed. and trans. Hans H. Gerth and C. Wright Mills (New York: Oxford University Press, 1958), 323–59.

51. See Bryan Wilson, *Religion in Secular Society: A Sociological Comment* (Baltimore: Penguin Books, 1966).

52. These three themes show up in scores of sociological analyses, but some of the books that have captured them most clearly and succinctly are: James A. Beckford, *Religion in Advanced Industrial Society* (London: Unwin Hyman, 1989); Peter

L. Berger, *The Sacred Canopy: Elements of a Sociological Theory of Religion* (Garden City, N.Y.: Doubleday, 1967); James Davison Hunter, *American Evangelicalism: Conservative Religion and the Quandary of Modernity* (New Brunswick, N.J.: Rutgers University Press, 1983); Meredith B. McGuire, *Religion: The Social Context* (Belmont, Calif.: Wadsworth, 1987); Marsha G. Witten, *All Is Forgiven: The Secular Message in American Protestantism* (Princeton: Princeton University Press, 1993).

53. Max Weber, "Science As a Vocation," in Gerth and Mills, *From Max Weber*, 155.

54. Robert Wuthnow's *Producing the Sacred* was extremely helpful for allowing me to see this. See his fourth chapter, "Special Interests," 88–104.

55. Ibid., 100.

56. Berger, *The Sacred Canopy*, 127–53.

57. Peter L. Berger, *The Heretical Imperative: Contemporary Possibilities of Religious Affirmation* (Garden City, N.Y.: Doubleday, 1979), 10.

58. See Bellah et al., *Habits of the Heart*; Peter Clecak, *America's Quest of the Ideal Self: Dissent and Fulfillment in the Sixties and Seventies* (New York: Oxford University Press, 1983); Richard A. Kulka, *The Inner American: A Self-Portrait from 1957–1976* (New York: Basic Books, 1981); Christopher Lasch, *The Culture of Narcissism* (New York: Norton, 1979); Philip Rieff, *The Triumph of the Therapeutic: The Uses of Faith after Freud* (New York: Harper and Row, 1966); and Steven M. Tipton, *Getting Saved from the Sixties: Moral Meaning in Conversion and Cultural Change* (Berkeley: University of California Press, 1982).

59. Wade Clark Roof and William McKinney, *American Mainline Religion: Its Changing Shape and Future* (New Brunswick, N.J.: Rutgers University Press, 1987), 49–50.

60. Ibid., 40–71.

61. John Murray Cuddihy, *No Offense: Civil Religion and Protestant Taste* (New York: Seabury Press, 1978), 16.

62. Thomas Luckmann, *The Invisible Religion: The Problem of Religion in Modern Society* (New York: Macmillan, 1967), 6.

63. Nowhere is this duality between constraint and enablements better explicated than in Anthony Giddens's structuration theory. See, for example, his *The Constitution of Society: Outline of the Theory of Structuration* (Berkeley: University of California Press, 1984).

Chapter Two

1. This was the eleventh Jimmy Carter Work Project. The first two, which took place in 1984 and 1985, were renovations of a six-story, nineteen-unit building in New York's Lower East Side. Subsequent projects, which were progressively larger, occurred in Chicago (June 1986), Charlotte (July 1987), Philadelphia (June 1988), Milwaukee (June 1989), Tijuana/San Diego (June 1990), Miami (June 1991), Baltimore/Washington, D.C. (June 1992), and Winnipeg, Manitoba/Waterloo, Ontario (July 1993). More recent projects took place in Los Angeles (July 1995), Vac, Hungary (August 1996), the Appalachian Mountain region of eastern Kentucky and Tennessee (1997), Houston (1998), and the Philippines (1999).

2. William James, "The Moral Equivalent of War," *Essays on Faith and Morals,* ed. Ralph Barton Perry (New York: Meridian Books, 1962), 325.

3. See Victor W. Turner, *The Ritual Process: Structure and Anti-Structure* (Chicago: Aldine, 1969), and also his *Dramas, Fields, and Metaphors: Symbolic Action in Human Society* (Ithaca, N.Y.: Cornell University Press, 1974).

4. Reported by Frye Gaillard, another observer of the blitz build, in *If I Were a Carpenter: Twenty Years of Habitat for Humanity* (Winston-Salem, N.C.: John F. Blair, 1996), xiv.

5. Karen Free, "Eagle Butte Revisited," *Habitat World,* August/September 1995, 9.

6. Millard Fuller and Diane Scott, *Love in the Mortar Joints: The Story of Habitat for Humanity* (Clinton, N.J.: New Win Publishing, 1980), 53.

7. For an interesting history of the community, see Dallas Lee, *The Cotton Patch Evidence: The Story of Clarence Jordan and the Koinonia Farm Experiment, 1942–1970* (Americus, Ga.: Koinonia Partners, 1971).

8. Millard Fuller, *Bokotola* (Clinton, N.J.: New Win Publishing, 1977), 21.

9. Arthur Boers, "The Prophet or the President?" *The Other Side,* January/February 1988, 33.

10. Lee, *The Cotton Patch Evidence,* 186.

11. Ibid.

12. Boers, "The Prophet or the President," 34.

13. Lee, *The Cotton Patch Evidence,* 208.

14. Fuller, *Bokotola,* 17.

15. Fuller and Scott, *Love in the Mortar Joints,* 65.

16. Fuller, *Bokotola,* 17.

17. Ibid., 18.

18. In Fuller's books, this scripture passage, along with most others, is taken from *Today's English Version of the Bible,* 2d ed. (New York: American Bible Society, 1992). Another frequently quoted passage, similarly denunciatory of usury, is Leviticus 25:35–37, which reads: "And if your brother becomes poor, and cannot maintain himself with you, you shall maintain him; as a stranger and a sojourner he shall live with you. Take no interest from him or increase, but fear your God; that your brother may live beside you. You shall not lend him your money at interest, nor give him your food for profit."

19. Fuller and Scott, *Love in the Mortar Joints,* 82.

20. Quoted from the minutes taken during the Habitat for Humanity conference, Koinonia Farm, September 24–26, 1976.

21. Uttered repeatedly (and in disparate versions) by Burnham, these well-known lines—not originally in the poetic form in which they appear in the minutes of the 1976 conference at Koinonia Farm—are recorded in Charles Moore, *Daniel H. Burnham: Architect and Planner of Cities* (Boston: Houghton Mifflin Company, 1921), 147.

22. Patrick O'Toole, "Housing's Giants: Market Says More and the Industry's Biggest Deliver," *Professional Builder* 65, no. 5 (April 2000): 61–110.

23. Quoted from the minutes taken during the Habitat for Humanity conference, September 24–26, 1976.

24. Habitat for Humanity International, *Affiliate Operations Manual*, 5 vols. (Americus, Ga.: Habitat for Humanity International, 1993), 1:145.

25. Millard Fuller and Diane Scott, *No More Shacks! The Daring Vision of Habitat for Humanity* (Waco, Texas: Word Books, 1986), 22.

26. Ibid., 20.

27. *Church Relations News*, January 1995, 7.

28. Taken from a promotional brochure for Habitat for Humanity International. Entitled "Opportunities for International Service," it circulated between 1988 and 1990.

29. See Fuller and Scott's chapter, "A Conscience for the World," in *No More Shacks!* 188–95.

30. *Habitat World*, December 1984, 3.

31. For a thoughtful explanation of the role of the prophet as "criticizing" injustices and "energizing" people for the task of establishing justice with an alternative vision of the world, see Walter Brueggemann, *The Prophetic Imagination* (Philadelphia: Fortress Press, 1978).

32. Habitat for Humanity International, *Affiliate Operations Manual*, 4:50.

33. John R. Alexander, ed., *How to Start a Habitat for Humanity Affiliate: Guidelines for Developing an Effective Partnership Housing Program* (Americus, Ga.: Habitat for Humanity International, 1989), 18.

34. Bonnie Watson, "Reaching Our Neighbors Worldwide," *The Affiliate Update: A Resource for Affiliate Board Members of Habitat for Humanity*, May/June 1996, 5.

35. Carl Umland, "A Tithing Perspective," *The Affiliate Update*, December 1996, 11.

36. For a classic discussion of the importance of utopian visions to spur social action, see Karl Mannheim, *Ideology and Utopia: An Introduction to the Sociology of Knowledge* (New York: Harcourt Brace Jovanovich, 1936).

37. Millard Fuller, "Building the Kingdom of God," in *Kingdom Building: Essays from the Grassroots of Habitat*, ed. David Johnson Rowe and Robert William Stevens (Americus, Ga.: Habitat for Humanity International, 1984), 14.

38. This sort of dichotomy is also evident in the Gospel accounts of Jesus' ministry. At certain points, he is portrayed as preaching an already existent kingdom, as in the line from Mark, "The time is fulfilled, and the Kingdom of God is at hand; repent, and believe in the gospel" (Mark 1:14). However, at other times, the Gospels seem to suggest that he understood the kingdom as not yet an earthly reality; for example, the Lord's Prayer includes the line, "Thy Kingdom come. Thy will be done, on earth as it is in heaven" (Matt. 6:19).

39. For an elaboration of this dual function of symbols, especially as it pertains to religious symbolism, see Clifford Geertz, "Religion as a Cultural System," in his *The Interpretation of Cultures* (New York: Basic Books, 1973), 87–125.

40. Bob Stevens, "What Has the Building of Houses to Do with the Gospel?" in Rowe and Stevens, *Kingdom Building*, 62.

41. Quoted in Millard Fuller and Linda Fuller, *The Excitement Is Building: How Habitat for Humanity Is Putting Roofs over Heads and Hope in Hearts* (Dallas: Word Publishing, 1990), 15.

42. Dallas Lee, ed., *The Substance of Faith and Other Sermons by Clarence Jordan* (New York: Association Press, 1972), 33.

43. For an influential explanation of the various dimensions of religiosity (belief, practice, knowledge, experience, and consequences), see Rodney Stark and Charles Y. Glock, *American Piety: The Nature of Religious Commitment*, vol. 1 (Berkeley: University of California Press, 1970).

44. *The Excitement is Building*, 18 min., Habitat for Humanity International, 1989, videocassette.

45. See Leonardo Boff and Clodovis Boff, *Introducing Liberation Theology* (Maryknoll, N.Y.: Orbis Books, 1989), 49–50.

46. Robert G. Bratcher, "The Biblical Mandate for Habitat," in Rowe and Stevens, *Kingdom Building*, 32.

47. Millard Fuller, "Sunday's a Coming," ibid., 46.

48. Clyde Tilley, "Habitat for Humanity: A Holistic Ministry," ibid., 34–35.

49. Fuller and Scott, *No More Shacks!* 127–28.

50. Fuller and Scott, *Love in the Mortar Joints*, 89.

51. See Fuller and Scott's chapter "The Economics of Jesus," ibid., 85–99.

52. This change in policy has allowed Habitat to make use of VISTA and AmeriCorps volunteers, who are increasingly found on affiliate staff rosters.

53. Fuller and Fuller, *The Excitement is Building*, 40.

Chapter Three

1. Andrew Slavitt, "Habitat for Humanity International" (unpublished paper, Harvard Business School, 1993).

2. Personal communication with a staff member in Habitat International's Campus Chapters Department.

3. *1999 Annual Report* (Americus, Ga.: Habitat for Humanity International, 2000), 6.

4. These affiliates are: Greater Cleveland Habitat for Humanity (HFH); Sandtown HFH (Baltimore); North Central Philadelphia HFH; and Newark HFH.

5. Data from a 1993 self-study undertaken by Habitat show that among volunteers who serve on affiliate boards of directors, 84 percent are white, 12 percent are black, 2 percent are Hispanic, and fewer than 1 percent are either Native American, Asian, or Pacific Islander. The one-third of all U.S. affiliates with paid staff evince a comparable racial profile among their employees: 87 percent white, 9 percent black, and 2 percent Hispanic, with Native Americans, Asians, and Pacific Islanders each representing less than 1 percent of affiliate staff members. Because Habitat works so extensively in minority communities, one might expect to see greater numbers of their residents partnering with local affiliates. Given that 56 percent of all Habitat homeowners are black and another 12 percent are Hispanic, the organization's ideal of working *with* rather than *for* those in need certainly calls for greater representation of those communities on staff and volunteer rosters. Moving closer to that ideal is an important and frequently discussed goal for the organization's future, as the existence of the Diversity Department indicates. "Affiliate Survey," Habitat for Humanity International, 1993.

6. For the sake of completeness, brief mention of the other initiatives within the domain of Public Awareness and Education may be helpful. The duties of the Media Relations Department are probably obvious. Given the increasing media coverage of Habitat events, however, handling the media skillfully has become both more complicated and more critical for the organization. The Department of the Environment helps affiliates locate the most appropriate building materials for their projects and tries to ensure that all Habitat construction remains low-cost, energy efficient, and environmentally benign. Habitat for Humanity with Disabilities provides technical and financial assistance to affiliates who are building barrier-free homes. Other relatively minor services and projects exist and others have come and gone. All told, this listing suggests what informing people's consciences about the problem of inadequate housing means in practice and indicates the sizable resources Habitat is willing to mobilize in order to do so.

7. This is also a role that is recognized by the local U.S. affiliates. According to Habitat's 1993 self-study, 83 percent of affiliates had someone representing them at an annual conference and 61 percent sent someone to a state meeting. Fifty-six percent sent someone to a one-day training session, and 49 percent of affiliates were represented at a two-to four-day training event. Also, individuals from a full 21 percent of all affiliates reported attending a nationwide conference sponsored by Habitat International. "Affiliate Survey," Habitat for Humanity International, 1993.

8. *Habitat World*, with a circulation exceeding one million, is an educational and promotional magazine published six times per year. It is mailed free of charge to contributors and to those who request it. The *Affiliate Update* is a free publication that provides nuts-and-bolts administrative and policy information for people who are active in Habitat affiliates, especially board members. Other free departmental newsletters are *Church Relations News*, Campus Chapters' *Frameworks*, Global Village's *Habitat Global Adventure*, and *News from Africa*.

9. So successful was this event that other fund- and consciousness-raising walks were undertaken afterward. Habitat's tenth anniversary was celebrated with a thousand-mile walk from Americus to Kansas City; a much-publicized, twelve-hundred-mile walk from Portland, Maine, to Atlanta marked its twelfth year of existence. These walks were also accompanied by various blitz builds and other promotional events scheduled to coincide with the walkers' progress along their routes.

10. Fuller and Scott describe the beginnings of his relationship with Carter in a chapter entitled "A Presidential Partner" in *No More Shacks!* 73–83.

11. Gaillard, *If I Were a Carpenter*, 47.

12. Jim Newton, "Habitat for Humanity: The Hope Homes," *Missions USA* (November/December 1984), 37.

13. Ibid. The passage Carter chose is from Matthew 6:2–3, which reads, "Thus, when you give alms, sound no trumpet before you, as the hypocrites do in the synagogues and in the streets, that they may be praised by men. Truly, I say to you, they have received their reward. But when you give alms, do not let your left hand know what your right hand is doing" (RSV).

14. That cost, however, varies significantly with relation to location. For example, Habitat houses in Maine are the least expensive with an average cost of $12,711, while they cost an average of $61,250 in the state of Nevada. Similar discrepancies

are found between houses built in rural areas and the more expensive projects undertaken by urban affiliates. Also, while the average cost of Habitat houses in the United States has increased slowly over the past couple of decades, this has been less true abroad. Houses built by international affiliates still cost an average of $2,000.

15. Department of Housing and Urban Development, *Making Homeownership a Reality: Survey of Habitat for Humanity International Homeowners and Affiliates* (Washington, D.C.: Government Printing Office, 1998).

16. "Affiliate Survey," Habitat for Humanity International, 1993.

17. Peter Dreier, "The New Politics of Housing," *Journal of the American Planning Association* 63, no. 1 (Winter 1997).

18. Department of Housing and Urban Development, *Rental Housing Assistance at a Crossroads: A Report to Congress on Worst Case Housing Needs* (Washington, D.C.: Government Printing Office, 1996).

19. Jason DeParle, "Slamming the Door," *New York Times Magazine*, October 20, 1996.

20. For his classic discussion of manifest and latent functions, see Robert K. Merton, *Social Theory and Social Structure* (New York: Free Press, 1968), 73–138.

Chapter Four

1. This sort of organizational structure, by which the affiliate is divided into separate (though not separately incorporated) chapters, is rare, but it seems to work in large metropolitan areas, where a number of affiliates would tend to compete with one another for community support. In addition to the St. Paul chapter, the Twin Cities affiliate consists of Southside Minneapolis, Northside Minneapolis, Northeast Suburban, and the Dakota County chapters.

2. This is mostly because of the financial complexities and potential legalities involved. Indeed, at the time of my visit the Twin Cities affiliate had just begun foreclosing on a defaulted homeowner from the Southside Minneapolis chapter. The affiliate's executive director felt confident that they could work with the homeowner family and perhaps grant them another extension. He was also concerned that, should the family default, they would have to be evicted during the Christmas season, an outcome that would benefit neither the family nor the affiliate's public relations efforts.

3. Michael Walzer, "The Problem of Citizenship," *Obligations: Essays on Disobedience, War, and Citizenship* (Cambridge, Mass.: Harvard University Press, 1970), 225.

4. According to Aristotle's classic definition, "The citizen in this strict sense is best defined by the one criterion, 'a man who shares in the administration of justice and in the holding of office.'" *Politics*, trans. Ernest Barker (New York: Oxford University Press, 1962), bk. III, chap. 1, 93.

5. Ibid., bk. VII, chap. 4, 292. It is important to recognize, however, that in Athens this pluralist ideal excluded women, foreign-born "metics," and slaves from the status and responsibility of citizenship.

6. See Robert A. Dahl's discussion of the "second democratic transformation" from the city-state to the nation-state in *Democracy and Its Critics* (New Haven: Yale University Press, 1989), 213–24.

7. See, for example, Herbert Gans, *Middle-American Individualism: The Future of Liberal Democracy* (New York: Free Press, 1988).

8. Sara M. Evans and Harry C. Boyte, *Free Spaces: The Sources of Democratic Change in America* (New York: Harper and Row, 1986).

9. I will refrain from discussing the outcomes of those four family-selection decisions for two reasons. First, it was the tenor of the actual discursive process that I most wanted to convey to the reader. Second, given the autonomy of local affiliates, the decisions of the St. Paul board would almost certainly differ from those of affiliate boards in other locations, both in the United States and especially abroad.

10. I use the qualifier "benign" lest we forget that the voluntary sector is also the seedbed of such malign, uncivil groups such as the Ku Klux Klan and, more recently, gun-toting militia groups.

11. *The Federalist Papers*, ed. Roy P. Fairfield (Garden City, N.Y.: Anchor Books, 1966), no. 51, 162. It should also be mentioned that this compilation of papers arguing in support of a federal constitution was written by Madison as well as Alexander Hamilton and John Jay. The authorship of some of the eighty-five papers has been disputed, but Douglass Adair has made the convincing claim that Hamilton wrote fifty-one papers, Madison twenty-nine, and Jay, due to illness, only five. See Adair, "A Note on Certain of Hamilton's Pseudonyms," *William and Mary Quarterly*, 3d ser., 12 (April 1955).

12. Kara Van Vonderen, "Habitat for Humanity: An Examination of the Process and Effects of Homeownership," master's thesis, Bethel College, 1996. This study focused on the Twin Cities affiliate.

13. Tilly Grey, "This Lady Is Really Cookin' Now: Habitat Homeowner Proves That Dreams Can Come True," *Habitat World*, April 1994, 6.

14. Terri Franklin, "Catch a Rising Star: Imelda Jackson's Day Care Center Brings New Hope for the Future," *Habitat World*, December 1994, 6.

15. Jim Purks, "Love the Lord . . . and Pay Your Bills: Habitat Homeowner Mary Stone Is Getting Her Family Out of Debt," *Habitat World*, April 1992, 12.

16. Sharon McPerson-Mullins, "The Mullins Miracle: Going from Homeless to Fearless and Taking Habitat Along," *Habitat World*, August 1990, 13.

17. Karen Free, "This Family's Going Places," *Habitat World*, April/May 1996, 6–7.

18. Terri Franklin, "What Is a Habitat House? More Than Roofs and Floors or Windows and Doors," *Habitat World*, June 1994, 12–13.

19. These figures, based on the study done by Kim Koscianski of Augsburg College in Minnesota, are reported in *The Affiliate Update*, June 1994, 1–2.

20. Amitai Etzioni, *A Comparative Analysis of Complex Organizations*, rev. ed. (New York: Free Press, 1975).

21. See, for example, Kevin Phillips, *The Politics of Rich and Poor: Wealth and the American Electorate in the Reagan Aftermath* (New York: Harper Collins, 1990).

22. Henry David Thoreau, *Walden* (New York: New American Library, 1980), 56.

23. Jean-Jacques Rousseau, *The Social Contract and the Discourse on the Origin of Inequality*, ed. Lester G. Crocker (New York: Pocket Books, 1967).

24. The practitioner of "telescopic philanthropy" in Dickens's *Bleak House* (New York: Bantam, 1983) is Mrs. Jellyby, a woman devoted to improving the economy and education of the denizens of Borrioboola-Gha, on the bank of the Niger River. In pursuing this passion, though, she neglected her more proximate responsibilities, which, alas, included tending to her own children.

25. For a discussion of why this polarization of political opinion leads to "absurd bifurcations," see Jim Wallis, *The Soul of Politics: Beyond "Religious Right" and "Secular Left"* (New York: Harcourt Brace, 1995). Cornel West's essay "Nihilism in Black America" in *Race Matters* (New York: Vintage Books, 1994), pp. 17–31, is also useful for distinguishing between what he calls "conservative behaviorists" and "liberal structuralists."

26. E. J. Dionne, Jr., *Why Americans Hate Politics* (New York: Touchstone, 1991).

27. Douglas S. Massey and Nancy A. Denton, *American Apartheid: Segregation and the Making of the Underclass* (Cambridge: Harvard University Press, 1993), 16.

28. Robert B. Reich, *The Work of Nations: Preparing Ourselves for Twenty-First-Century Capitalism* (New York: Vintage Books, 1992), 302–3.

29. For insightful discussion regarding the relation of voluntarism to leisure, see Roger A. Lohmann, *The Commons: New Perspectives on Nonprofit Organizations and Voluntary Action* (San Francisco: Jossey-Bass, 1992).

Chapter Five

1. Jurgen Habermas, *The Theory of Communicative Action*, vol. 2, *Lifeworld and System*, trans. Thomas McCarthy (Boston: Beacon Press, 1987).

2. John Stuart Mill, *Representative Government* (New York: Everyman, 1910), 217.

3. John Stuart Mill, *Utilitarianism, On Liberty, Essay on Bentham* (New York: Meridian, 1974), 243.

4. One thinks of Robert Michels's discussion of the "iron law of oligarchy" by which organizations inevitably become "divided into a minority of directors and a majority of directed." See his classic *Political Parties: A Sociological Study of the Oligarchical Tendencies of Modern Democracy* (New York: Free Press, 1962).

5. For a discussion of the tensions that can occur between executive directors of nonprofits and volunteers, see Steven Rathgeb Smith and Michael Lipsky, *Nonprofits for Hire: The Welfare State in the Age of Contracting* (Cambridge, Mass.: Harvard University Press, 1993), 72–97.

6. Quoted in Andrew Slavitt, "Habitat for Humanity International" (unpublished paper, Harvard Business School, 1993).

7. Max Weber, *Economy and Society: An Outline of Interpretive Sociology*, ed. Guenther Roth and Claus Wittich (Berkeley: University of California Press), 246–54.

8. For an excellent discussion of the problematic necessity of institutionalization for religious groups, see Thomas F. O'Dea and Janet O'Dea Aviad, "Five Dilemmas in the Institutionalization of Religion," *The Sociology of Religion*, 2d ed. (Englewood Cliffs, N.J.: Prentice-Hall, 1983), 56–64.

9. Lester M. Salamon, *Partners in Public Service: Government-Nonprofit Relations in the Modern Welfare State* (Baltimore: Johns Hopkins University Press, 1995), 33–49.

10. Tocqueville, *Democracy in America*, 517.

11. Ibid., 692.

12. Ibid., 254.

13. My understanding of commercialization, as used in this context, has been significantly influenced by the concept of "institutional isomorphism" as peerlessly described by Paul J. DiMaggio and Walter W. Powell in their essay "The Iron Cage Revisited: Institutional Isomorphism and Collective Rationality in Organizational Fields," in *The New Institutionalism in Organizational Analysis*, ed. Walter W. Powell and Paul J. DiMaggio (Chicago: University of Chicago Press, 1991), 63–82.

14. The geographic distribution of the remainder of its U.S. affiliates is as follows: Northeast (15 percent); Midwest (21 percent); Southwest (12 percent), and West (8 percent).

15. Information about how to gain access to these types of resources is plentiful in Habitat's organizational literature intended for affiliate volunteers, boards, and staffs. See, for example, Sarah Birmingham, "Land Acquisition: Government Sources of Property," *The Affiliate Update*, August 1994, 6.

16. "Habitat, HUD, HOPE III, and HOME Partnership," *The Affiliate Update*, March 1994, 5.

17. Michael Willard, "A '1,000-Pound Gorilla' but a Golden Opportunity," *The Affiliate Update*, August/September 1996, 1 3.

18. Affiliates that receive this money must send two representatives to a Habitat International training session on record keeping and program compliance; and once they actually receive the money, affiliates must provide Americus with quarterly reports. This is to ensure that affiliates comply with a multitude of HUD requirements regarding property acquisition, environmental provisions, equal employment opportunity, minority and women's business opportunities, lobbying, drug-free workplaces, lead-based paint removal, and still other issues.

19. Drew Cathell, "Building Costlier Houses: A New Perspective," *The Affiliate Update*, August/September, 1996, 6.

20. The term *de-commodification* is used by Gøsta Esping-Andersen to describe how social welfare policies pry the distribution of social goods from the cash nexus. See his chapter "De-Commodification in Social Policy" in *The Three Worlds of Welfare Capitalism* (Princeton: Princeton University Press, 1990), 35–54.

21. Jon Van Til, *Mapping the Third Sector: Voluntarism in a Changing Social Economy* (New York: Foundation Center, 1988), 215.

22. That phrase, in fact, is quoted from Fuller's chapter on corporate partnerships in his *A Simple, Decent Place to Live*, 181–92.

23. For two excellent analyses of corporate power in the United States that express such suspicions, see Edward S. Herman, *Corporate Control, Corporate Power* (New York: Cambridge University Press, 1981), and G. William Domhoff, *Who Rules America? Power and Politics in the Year 2000* (Mountain View, Calif.: Mayfield Publishing, 1998).

24. Fuller, *A Simple, Decent Place to Live*, 181.

25. Habitat for Humanity International, *Affiliate Operations Manual*, vol. 3 (Americus: Habitat for Humanity International, 1993), 26.

26. Sonja D. Lewis, "The New Campus Chapters Covenant," *The Affiliate Update*, February/March 1996, 11.

27. These are discussed in Jim Purks, "Four Core Messages to Communicate," *The Affiliate Update*, February/March 1996, 3.

28. Doug Bright, "To Plan for the Future, You've Got to Know Where You Are Today," *The Affiliate Update*, November/December 1995, 4.

Chapter Six

1. Juliet B. Schor, *The Overworked American: The Unexpected Decline of Leisure* (New York: Basic Books, 1991).

2. Clifford Geertz, "Thick Description: Toward an Interpretive Theory of Culture," in *The Interpretation of Cultures* (New York: Basic Books, 1973), 5.

3. As Fuller puts it in his *The Theology of the Hammer*, "Churches are the primary partners that work with Habitat in an almost infinite variety of creative overlapping circles. We cherish these partnerships with churches because ... I have always seen Habitat for Humanity as a servant of the church and as a vehicle through which the church and its people can express their love, faith, and servanthood to needy people in a very tangible and concrete (literally!) way" (p. 53).

4. This frequently quoted statement first appeared in *The Excitement is Building*, 18 min., Habitat for Humanity International, 1989, videocassette.

5. Regarding the tight budgets of the churches, see Robert Wuthnow, *Crisis in the Church: Spiritual Malaise and Fiscal Woes* (New York: Oxford University Press, 1997).

6. For these figures, see *Church Relations News*, July 1996, 4–5. Contributions from conservative churches for the same year were: Assemblies of God ($17,000); Churches of Christ ($141,000); Church of God in Christ ($5,000); Church of the Nazarene ($2,500); Seventh-Day Adventist ($16,000); and United Pentecostal Church ($13,000). Contributions that year from the historically black churches were: African Methodist Episcopal ($23,000); African Methodist Episcopal Zion ($2,000); Christian Methodist Episcopal ($15,000); National Baptist Convention of America ($17,000); and National Baptist Convention, USA ($10,000).

7. This is a marked increase over the forty-five houses that were built during the inaugural "Building on Faith" week in 1995.

8. Quoted in Fuller, *The Theology of the Hammer*, 63.

9. This is one of Fuller's frequently used expressions (quoted in Fuller and Fuller, *The Excitement is Building*, 40).

Chapter Seven

1. B'nai B'rith Hillel Foundations provide social, community service, and worship opportunities to Jewish students and faculty on more than four hundred university campuses worldwide. Habitat's partnership with them, as with the rest of the Jewish community in the United States, has been growing in recent years.

2. Wade Clark Roof and William McKinney, *American Mainline Religion: Its Changing Shape and Future* (New Brunswick, N.J.: Rutgers University Press, 1987), 40–71.

3. Robert Wuthnow, *The Restructuring of American Religion*, 71–99.

4. *Presbyterian Panel Report*, cited in Wuthnow, *Christianity in the Twenty-first Century*, 40.

5. George Gallup, Jr., and Jim Castelli, *The People's Religion: American Faith in the Nineties* (New York: Macmillan, 1989), 48.

6. Ibid., 46.

7. George Gallup, Jr., *The Unchurched American—Ten Years Later* (Princeton, N.J.: Princeton Religion Research Center, 1988); cited in Robert Wuthnow, *Sharing the Journey: Support Groups and America's New Quest for Community* (New York: Free Press, 1994), 39.

8. Wade Clark Roof, *A Generation of Seekers: The Spiritual Journeys of the Baby Boom Generation* (San Francisco: Harper Collins, 1993), 235.

9. Dean R. Hoge, Benton Johnson, and Donald A. Luidens, *Vanishing Boundaries: The Religion of Mainline Protestant Baby Boomers* (Louisville, Ky.: Westminster/John Knox Press, 1994).

10. Roof, *A Generation of Seekers*, 67–72.

11. See Dean M. Kelley, *Why Conservative Churches Are Growing: A Study in Sociology of Religion* (New York: Harper and Row, 1972).

12. For a discussion of the manageable limits that volunteer roles can place on people's dedication to community service, see Robert Wuthnow's chapter "Bounded Love" in *Acts of Compassion: Caring for Ourselves and Helping Others* (Princeton, N.J.: Princeton University Press, 1991), 191–220.

13. It should be noted that evangelicalism in the United States is not a monolithic movement. For discussions of the more socially progressive "new evangelicals," see Richard Quebedeaux, *The Worldly Evangelicals* (San Francisco: Harper and Row, 1978), and James Davison Hunter, *Evangelicalism: The Coming Generation* (Chicago: University of Chicago Press, 1987).

14. Habitat for Humanity International, *Affiliate Operations Manual*, vol. 1 (Americus, Ga.: Habitat for Humanity International, 1993), 18.

15. See, for example, Andrew Greeley, *The Denominational Society: A Sociological Approach to Religion in America* (Glenview, Ill.: Scott, Foresman, 1972), 5–29. Regarding these two foci, Greeley writes: "Not everything that man perceives as extraordinary becomes sacred, but when the extraordinary touches on ultimate meaning or ultimate belonging, on the answers to the basic questions and the relationships which constitute the basic fellowship, man is so impressed by their importance that he treats them as though they were very different from anything else that happens in his life. Religion is nothing more than a set of symbols—doctrinal, moral, ritual, and organizational—that man has evolved for organizing his relationship with the sacred" (p. 28).

16. Philip Rieff, *The Triumph of the Therapeutic: Uses of Faith after Freud* (Chicago: University of Chicago Press, 1966), 252.

17. Quoted in Bellah et al., *Habits of the Heart*, 233.

18. Gallup and Castelli, *The People's Religion*, 46.

19. Amos 6:21–24.

20. Roof discusses the impressive diffusion of tolerance among baby boomers; a full 87 percent in his survey said there should be more acceptance of different lifestyles in society. See *Generation of Seekers*, 45.

21. Ibid., 80.

22. George Gallup, Jr., *Faith Development and Your Ministry* (Princeton, N.J.: Princeton Religion Research Center, 1985). A discussion of these figures and the "yearning for the spiritual" in modern American culture appears in Robert Wuthnow's *Sharing the Journey*, 32–33.

23. Paul Tillich, *Systematic Theology*, vol. 1 (Chicago: University of Chicago Press, 1951), 11–15.

24. See "The Virtues, the Unity of a Human Life and the Concept of a Tradition," in Alasdair MacIntyre, *After Virtue: A Study in Moral Theory* (Notre Dame, Ind.: University of Notre Dame Press, 1981), 190–209.

25. See Robert J. Lifton, *The Protean Self* (New York: Basic Books, 1993).

26. Anthony Giddens, *Modernity and Self-Identity: Self and Society in the Late Modern Age* (Stanford, Calif.: Stanford University Press, 1991), 5.

27. Peter L. Berger, *A Rumor of Angels: Modern Society and the Rediscovery of the Supernatural* (Garden City, N.Y.: Doubleday, 1969), 61–94. Writes Berger, "By signals of transcendence I mean phenomena that are to be found within the domain of our 'natural' reality but that appear to point beyond that reality" (pp. 65–66).

28. The classic text is William James's *The Varieties of Religious Experience* (1902; reprint, New York: New American Library, 1958). For Cox's analysis of how the desire for religious experience has fueled the Pentecostal movement in the United States, see his *Fire from Heaven: The Rise of Pentecostal Spirituality and the Reshaping of Religion in the Twenty-First Century* (New York: Addison-Wesley, 1995).

29. Tex Sample, *U.S. Lifestyles and Mainline Churches: A Key to Reaching People in the Nineties* (Louisville, Ky.: Westminster/John Knox Press, 1990).

30. Daniel Yankelovich, *New Rules: Searching for Self-Fulfillment in a World Turned Upside Down* (New York: Random House, 1981).

31. Troeltsch, *The Social Teachings of the Christian Churches*, 991–1013.

32. Karl Marx and Friedrich Engels, *The Communist Manifesto* (New York: Oxford University Press, 1998), 16.

Chapter Eight

1. Quoted in Jeremy Rifkin, *The End of Work: The Decline of the Global Labor Force and the Dawn of the Post-Market Era* (New York: Tarcher/Putnam, 1995), 245.

2. Wuthnow, *Acts of Compassion*, 10.

3. Quoted in Morton Hunt, *The Compassionate Beast: The Scientific Inquiry into Human Altruism* (New York: Doubleday, 1990), 12.

4. Alfie Kohn, *The Brighter Side of Human Nature: Altruism and Empathy in Everyday Life* (New York: Basic Books, 1990), 204.

5. Charles Horton Cooley, *Social Organization: A Study of the Larger Mind* (New York: Scribner's, 1909); cited in Kohn, *The Brighter Side of Human Nature*, v.

6. For a fuller explanation of this view of institutions—"normative patterns embedded in and enforced by laws and mores (informal customs and practices)"—see Bellah et al., *The Good Society*, 4–18, 287–93. Other instructive treatments of institutions are found in Mary Douglas, *How Institutions Think* (Syracuse, N.Y.: Syracuse University Press, 1986), and W. Richard Scott, *Institutions and Organizations* (Thousand Oaks, Calif.: Sage Publications, 1995).

7. E. J. Dionne, *Why Americans Hate Politics* (New York: Touchstone, 1992), 20.

8. Martin E. Marty, *The Public Church: Mainline-Evangelical-Catholic* (New York: Crossroad Publishing, 1981).

9. Philip Selznick, *The Moral Commonwealth: Social Theory and the Promise of Community* (Berkeley: University of California Press, 1992), 387–427.

10. Bellah et al., *Habits of the Heart*, 47.

11. See Rosabeth Moss Kanter, *Commitment and Community: Communes and Utopias in Sociological Perspective* (Cambridge, Mass.: Harvard University Press, 1972).

12. Robert Wuthnow, "Tocqueville's Question Reconsidered: Voluntarism and Public Discourse in Advanced Industrial Societies," in Robert Wuthnow, ed., *Between States and Markets: The Voluntary Sector in Comparative Perspective* (Princeton, N.J.: Princeton University Press, 1991), 305.

13. T. H. Marshall, *Citizenship and Social Class and Other Essays* (Cambridge: Cambridge University Press, 1950).

14. Katherine T. Beddingfield, "Sizing Up the Biggest: Stories and Stats of 50 American Charities," *U.S. News and World Report*, December 4, 1995, 88–95.

15. Quoted from Brian O'Connell, *America's Voluntary Spirit: A Book of Readings* (New York: The Foundation Center, 1983). The original citation is from Jane Addams, *Democracy and Social Ethics*, ed. Anne Firor Scott (Cambridge, Mass.: Belknap Press, 1964).

16. For a discussion of such "voluntary failures" as "philanthropic particularism" and "philanthropic insufficiency," see Salamon, *Partners in Public Service*, 33–52.

17. William M. Sullivan, "Reinstitutionalizing Virtue in Civil Society," in *Seedbeds of Virtue: Sources of Competence, Character, and Citizenship in American Society*, ed. Mary Ann Glendon and David Blankenhorn (New York: Madison Books, 1995), 192.

18. Bellah et al., *Habits of the Heart*, 219.

19. Quoted in Laurent A. Parks Daloz et al., *Common Fire: Lives of Commitment in a Complex World* (Boston: Beacon Press, 1996), 202. The original citation is from William Sloane Coffin, *Alive Now!* May/June 1993, 37.

20. Quoted in Theodore Draper, "Hume and Madison: The Secrets of Federalist Paper No. 10," *Encounter* 58 (1982): 47; cited in Bellah et al., *Habits of the Heart*, 254.

21. Cited in Linell E. Cady, *Religion, Theology, and American Public Life* (Albany: State University of New York Press, 1993), 19.

22. Wolfe, *Whose Keeper?* 30.

Selected Bibliography

Primary Sources

Alexander, John R., ed. *How to Start a Habitat for Humanity Affiliate: Guidelines for Developing an Effective Partnership Housing Program*. Americus, Ga.: Habitat for Humanity International, 1989.

Fuller, Millard. *Bokotola*. Clinton, N.J.: New Win Publishing, 1977.

———. "Habitat for Humanity: Changing the World One House at a Time." In *Housing America: Mobilizing Bankers, Builders and Communities to Solve the Nation's Affordable Housing Crisis*, ed. Jess Lederman. Chicago: Probus Publishing, 1993.

———. *The Theology of the Hammer*. Macon, Ga.: Smyth and Helwys, 1994.

———. *A Simple, Decent Place to Live: The Building Realization of Habitat for Humanity*. Americus, Ga.: Habitat for Humanity International, 1995.

———. *More Than Houses: How Habitat for Humanity Is Transforming Lives and Neighborhoods*. Nashville: Word Publishing, 2000.

Fuller, Millard, and Linda Fuller. *The Excitement Is Building*. Dallas: Word Publishing, 1990.

Fuller, Millard, and Diane Scott. *Love in the Mortar Joints: The Story of Habitat for Humanity*. Clinton, N.J.: New Win Publishing, 1980.

———. *No More Shacks! The Daring Vision of Habitat for Humanity*. Waco: Word Books, 1986.

Gaillard, Frye. *If I Were a Carpenter: Twenty Years of Habitat for Humanity*. Winston-Salem, N.C.: John F. Blair, 1996.

Habitat for Humanity International. *Affiliate Operations Manual*, vols. 1–5. Americus, Ga.: Habitat for Humanity International, 1993.

———. *Habitat for Humanity International: 1993 Annual Report*. Americus, Ga.: Habitat for Humanity International, 1993.

———. *Habitat for Humanity Five-Year Plan*. Americus, Ga.: Habitat for Humanity International, 1994.

———. *Habitat for Humanity International: 1994 Annual Report*. Americus, Ga.: Habitat for Humanity International, 1994.

———. *Habitat for Humanity International: 1995 Annual Report*. Americus, Ga.: Habitat for Humanity International, 1995.

———. *Habitat for Humanity International: 1996 Annual Report.* Americus, Ga.: Habitat for Humanity International, 1996.

———. *Building the Future: 1995 Year Book.* Americus, Ga.: Habitat for Humanity International, 1996.

———. *Habitat World.* Americus, Ga.: Habitat for Humanity International, 1976–1999.

———. *The Affiliate Update.* Americus, Ga.: Habitat for Humanity International, 1990–1999.

———. *Church Relations News.* Americus, Ga.: Habitat for Humanity International, 1993–1999.

Lee, Dallas. *The Cotton Patch Evidence: The Story of Clarence Jordan and the Koinonia Farm Experiment (1942–1970).* Americus, Ga.: Koinonia Partners, 1971.

Rowe, David Johnson, and Robert William Stevens. *Kingdom Building: Essays from the Grassroots of Habitat.* Americus, Ga.: Habitat for Humanity International, 1984.

Secondary Sources

Adams, James Luther. *The Prophethood of All Believers.* Boston: Beacon Press, 1986.

———. *Voluntary Associations: Socio-cultural Analyses and Theological Interpretation,* ed. J. Ronald Engel. Chicago: Exploration Press, 1986.

Ahlstrom, Sydney E. *A Religious History of the American People.* New Haven: Yale University Press, 1972.

Albanese, Catherine L. *America: Religions and Religion.* 2d ed. Belmont, Calif.: Wadsworth Publishing Company, 1992.

Ammerman, Nancy Tatom. *Congregation and Community.* New Brunswick, N.J.: Rutgers University Press, 1997.

Anheier, Helmut K., and Wolfgang Seibel, eds. *The Third Sector: Comparative Studies of Nonprofit Organizations.* Berlin: De Gruyter, 1990.

Arendt, Hannah. *The Human Condition.* Chicago: University of Chicago Press, 1958.

Barbalet, J. M. *Citizenship: Rights, Struggle, and Class Inequality.* Minneapolis: University of Minnesota Press, 1988.

Barber, Benjamin. *Strong Democracy: Participatory Politics for a New Age.* Berkeley: University of California Press, 1984.

Beckford, James A. *Religion and Advanced Industrial Society.* Boston: Unwin Hyman, 1989.

Bellah, Robert N. *Beyond Belief: Essays on Religion in a Post-Traditionalist World.* Berkeley: University of California Press, 1970.

Bellah, Robert N., Richard Madsen, William M. Sullivan, Ann Swidler, and Steven M. Tipton. *Habits of the Heart: Individualism and Commitment in American Life.* Berkeley: University of California Press, 1985.

———. *The Good Society.* New York: Vintage Books, 1991.

Berger, Peter L. *The Sacred Canopy: Elements of a Sociological Theory of Religion.* Garden City, N.Y.: Doubleday, 1967.

———. *A Rumor of Angels: Modern Society and the Rediscovery of the Supernatural.* New York: Doubleday, 1969.

———. *The Heretical Imperative: Contemporary Possibilities of Religious Affirmation.* Garden City, N.Y.: Anchor Books, 1979.

Berger, Peter L., Brigitte Berger, and Hansfried Kellner. *The Homeless Mind: Modernization and Consciousness.* New York: Vintage Books, 1973.

Berger, Peter L., and Richard John Neuhaus. *To Empower the People: The Role of Mediating Structures in Public Policy.* Washington, D.C.: AEI Press, 1977.

Bloom, Harold. *The American Religion: The Emergence of the Post-Christian Nation.* New York: Touchstone, 1992.

Borgmann, Albert. *Crossing the Postmodern Divide.* Chicago: University of Chicago Press, 1992.

Bratt, Rachel G., Langley C. Keyes, Alex Schwartz, and Avis C. Vidal. *Confronting the Management Challenge: Affordable Housing in the Nonprofit Sector.* New York: Community Development Research Center, 1994.

Bremmer, Robert H. *American Philanthropy,* 2d ed. Chicago: University of Chicago Press, 1988.

Brown, H. James, and others. *The State of the Nation's Housing.* Cambridge: Harvard University Joint Center for Housing Studies, 1995.

Bulmer, Martin. *The Social Basis of Community Care.* Boston: Allen and Unwin, 1987.

Burke, Edmund. *Reflections on the Revolution in France.* New York: Penguin Books, 1969

Cady, Linell E. *Religion, Theology, and American Public Life.* Albany: State University of New York Press, 1993.

Calhoun, Craig, ed. *Habermas and the Public Sphere.* Cambridge, Mass.: MIT Press, 1992

Carter, Stephen L. *The Culture of Disbelief: How American Law and Politics Trivialize Religious Devotion.* New York: Anchor Books, 1993.

Casanova, Jose. *Public Religions in the Modern World.* Chicago: University of Chicago Press, 1994.

Cass, Rosemary Higgins, and Gordon Manser. *Voluntarism at the Crossroads.* New York: Family Service Association of America, 1976.

Cherry, Conrad, and Rowland A. Sherrill, eds. *Religion, the Independent Sector, and American Culture.* Atlanta: Scholars Press, 1992.

Clecak, Peter. *America's Quest for the Ideal Self: Dissent and Fulfillment in the Sixties and Seventies.* New York: Oxford University Press, 1983.

Coates, Roger. *Making Room at the Inn: Congregational Investment in Affordable Housing.* Washington, D.C.: Churches Conference on Shelter and Housing, 1991.

Cohen, Jean L., and Andrew Arato. *Civil Society and Political Theory.* Cambridge, Mass.: MIT Press, 1992.

Cohen, Joshua, and Joel Rogers, eds. *Associations and Democracy.* New York: Verso, 1995.

Cohen, Ronald. "Altruism and the Evolution of Civil Society." In *Embracing the Other: Philosophical, Psychological, and Historical Perspectives on Altruism,* ed. Pearl M. Oliner and others. New York: New York University Press, 1992.

Colby, Anne, and William Damon. *Some Do Care: Contemporary Lives of Moral Commitment.* New York: Free Press, 1992.

Coleman, John A., S.J. *An American Strategic Theology.* New York: Paulist Press, 1982.

———. "The Two Pedagogies: Discipleship and Citizenship." In *Education for Citizenship and Discipleship*, ed. Mary C. Boys. New York: Pilgrim Press, 1989.

———. "Under the Cross and the Flag: Reflections on Discipleship and Citizenship in America." *America* 174, no. 16 (May 11, 1996): 6–14.

Coles, Robert. *The Call of Service: A Witness to Idealism.* New York: Houghton Mifflin, 1993.

Cuddihy, John Murray. *No Offense: Civil Religion and Protestant Taste.* New York: Seabury Press, 1978.

Dahl, Robert A. *Democracy and Its Critics.* New Haven: Yale University Press, 1989.

Daloz, Laurent A. Parks, Cheryl H. Keen, James P. Keen, and Sharon Daloz Parks. *Common Fire: Lives of Commitment in a Complex World.* Boston: Beacon Press, 1996.

Davidson, James D. *Mobilizing Social Movement Organizations: The Formation, Institutionalization, and Effectiveness of Ecumenical Urban Ministries.* Storrs, Conn.: Society for the Scientific Study of Religion, 1985.

Davis, Bertha. *America's Housing Crisis.* New York: Impact Books, 1990.

Delaat, Jacqueline. "Volunteering as Linkage in the Three Sectors." *Journal of Voluntary Action Research* 16 (1987): 97–111.

Dionne, E. J., Jr. *Why Americans Hate Politics.* New York: Touchstone, 1992.

———, ed. *Community Works: The Revival of Civil Society in America.* Washington, D.C.: Brookings Institution Press, 1998.

Douglas, James. *Why Charity? The Case for a Third Sector.* Beverly Hills: Sage Publications, 1983.

Douglas, Mary. *How Institutions Think.* Syracuse, N.Y.: Syracuse University Press, 1986.

Douglas, Mary, and Steven Tipton, eds. *Religion in America: Spiritual Life in a Secular Age.* Boston: Beacon Press, 1982.

Durkheim, Emile. *The Elementary Forms of the Religious Life.* Trans. Karen E. Fields. New York: Free Press, 1995.

Ellis, Susan J., and Katherine H. Noyes. *By the People: A History of Americans as Volunteers.* Rev. ed. San Francisco: Jossey-Bass, 1990.

Elshtain, Jean Bethke. *Democracy on Trial.* New York: Basic Books, 1995.

Esping-Andersen, Gøsta. *The Three Worlds of Welfare Capitalism.* Princeton, N.J.: Princeton University Press, 1990.

Etzioni, Amitai. *Modern Organizations.* Englewood Cliffs, N.J.: Prentice-Hall, 1964.

Evans, Sara M., and Harry C. Boyte. *Free Spaces: The Sources of Democratic Change in America.* New York: Harper and Row, 1986.

Finke, Roger, and Rodney Stark. *The Churching of America: 1776–1990.* New Brunswick, N.J.: Rutgers University Press, 1992.

Fuller, Robert C. *Ecology of Care: An Interdisciplinary Analysis of the Self and Moral Obligation.* Louisville, Ky.: Westminster/John Knox Press, 1992.

Gallup, George, Jr., and Jim Castelli. *The People's Religion: American Faith in the Nineties.* New York: Macmillan, 1989.

Gamwell, Franklin I. *Beyond Preference: Liberal Theories of Independent Association.* Chicago: University of Chicago Press, 1984.

Geertz, Clifford. *The Interpretation of Cultures.* New York: Basic Books, 1973.

Gellner, Ernest. *Conditions of Liberty: Civil Society and Its Rivals.* New York: Penguin Books, 1994.

Giddens, Anthony. *The Constitution of Society: Outline of the Theory of Structuration.* Berkeley: University of California Press, 1984.

———. *The Consequences of Modernity.* Stanford: Stanford University Press, 1990.

———. *Modernity and Self-Identity: Self and Society in the Late Modern Age.* Stanford: Stanford University Press, 1991.

Gidron, Benjamin, Ralph M. Kramer, and Lester Salamon, eds. *Government and the Third Sector: Emerging Relationships in Welfare States.* San Francisco: Jossey-Bass, 1992.

Gilbert, Neil. *Capitalism and the Welfare State: Dilemmas of Social Benevolence.* New Haven: Yale University Press, 1983.

Gitlin, Todd. *The Twilight of Common Dreams: Why America Is Wracked by Culture Wars.* New York: Metropolitan Books, 1995.

Glendon, Mary Ann, and David Blankenhorn, eds. *Seedbeds of Virtue: Sources of Competence, Character, and Citizenship in American Society.* New York: Madison Books, 1995.

Greeley, Andrew M. *The Denominational Society: A Sociological Approach to Religion in America.* Glenview, Ill.: Scott, Foresman, 1972.

———. *Religion: A Secular Theory.* New York: Free Press, 1982.

———. *Religious Change in America.* Cambridge, Mass.: Harvard University Press, 1989.

Gronbjerg, Kristen A. "Patterns of Institutional Relations in the Welfare State: Public Mandates and the Nonprofit Sector." *Journal of Voluntary Action Research* 16 (1987): 64–80.

Habermas, Jurgen. *Legitimation Crisis.* Boston: Beacon Press, 1975.

———. *The Theory of Communicative Action,* vol. 1, *Reason and the Rationalization of Society.* Trans. Thomas McCarthy. Boston: Beacon Press, 1984.

———. *The Theory of Communicative Action,* vol. 2, *Lifeworld and System.* Trans. Thomas McCarthy. Boston: Beacon Press, 1987.

———. *Moral Consciousness and Communicative Action.* Trans. Christian Lenhardt and Shierry Weber Nicholsen. Cambridge, Mass.: MIT Press, 1990.

———. *The Structural Transformation of the Public Square: An Inquiry into a Category of Bourgeois Society.* Trans. Thomas McCarthy. Cambridge, Mass.: MIT Press, 1993.

Hall, Peter Dobkin. "Abandoning the Rhetoric of Independence: Reflections on the Nonprofit Sector in the Post-Liberal Era." *Journal of Voluntary Action Research* 16 (1987): 11–28.

———. *Inventing the Nonprofit Sector: And Other Essays on Philanthropy, Voluntarism, and Nonprofit Organizations.* Baltimore: Johns Hopkins University Press, 1994.

Hammond, Phillip E., ed. *The Sacred in a Secular Age*. Berkeley: University of California Press, 1985.

Hansmann, Henry. "The Role of Nonprofit Enterprise." *Yale Law Review* 89 (1987): 835–901.

Harman, John D., ed. *Volunteerism in the Eighties: Fundamental Issues in Voluntary Action*. Washington, D.C.: University Press of America, 1982.

Hart, Stephen. *What Does the Lord Require? How American Christians Think about Economic Justice*. New York: Oxford University Press, 1992.

Hatch, Nathan O. *The Democratization of American Christianity*. New Haven: Yale University Press, 1989.

Hausknecht, Murray. *The Joiners: A Sociological Description of Voluntary Association Membership in the United States*. New York: Bedminster Press, 1962.

Havel, Vaclav, and others. *The Power of the Powerless: Citizens against the State in Central-Eastern Europe*. Armonk, N.Y.: M. E. Sharpe, 1985.

Hays, R. Allen. *The Federal Government and Urban Housing: Ideology and Change in Public Policy*. 2d ed. Albany: State University of New York Press, 1995.

Hirschman, A. O. *Exit, Voice, and Loyalty*. Cambridge: Harvard University Press, 1970.

Hodgkinson, Virginia Ann. *Motivations for Giving and Volunteering*. New York: Foundation Center, 1990.

Hodgkinson, Virginia Ann, Murray S. Weitzman, and Arthur D. Kirsch. *From Belief to Commitment: The Community Service Activities and Finances of Religious Congregations in the United States*. Washington, D.C.: Independent Sector, 1993.

Hodgkinson, Virginia Ann, Murray S. Weitzman, Christopher M. Toppe, and Stephen M. Noga. *Dimensions of the Independent Sector: A Statistical Profile*. Washington, D.C.: Independent Sector, 1994.

———. *Giving and Volunteering in the United States: Findings from a National Survey*. Washington, D.C.: Independent Sector, 1996.

Hoge, Dean R., Benton Johnson, and Donald A. Luidens. *Vanishing Boundaries: The Religion of Mainline Baby Boomers*. Louisville: Ky.: Westminster/John Knox Press, 1994.

Hohendahl, Peter Uwe. "Critical Theory, Public Sphere, and Culture." *New German Critique* 16 (1979): 89–118.

Hunter, James Davison. *Culture Wars: The Struggle to Define America*. New York: Basic Books, 1991.

Jeavons, Thomas H. *When the Bottom Line Is Faithfulness: Management of Christian Service Organizations*. Indianapolis: Indiana University Press, 1994.

Kanter, Rosabeth Moss. *Commitment and Community: Communes and Utopias in Sociological Perspective*. Cambridge, Mass.: Harvard University Press, 1972.

Knoke, David, and James R. Wood. *Organized for Action: Commitment in Voluntary Associations*. New Brunswick, N.J.: Rutgers University Press, 1981.

Kohn, Alfie. *The Brighter Side of Human Nature: Altruism and Empathy in Everyday Life*. New York: Basic Books, 1990.

Kornhauser, William. *The Politics of Mass Society*. Glencoe, Ill.: Free Press, 1959.

Kosmin, Barry A., and Seymour P. Lachman. *One Nation under God: Religion in Contemporary American Society*. New York: Harmony Books, 1993.

Kramer, Ralph M. *Voluntary Agencies in the Welfare State.* Berkeley: University of California Press, 1984.

Kymlicka, Will, and Wayne Norman. "Return of the Citizen: A Survey of Recent Work on Citizen Theory." *Ethics* 104 (January 1994): 352–81.

Lasch, Christopher. *The Culture of Narcissism: American Life in an Age of Diminishing Expectations.* New York: W. W. Norton, 1978.

Leege, David C., and Lyman A. Kellstedt. *Rediscovering the Religious Factor in American Politics.* Armonk, N.Y.: M. E. Sharpe, 1993.

Lindblom, Charles E. *Politics and Markets: The World's Political-Economic Systems.* New York: Basic Books, 1977.

Lohmann, Roger A. *The Commons: New Perspectives on Nonprofit Organizations and Voluntary Action.* San Francisco: Jossey-Bass, 1992.

Lovin, Robin W., ed. *Religion and American Public Life. Interpretations and Explorations.* New York: Paulist Press, 1986.

Luckmann, Thomas. *The Invisible Religion: The Problem of Religion in Modern Society.* New York: Macmillan, 1967.

Macedo, Stephen. *Liberal Virtues: Citizenship, Virtue and Community.* New York: Oxford University Press, 1990.

MacIntyre, Alasdair. *After Virtue: A Study in Moral Theory.* Notre Dame, Ind.: University of Notre Dame Press, 1981.

Madison, James, et al. *The Federalist Papers.* Ed. Roy P. Fairfield. Garden City, N.Y.: Doubleday, 1966.

Mannheim, Karl. *Ideology and Utopia: An Introduction to the Sociology of Knowledge.* Trans. Louis Wirth and Edward Shils. New York: Harcourt Brace Jovanovich, 1985.

Mansbridge, Jane J., ed. *Beyond Self-Interest.* Chicago: University of Chicago Press, 1990.

Marshall, T. H. *Citizenship and Social Class and Other Essays.* Cambridge: Cambridge University Press, 1950.

Martin, Mike W. *Virtuous Giving: Philanthropy, Voluntary Service, and Caring.* Indianapolis: Indiana University Press, 1994.

Marty, Martin E. *The Public Church: Mainline-Evangelical-Catholic.* New York: Crossroad Publishing, 1981.

———. *Pilgrims in Their Own Land: Five Hundred Years of Religion in America.* New York: Penguin Books, 1984.

McGuire, Meredith B. *Religion: The Social Context.* 2d ed. Belmont, Calif.: Wadsworth Publishing, 1987.

McKnight, John. *The Careless Society: Community and Its Counterfeits.* New York: Basic Books, 1995.

Meister, Albert. *Participation, Associations, Development, and Change.* New Brunswick, N.J.: Transaction Books, 1984.

Michels, Robert. *Political Parties: A Sociological Study of the Oligarchical Tendencies of Modern Democracy.* New York: Free Press, 1962.

Mill, John Stuart. *Utilitarianism, On Liberty, Essay on Bentham.* Ed. Mary Warnock. New York: Meridian, 1974.

Miller, Donald E. *Reinventing American Protestantism: Christianity in the New Millennium.* Berkeley: University of California Press, 1997.

Monsma, Stephen V. *When Sacred and Secular Mix: Religious Nonprofit Organizations and Public Money.* Lanham, Md.: Rowman and Littlefield, 1996.

Mooney, Christopher F., S.J. *Public Virtue: Law and the Social Character of Religion.* Notre Dame, Ind.: University of Notre Dame Press, 1986.

Neuhaus, Richard John. *The Naked Public Square: Religion and Democracy in America.* Grand Rapids, Mich.: Eerdmans Publishing, 1984.

Niebuhr, H. Richard. *Christ and Culture.* New York: Harper and Brothers, 1951.

Nielsen, Waldemar A. *The Endangered Sector.* New York: Columbia University Press, 1979.

Nisbet, Robert. *The Quest for Community: A Study in the Ethics of Order and Freedom.* San Francisco: ICS Press, 1990.

Noddings, Nel. *Caring: A Feminine Approach to Ethics and Moral Education.* Berkeley: University of California Press, 1984.

O'Connell, Brian. *America's Voluntary Spirit: A Book of Readings.* New York: Foundation Center, 1983.

O'Dea, Thomas F., and Janet O'Dea Aviad. *The Sociology of Religion.* 2d ed. Englewood Cliffs, N.J.: Prentice-Hall, 1983.

Oliner, Pearl M., and Samual P. Oliner. *Toward a Caring Society: Ideas into Action.* Westport, Conn.: Praeger, 1995.

Olson, Mancur. *The Logic of Collective Action: Public Goods and the Theory of Groups.* Cambridge: Harvard University Press, 1971.

O'Neill, Michael. *The Third America: The Emergence of the Nonprofit Sector in the United States.* San Francisco: Jossey-Bass, 1989.

Palmer, Parker J. *The Company of Strangers: Christians and the Renewal of America's Public Life.* New York: Crossroad, 1981.

Pateman, Carole. *Participation and Democratic Theory.* Cambridge: Cambridge University Press, 1970.

Paul, Ellen Frankel, ed. *Beneficence, Philanthropy, and the Public Good.* New York: Basil Blackwell, 1987.

Payton, Robert L. *Voluntary Action for the Public Good.* New York: Macmillan, 1988.

Pearce, Jone L. *Volunteers: The Organizational Behavior of Unpaid Workers.* New York: Routledge, 1993.

Pennock, J. Roland, and John W. Chapman, eds. *Voluntary Associations.* New York: Atherton Press, 1969.

Perrow, Charles. *Complex Organizations: A Critical Essay.* 3d ed. New York: Random House, 1986.

Petersen, Rodney L., ed. *Christianity and Civil Society: Theological Education for Public Life.* Maryknoll, N.Y.: Orbis Books, 1995.

Powell, Walter W., ed. *The Nonprofit Sector: A Research Handbook.* New Haven: Yale University Press, 1987.

Powell, Walter W., and Paul J. DiMaggio, eds. *The New Institutionalism in Organizational Analysis.* Chicago: University of Chicago Press, 1991.

Putnam, Robert D. *Making Democracy Work: Civic Traditions in Modern Italy.* Princeton: Princeton University Press, 1993.

————. "Bowling Alone: America's Declining Social Capital." *Journal of Democracy* 6 (Jan. 1995): 65–78.

Radest, Howard B. *Community Service: Encounter with Strangers.* Westport, Conn.: Praeger, 1993.

Reichley, James A. *Religion in American Public Life.* Washington, D.C.: Brookings Institution, 1985.

Rieff, Philip. *The Triumph of the Therapeutic: Uses of Faith after Freud.* Chicago: University of Chicago Press, 1966.

Rifkin, Jeremy. *The End of Work: The Decline of the Global Labor Force and the Dawn of the Post-Market Era.* New York: Tarcher/Putnam, 1995.

Robertson, D. B., ed. *Voluntary Associations: A Study of Groups in Free Societies.* Richmond, Va.: John Knox Press, 1966.

Roof, Wade Clark. *A Generation of Seekers: The Spiritual Journeys of the Baby Boom Generation.* New York: HarperCollins, 1993.

Roof, Wade Clark, and William McKinney. *American Mainline Religion: Its Changing Shape and Future.* New Brunswick, NJ: Rutgers University Press, 1987.

Roozen, David A., William McKinney, and Jackson W. Carroll. *Varieties of Religious Presence: Mission in Public Life.* New York: Pilgrim Press, 1984.

Rousseau, Jean-Jacques. *The Social Contract and the Discourse on the Origin of Inequality.* Ed. Lester G. Crocker. New York: Pocket Books, 1967.

Salamon, Lester M. "Of Market Failure, Voluntary Failure, and Third-Party Government: Toward a Theory of Government-Nonprofit Relations in the Modern Welfare State." *Journal of Voluntary Action Research* 16 (1987): 29–49.

————. *America's Nonprofit Sector: A Primer.* New York: Foundation Center, 1992.

————. *Partners in Public Service: Government-Nonprofit Relations in the Modern Welfare State.* Baltimore: Johns Hopkins University Press, 1995.

Salins, Peter D. *Housing America's Poor.* Chapel Hill, N.C.: University of North Carolina Press, 1987.

Schervish, Paul G., Virginia A. Hodgkinson, and Margaret Gates, eds. *Care and Community in Modern Society: Passing on the Tradition of Service to Future Generations.* San Francisco: Jossey-Bass, 1995.

Schmidt, J. David, Martyn Smith, and Wesley Kenneth Wilmer. *The Prospering Parachurch: Enlarging the Boundaries of God's Kingdom.* San Francisco: Jossey-Bass, 1998.

Scott, W. Richard. *Institutions and Organizations.* Thousand Oaks, Calif.: Sage Publications, 1995.

Seligman, Adam B. *The Idea of Civil Society.* Princeton: Princeton University Press, 1992.

Selznick, Philip. *The Moral Commonwealth: Social Theory and the Promise of Community.* Berkeley: University of California Press, 1992.

Sennett, Richard. *The Fall of the Public Man.* New York: Knopf, 1977.

Shklar, Judith N. *American Citizenship: The Quest for Inclusion.* Cambridge, Mass.: Harvard University Press, 1991.

Sills, David L., "Voluntary Associations: Sociological Aspects." In David L. Sills, ed. *International Encyclopedia of the Social Sciences.* New York: Free Press, 1968.

Smith, Bruce L. R., ed. *The New Political Economy: The Public Use of the Private Sector.* New York: John Wiley and Sons, 1975.

Smith, Steven Rathgeb, and Michael Lipsky. *Nonprofits for Hire: The Welfare State in the Age of Contracting.* Cambridge, Mass.: Harvard University Press, 1993.

Stone, Michael E. *Shelter Poverty: New Ideas on Housing Affordability.* Philadelphia: Temple University Press, 1993.

Stout, Jeffrey. *Ethics after Babel: The Languages of Morals and Their Discontents.* Boston: Beacon Press, 1988.

Swidler, Ann. "Culture in Action." *American Sociological Review* 51 (1986): 273–86.

Taylor, Charles. *The Sources of the Self: The Making of Modern Identity.* Cambridge, Mass.: Harvard University Press, 1989.

Tipton, Steven M. *Getting Saved from the Sixties: Moral Meaning in Conversion and Cultural Change.* Berkeley: University of California Press, 1982.

Tocqueville, Alexis de. *Democracy in America.* Trans. George Lawrence. New York: Doubleday, 1969.

Toennies, Ferdinand. *Community and Society.* Ed. and trans. Charles P. Loomis. East Lansing: Michigan State University, 1957.

Troeltsch, Ernst. *The Social Teaching of the Christian Churches.* 2 vols. Trans. Olive Wyon. Louisville, Ky.: Westminster/John Knox Press, 1931.

Van Til, Jon. *Mapping the Third Sector: Voluntarism in a Changing Social Economy.* New York: Foundation Center, 1988.

———, ed. *Critical Issues in American Philanthropy: Strengthening Theory and Practice.* San Francisco: Jossey-Bass, 1990.

Verba, Sydney, Kay Lehman Schlozman, and Henry E. Brady. *Voice and Equality: Civic Voluntarism in American Politics.* Cambridge: Harvard University Press, 1995.

Wald, Kenneth D. *Religion and Politics in the United States.* 2d ed. Washington, D.C.: Congressional Quarterly, 1992.

Wallis, Jim. *The Soul of Politics: Beyond "Religious Right" and "Secular Left."* New York: Harcourt Brace, 1995.

Walzer, Michael. *Obligations: Essays on Disobedience, War and Citizenship.* Cambridge: Harvard University Press, 1970.

———. *Spheres of Justice: A Defense of Pluralism and Equality.* New York: Basic Books, 1983.

———. "The Idea of Civil Society." *Dissent* (Spring 1991): 293–304.

Ware, Alan. *Between Profit and the State: Intermediate Organizations in Britain and the United States.* Princeton: Princeton University Press, 1989.

Warner, Stephen R. "Work in Progress toward a New Paradigm for the Sociological Study of Religion in the United States." *American Journal of Sociology* 98, no. 5 (1993): 1044–93.

Weber, Max. *From Max Weber: Essays in Sociology.* Ed. and trans. H. H. Gerth and C. W. Mills. New York: Oxford University Press, 1946.

———. *Economy and Society: An Outline of Interpretive Sociology.* Ed. Guenther Roth and Claus Wittich. Berkeley: University of California Press, 1978.

Weisbrod, Burton A. *The Nonprofit Economy.* Cambridge: Harvard University Press, 1988.

Wilson, John F. *Public Religion in American Culture.* Philadelphia: Temple University Press, 1979.

Witten, Marsha G. *All Is Forgiven: The Secular Message in American Protestantism.* Princeton: Princeton University Press, 1993.

Wolch, Jennifer R. *The Shadow State: Government and Voluntary Sector in Transition.* New York: Foundation Center, 1990.

Wolfe, Alan. *Whose Keeper? Social Science and Moral Obligation.* Berkeley: University of California Press, 1989.

————. *One Nation, After All: What Middle-Class Americans Really Think about God, Country, Family, Racism, Welfare, Immigration, Homosexuality, Work, the Right, the Left, and Each Other.* New York: Viking Press, 1998.

Wood, James R. *Leadership in Voluntary Organizations: The Controversy over Social Action in Protestant Churches.* New Brunswick, N.J.: Rutgers University Press, 1981.

Wuthnow, Robert. *The Restructuring of American Religion: Society and Faith since World War II.* Princeton: Princeton University Press, 1988.

————. *Acts of Compassion: Caring for Ourselves and Helping Others.* Princeton: Princeton University Press, 1991.

————. *Producing the Sacred: An Essay on Public Religion.* Urbana: University of Illinois Press, 1994.

————. *Sharing the Journey: Support Groups and America's New Quest for Community.* New York: The Free Press, 1994.

————. *Learning to Care: Elementary Kindness in an Age of Indifference.* New York: Oxford University Press, 1995.

————. *Christianity and Civil Society: The Contemporary Debate.* Valley Forge, Pa.: Trinity Press International, 1996.

————. *After Heaven: Spirituality in America since the 1950s.* Berkeley: University of California Press, 1998.

————, ed. *Between States and Markets: The Voluntary Sector in Comparative Perspective.* Princeton: Princeton University Press, 1991.

Wuthnow, Robert, Virginia A. Hodgkinson, and Associates. *Faith and Philanthropy in America: Exploring the Role of Religion in America's Voluntary Sector.* San Francisco: Jossey-Bass, 1990.

Yarnold, Barbara M. *The Role of Religious Organizations in Social Movements.* New York: Praeger, 1991.

Young, Dennis R. *If Not for Profit, for What? A Behavioral Theory of the Nonprofit Sector Based on Entrepreneurship.* Lexington, Mass.: D. C. Heath, 1983.

Zarembka, Arlene. *The Urban Housing Crisis: Social Economic, and Legal Issues and Proposals.* New York: Greenwood Press, 1990.

Index